The Act of

READING

"The Act of
READING"

ALAN CASTY
Santa Monica City College

PRENTICE-HALL, INC.   *Englewood Cliffs, N.J.*

Library of Congress Catalog Card No.: 62-8175

First printing . . . . January, 1962
Second printing . . . . January, 1963

Printed in the United States of America
00373–C

Acknowledgments

"The Great Texas Crash"
From *Coronet*, August, 1956. © 1956 by Esquire, Inc.
Reprinted by permission of the publishers.

"Is Football a Substitute for Motherhood?"
From *Sports Illustrated*, March 23, 1959.
Reprinted by special permission from *Sports Illustrated*.

"Concerning a Rumor in August"
From *Saturday Review*, August 2, 1958. Excerpted and Edited by John Lear, science editor
of *Saturday Review*. Reprinted by permission of Saturday Review.

"The Jet That Crashed before Take-off"
Copyright © 1957 by Beirne Lay, Jr.
Reprinted by permission of Harold Ober Associates Incorporated.

"The Civil War"
From *Holiday*, May, 1953. Copyright 1953 by The Curtis Publishing Company.
Reprinted by permission of Harold Matson Company.

"Too Early Spring"
From *The Selected Works of Stephen Vincent Benet*. Holt, Rinehart and Winston, Inc.
Copyright, 1933, by The Butterick Company. Reprinted by permission of Brandt and Brandt.

"My Average Uncle"
From *Book of Uncles* by R. P. T. Coffin.
Copyright 1942 by The MacMillan Company and used with their permission.

"New York"
From *New York—A Serendipiter's Journey* by Gay Talese. Copyright © 1961 by Gay Talese.
Reprinted by permission of Harper and Brothers. Originally published in *Esquire*.

"Miami—Florida's Gold Coast"
From *Holiday*, January, 1952. Reprinted by permission of the author.

"Miami"
From *Red, Black, Blond and Olive* by Edmund Wilson. © 1956, Oxford University Press.
Reprinted by permission of Edmund Wilson.

"The Innocence of Marilyn Monroe"
From *Encounter*, March, 1955. Reprinted by permission of David Sylvester and *Encounter*.

"Brando: The Gilded Image"
From *Playboy*: Copyright © 1961 by HMH Publishing Co., Inc.
Reprinted by permission of Jerry Tallmer and *Playboy*.

"Disneyland and Las Vegas"
From *The Nation*, June 7, 1958. Reprinted by permission of *The Nation*.

"What is History?"
From *Modern History* by Carl Becker. Copyright 1958, Frederick D. Becker.
Publisher, Silver Burdett Company and used with their permission.

"The Individual and The Group"
From *Sociology* by John F. Cuber. Fourth Edition copyright © 1959, Appleteon Century-Crofts, Inc. and used with their permission.

"Thinking Machines Are Getting Smarter"
From *Mechanix Illustrated*, October, 1958. Reprinted by permission of *Mechanix Illustrated*.

"Why They Race With Fate"
From *The New York Times Magazine*, May 24, 1959.
Reprinted with the permission of *The New York Times*.

"The Place of Jazz"
From *A Handbook of Jazz* by Barry Ulanov. Copyright © 1957 by Barry Ulanov.
Reprinted by permission of The Viking Press, Inc.

"The Science of Dreams"
From *Newsweek*, April 6, 1959. Reprinted by permission of *Newsweek*.

"The Push into Space"
From *Time*, January 19, 1959. Reprinted by permission from *Time The Weekly Newsmagazine*; copyright Time Inc., 1959.

"Civil Defense Is a Farce"
From *The Philadelphia Bulletin*. Reprinted by permission of United Feature Syndicate.

"Go Western, Young Writer"
From *The New Republic*, March 2, 1959. Reprinted by permission of *The New Republic*.

"Good Grief, More Peanuts!"
From *The Reporter*, April 30, 1959. Copyright 1959 by The Reporter Magazine Company.
Reprinted by permission of *The Reporter* and Gerald Weales.

"The Egghead Vs. The Muttonhead"
From *The New York Times Magazine*, November 23, 1958.
Reprinted with the permission of *The New York Times*.

"Why Not Let Pay TV Have a Trial Run?"
From *The Saturday Evening Post*, January 31, 1959. Reprinted by special permission of *The Saturday Evening Post*. © 1959 by The Curtis Publishing Company.

"The Case Against Pay TV"
From *The New York Times Magazine*, October 6, 1957.
Reprinted with the permission of *The New York Times*.

"The Real Delinquent—The Parent?"
From *The New York Times Magazine*, December 22, 1946.
Reprinted with the permission of *The New York Times*.

"Parents and Juvenile Delinquency"
From *Holiday*, June, 1958. Reprinted by permission of Bergen Evans.

"Why Are Americans Unhappy?"
From *Contemporary Issues*, April-May, 1958.
Reprinted by permission of Contemporary Press and Alan Dutscher.

Introduction

Many textbooks and many courses, complete with complicated and expensive machinery, start by informing you that if you are going to read better, you have to improve the way you move your eyes over the printed page. Watch those pauses, watch those word groups, watch those backslidings. This is all useful advice, I am sure, as increasing your reading speed is a useful hobby.

This information is useful—but not the heart of the matter. For if you are like most troubled readers, your problem is not that you don't use your eyes properly. It is, rather, that your eyes are all you are using. Your eyes move along the page, but your mind, your thoughts, your imagination, your emotions—these are at rest. You are sitting back and absorbing through your eyes. You are the *passive* reader. You are not ready to pounce on the printed page and probe, question, and demand of it. You are not the *active* reader. And you should be. For reading is an act that you yourself must perform.

To be more accurate, I probably should say you are somewhere in between: a kind of neither-nor reader—neither completely passive, nor anywhere active enough. But the first thing to do is to recognize the importance of your *attitude* toward the printed page. Then decide where on this scale of reading action you yourself fall. This mental stance you take toward a page is going to determine what you acquire from that page. Probably the most convenient clue

to your own attitude is what you are left with when you finish. The passive reader is left with a grab bag of random facts or bits of stories, some amusing or shocking, and some even exciting. But he has no idea why all those random facts he remembers so well were there or what they add up to. His problem—and yours too, if the description fits—is that he does not comprehend what he reads.

You are, I am sure, familiar with the term "reading comprehension." This is what you want to increase. This is what books of this sort try to help you increase. But what does it really mean? What, for example, is the connection between the word *comprehensive* and the word *comprehension?* The connection (if you check the dictionary) should suggest to you that to comprehend doesn't mean to understand in pieces, but to understand as a unified whole that includes all the parts. This is the real goal.

There are no secret passwords to that goal, but there are three words which can suggest the direction. These words have to be asked as questions, and it is only by asking of a page that you become an active, comprehending reader. If you sit back and wait for the page to tell you something, your very attitude defeats you before you start.

These three words and questions, are *Why? What?* and *How?* The active reader asks them by habit, probably without even noticing. But what the passive reader has to do is ask them each time. Habits have to be shaped; they don't just happen.

Asking Why?

Why seeks a purpose. *Why* was an article, an essay, a story, or a book written? You can be sure that if the author was a professional he knew specifically why. The purpose shaped everything he said. So the first step to understand what he wrote is to determine why he wrote it.

For example, if you think a writer is giving you a commonly accepted *definition*, when he is actually attempting to force his *opinion* upon you, you are very likely to misunderstand his statement, if not actually be misled by it.

There are two ways to approach this matter of purpose. One is based on the attempted *effect* on the reader. Is it supposed to amuse you, move you, frighten you, amaze you, or maybe just let you know?

The second purpose is based on the type of writing. There are a number of ways to classify types of written material, but a simple and useful way is to set up four basic types: *story, description, explanation,* and *statement of opinion.* Just about anything written can be pigeonholed under one of these types without doing too much damage to its contents. You might have already noticed that this is the way I have organized the reading material in this book. What is generally involved in each of these types? What can a writer do with them? What do you as a reader have to do to comprehend them? These are the questions that the introduction to each section of the book will discuss.

Asking What?

A final *why* question actually leads us to the question of *what.* That is, when we ask, "Why was it written?" we are also asking, "What does it all add up to?" This is the most important question. This is what we seek to comprehend. What is its thesis? What is its basic controlling statement? What is its point? This thesis, this controlling statement, this point is what a piece is saying about its subject. You need to know more than just what the subject is. You need to know what is being said *about* the subject. You may know, for example, that the subject is jazz. But you don't really comprehend until you know what is being said *about* jazz, and just *what* jazz communicates.

You will not be able to tell what an article or book means unless you know what the individual words mean. Probably the best way to miss the point is to skip those words you are not quite sure of. More often than not, those are the words that carry the chief clues to the meaning of key sentences or paragraphs, or to the meaning of the whole thing. Without understanding them, you're fishing with a hole in your net, which is fine if you meant to doze and didn't want to catch anything. But if you do want to catch something or understand, you have to deal with those troubling words. A dictionary is of course vital, but even a dictionary has to be used intelligently and actively. For a word can mean a number of things, depending on its context, that is, the situation in which it is used. You have to adjust dictionary meanings to the word's place in a sentence or paragraph, and to its surroundings, to get its exact meaning.

Asking How?

To grasp fully *what* a work is saying, you must be able to notice and understand *how* the author produced the key statement. This does not mean you have to become an expert on how to put together a piece of writing, but you must be able to recognize and use certain basic elements in the finished product.

To know the difference between the major ideas and the minor, supporting ideas and details you have to be able to use the *clues of organization* the author provides. You have to notice how he produces emphasis and how he groups his ideas and evidence. You can often determine emphasis and organization merely by paying enough attention to the very beginning so that you know what the rest of the piece is supposed to show you.

Other methods of understanding *how* the author achieves his statement are explained in the introductions to the four parts of this book. Here, only one more point need be made. And that is how the author *uses details* to illustrate and support his main points and how these details fit into the whole. No single sentence or paragraph, no anecdote or scene or example in a good piece of writing is used merely for itself. All the parts are used to support the whole, the central statement. And you are not really reading comprehensively until you can determine just *how* any single illustration or example helps to make clearer some general idea that is behind all the illustrations or examples. If you find a little anecdote in an article about a man beating his wife, it's not enough to remember it. You have to know why the author is telling it to you, what it's supposed to be showing, and how it is contributing to the main idea or ideas of the whole work. An active reader can do this. Can you?

Using This Book

The contents of this book have been organized to assist you in asking and answering the questions *Why? What?* and *How?* The articles have been grouped according to the four types of writing (story, description, explanation, and statement of opinion) to enable you to see the different ways in which they work.

Within each of the four groups the selections proceed from shorter to longer in length, and easier to more difficult. This progression to greater length and complexity calls for you to grasp and put together more and more details as you go along through each section of the book.

To show how a work is organized, and how you should go about reading it, eight selections in the book have underscoring and marginal notes. These markings are not only to serve as a guide to a particular work, but are to show you how to mark up further reading material for better understanding and retention. The active reader is active with a pencil too; it's a habit you should develop.

The exercises (at the back) for each selection include vocabulary study and a multiple-choice section. Not until you have understood the key words can you hope to understand the whole work. The words I have chosen to ask you about are important to the work, and you will find that you are guided back to the original paragraphs to find the answers. In this way you are developing your understanding of the selection while you are improving your understanding of the words.

I suggest that when you are reading through the material for the first time, you mark all the words you have difficulty with and, if possible, check their meanings immediately. You will often find that the words you have marked are the words that are the answers to the vocabulary study. You will also find that the vocabulary exercises lead you through the essay in proper sequence; they don't jump around.

A thorough study of the vocabulary exercises is a step to understanding the article. The exercises to test your understanding of the contents of the article should complete the job. All these drills begin with questions on the basic purposes and statements of a piece. They then move to some of the important subdivisions and finally focus on important details. Their basic purpose is not to test your memory, although sometimes it will be helpful to answer them from memory. Their purpose is to get you to see how the selection is put together and what it all adds up to. They should make you look at the selection more closely and read it more actively. And so you should, at least part of the time, check back to the text itself as you answer the questions. You shouldn't have to guess; it's all in the text.

Table of Contents

The Act of

READING

PART 1

Reading the

STORY

INTRODUCTION

There are many kinds of stories or narratives. Some are true; some are fiction. In newspapers and magazines we find news stories, which tell us of events which have happened and things that people have done. In books we find history, the story of man's progress in the world, and biography, the story of a person's life. We also find novels and short stories, fictional accounts of imaginary people and imaginary happenings. Anything that is written to tell us "This is what happened" is called a story, whether it be fact or fiction.

As a reader, then, your first job is to notice that a story is being told, true ro imaginary. Whatever the type, all stories are similar in one way: the author has organized a series of events to show the cause and effect connections between them, to make them a unified whole, and, often, to show what *meaning* the occurrence should have for you.

Asking Why

Nevertheless, in reading stories, many people never bother to ask *why* the author is telling them "This is what happened." They never realize that there may be a real point to the whole thing, that the author may have presented a problem or made a statement that they should or could be interested in. Instead they read the details of what happened, enjoy them or don't, but never get to the meaning, to the reason the writer believed the story important enough to tell in the first place.

Why does anyone write a story? He writes it because he has some opinion about the actions or events in it; if nothing else, he has the opinion that they are unusual enough to interest you, the reader. Even in reading news stories and histories, which are supposedly direct, objective accounts of real events, you should recognize that often you are not merely informed, but are invited to form an opinion about whether the event was good or bad or about why it happened. Fiction stories, of course, are written to entertain you by presenting an amusing, frightening, mysterious, or otherwise interesting series of events. But by noticing what the writer considers to be amusing, frightening, mysterious, or interesting, you can find out what he thinks about the world and about people.

Asking What and How

To understand what a writer's point is, you must first be aware of his attitude toward the happenings in his story. Is he serious, or does he think the occurrences are funny? Does he appear disinterested (merely reporting the facts) or does he openly show his personal interest? In short, is he judging, and asking you to judge, the people and events in the story? If he is trying to make a judgment, and he usually is, you have not really understood the story until you know what that judgment is. Then you can make up your own mind as to the truth or falsity of the author's statement and decide whether his statement was important enough to be worth making.

Occasionally, but not often, the author directly tells you the point of the story, the theme. In old-time stories there was often a "moral" at the end telling the reader what he should think about what he had just read; for example, "The moral of this story is that a man whose wife is beautiful lies in constant danger of losing her." In modern stories, particularly in fiction, the writers usually leave it up to the reader to interpret the events of the narrative. You, the reader, are asked to judge the people in the story and the things they do while the author chooses words to describe their actions which he hopes will make you judge the occurrences in the same way that he does. Sometimes the author presents his ideas by letting them be directly discussed by the people in the story—by showing them talking or arguing about some point.

Since in fiction the theme usually is implied only, this type of story is often the hardest to interpret. Here too the themes are often more serious and complex. Of course, some stories are not intended to be significant; they are meant to be merely entertaining. But many stories (and these are considered the most valuable as literature) are meant not only to entertain but to illustrate some basic truth about people, about the meaning of life. In analyzing these stories which comment on people and life, you need to determine what such things as the plot, the setting, and the characters are supposed to represent. If you can follow the suggested clues to the themes, your enjoyment of the stories will be greatly increased.

IN READING THIS SECTION—

1. Be sure to determine *why* each of these stories was told.

2. Notice that as the stories get longer and more complex, they embody more definite comments about some aspect of life.

3. Notice *how* these comments are made, directly or indirectly.

The Great Texas Crash

ELWELL CRISSEY

[1] A westering sun slanted down upon 30,000 men, women, and children scattered over the raw, heat-baked slopes of a shallow natural amphitheater in Mc-Lennan County, Texas. All day long they had been arriving, on excursion trains, in farm wagons, surreys, and on horseback to witness the zaniest yet most spectacular drama in the boisterous history of early American railroading.

[2] They were hot, dusty, and tired, but all that was forgotten now as they fixed their attention on the twin ribbons of steel that crossed the amphitheater. On one rim stood a brilliantly painted locomotive and string of cars, the engine's diamond-shaped stack belching smoke. On the opposite rim, facing it some two miles away, waited a similar train.

[3] About midway between them, beside a telegraph pole bearing the freshly painted sign—"Point of Collision" —stood a tall man in a frock coat. He waved his sun helmet and a tense hush fell over the assemblage.

[4] The starting signal was flashed. The locomotives answered it with blasts from their whistles and the crowd broke into a cheer as the drive wheels turned and the trains started down the grades toward each other.

[5] It was ten minutes after five on Tuesday, September 15, 1896, and the great Missouri, Kansas & Texas collision party was under way.

[6] The idea for the M. K. & T.'s superspectacle originated in a collision staged for publicity purposes by an Ohio railroad the previous summer. Two ancient locomotives, each hauling a few decrepit freight cars, bumped noses and cracked up several cars. It wasn't much to watch.

[7] Among those disappointed by the poor show was young W. G. Crush of Dallas, Texas, general passenger agent for the M. K. & T., or "Katy" as the road was familiarly known. Mr. Crush believed that the lusty young Katy could stage a wreck really worth watching, and that Texas was the place to do it. He sold the idea to officials of the line and presently gaudy bill posters announcing the event appeared on Texas barns and fences.

[8] The Katy shops put a pair of locomotives of the '80's into perfect mechanical condition. Their cabs and wheels were painted bright green, the tenders red. Cowcatcher bars were alternate green and red, boilers enameled gleaming black.

[9] To give added weight, the cattle cars that were to make up the trains were filled with crossties, and their sides boarded over and covered with bill posters.

[10] The spot selected for the collision was at the bottom of a shallow depression from which the track sloped

5

upward in both directions. This increased momentum. The surrounding hills made a natural theater for the show, and officials assured everybody there was no danger.

[11]   Early on the morning of the great day, spectators began arriving from as far away as Parsons, Kansas, and Galveston on the Gulf; and before the day was over the Katy had pressed into service every passenger coach it owned.

[12]   At five o'clock, both trains coasted down to the collision point, put their pilots together, and were photographed; then backed slowly up the grades to their appointed stations.

[13]   "This was the moment we had waited for," James Virgil Montrief, late mayor of Bridgeport, Texas, remembered not long ago. "I'll admit I was nervous, so I found a place near the top of a hill probably 300 yards from the track. And I can tell you, I'm mighty thankful I did."

[14]   "On every vantage point in all directions spectators stood literally on tiptoes, fascinated. Those trains sure sound dizzy nowadays, but we thought they were downright beautiful."

[15]   Mr. Crush waved his sun helmet and, moments later, the show was on.

[16]   Black smoke rolling, safety valves hissing, the trains got under way. Each whistle cord had been rigged to a drive wheel, causing the whistles to shriek at every turn. In addition, torpedoes had been strapped to the rails at intervals, making a ghastly uproar that rose in crescendo as the trains gathered speed.

[17]   Faster and faster they raced down the incline toward each other. The suspense an instant before the collison was almost unendurable. Many turned away, unable to bear the sight, as the two locomotives crashed head on with a jar that shook the ground. They met within ten feet of the sign—but the result

was more than anybody had bargained for.

[18]   The front ends flattened out with the shock. There was the sickening sound of splintering wood and the tortured shriek of rending metal. Then, instead of upending as anticipated, the locomotives telescoped horizontally—and both boilers exploded with a monstrous roar.

[19]   Instantly, the collision point was enveloped in a cloud of scalding steam from which a deadly hail of steel fragments—some the size of postage stamps, others whole drive wheels—sprayed out over the terrified crowd.

[20]   The cap sheaf of a smokestack was blown a quarter of a mile and buried itself in the earth only 15 feet from screaming men and women struggling frantically to get out of its path. A pair of massive trucks weighing nearly a ton were lifted into the air, knocking down a telegraph pole as if it had been a weed.

[21]   A cylinder head with two feet of piston rod attached, sailing round and round, whistled directly over the photographer's stand. J. C. Dean, a Waco photographer, had his right eye destroyed by a two-inch bolt. Another hurtling bolt broke the leg of a 14-year-old boy.

[22]   Two lengths of heavy brake chain soared through the air, coiling and uncoiling like aerial serpents. One cracked the skull of 19-year-old Ernest Darnell of Bremond, who died shortly after. By some strange miracle his, and that of one other person who was fatally injured that day, were the only deaths attributable to the explosion.

[23]   A McLennan County farmer, watching the crash from a treetop, became so excited he fell from his perch, broke his left leg, and dislocated his right hip.

[24]   All that was left of the two trains, except for each rear car, was a smoking mass of broken metal and kin-

dling wood. "I doubt if there ever was more complete destruction in the world than of those two engines," a famous photographer from New York said later. "It did not seem to me as if a piece as big as a hat remained."

[25]   For a full minute after the explosion, the crowd stood stock still, literally stunned by the concussion. Then, with a yell, those that found themselves unhurt broke for the wreck to hunt souvenirs.

[26]   The Katy never again operated so many trains in one day. But though a huge sum was realized, heavy damages had to be paid out to the injured.

[27]   However, Mr. Crush always claimed his great collision show was a tremendous success. And the Katy is still proud of it—it made the road famous from coast to coast.

WRITING ASSIGNMENTS

1. Tell the story of a significant (exciting, horrifying, thrilling, amusing, etc.) public event in the same way that Mr. Crissey has told his story. That is, begin with a brief description of the situation and setting before the actual event begins, follow this with an explanation of why the event is being held, and then set forth in detail the significant actions that occurred. Finally, if there were any after-effects or results, present them.

2. Do you think there is any moral issue involved in this Great Texas crash? In other words, do you feel the railway officials were guilty of any wrong-doing? In a brief argument, prosecute them or defend them on this charge.

3. Tell an "I was there" kind of story about the most dangerous experience in which you personally were involved.

Is Football A Substitute For Motherhood?

[1]   If worded just right, a classified ad in Brown University's student newspaper, the DAILY HERALD, can release as much energy as a hydrogen bomb. The man who discovered the magic formula is Wade C. Thompson, an English instructor at Brown. Here is his ad:

CLASSIFIEDS

Will all students of Brown and Pembroke (undergraduate or graduate), all faculty members, library or administrative officials, who wish to sign a petition calling for the abolition of Intercollegiate Football at Brown, please contact Wade Thompson. PL. 1-6767.

[2] Thompson has red hair, a flair for controversy and a fine bass voice. He is six feet, four inches tall and has played basketball but not football. He once sang bass in the chorus of the Radio City Music Hall in order to support himself and his family while he worked for his doctorate at Columbia University. While at the Music Hall he organized the Rockettes into a labor union, and did the job so skillfully that he became a full-time labor organizer for a year.

Background on Thompson

[3] Thompson will soon receive his Ph.D from Columbia (his doctoral dissertation is on the aesthetic theories of Henry David Thoreau) and will soon move up to an assistant professorship at Brown—not, however, because of his anti-football ad. He is, temporarily and in a mild way, a national celebrity. For the DAILY HERALD, while running the ad in its classified section, ran a story about the ad on Page One (INSTRUCTOR ADVOCATES ABOLITION OF FOOTBALL) and PL 1-6767 became the busiest telephone in Providence, R.I.

[4] Thompson received bully-boy threats by telephone, a courteous visit from Brown's football captain (who offered physical protection against possible violence) and offers to sign his petition, which was imaginary anyway. The teacup storm became a gale which roared about the campus; Brown students turned fervently pro- or acidly anti-Thompson. Newspapers all over the country took up the story, and everybody enjoyed the wonderful nonsense except Wade Thompson, who got tired of answering the telephone and being interviewed.

Reactions to his ad

[5] The debate went on, informally but vigorously, for a week and then was made official by a panel discussion, followed by a question period, in Brown's stately Sayles Hall. Flanked by paintings of Brown worthies of the past 195 years, Thompson took one side, Athletic Director Paul F. Mackesey took the other and a few hundred students came to clap, boo and listen.

Final development

[6] "I have received hundreds of invitations to drop dead," Thompson began, admitting that he and his imaginary anti-football committee had found themselves "outnumbered approximately 40,000 to one. We hung out one surrender flag after another. Still the shooting continued. We resolved to retreat from one untenable position to another, but the hullabaloo went on."

His real point and purpose

[7] Thompson had called football anti-intellectual, he said, but what he was really opposed to was "the sanctification of football." The clamorous reaction to his advertisement had proved, he said, that even at Brown, which follows the Ivy League code of amateurism in athletics, football is sanctified.

[8] "It is preposterous to think that Brown is going to abolish football just because I said it should." But, he insisted, "football doesn't build character any more than tennis does, or chess. It is no substitute for motherhood. . . . It has been choked with clichés, mired in sentimental mush, drowned in tears and flap-doodle, until no football coach can go from one job to another without more idiotic fanfare than that which will accompany the Second Coming."

Thompson's argument

[9] Athletic Director Mackesey, a lawyer who speaks as persuasively

as Thompson, said he felt that the evening's discussion dignified the subject of anti-football beyond its deserts. "If athletics does not make a sensible and sound contribution to education as we understand it, then there is no justification for it in our college program. . . . Only those who have viewed education narrowly, with one eye, have considered that scholarship alone is enough to make the whole man. . . . College education is a four-year experience in preparation for the whole of life and not for one part of it.

Mackesey's argument

[10] "What better preparation for all of life than hard work and success both in the classroom and on the playing field? The scholar-athlete, the college football player, is not a divided, cross-eyed person but a man of twofold ability. . . . There are more things in heaven and earth, Mr. Thompson, than are dreamt of in your philosophy."

[11] What began as a joke and became a farce thus wound up almost soberly, with the students listening to both speakers as carefully as to a classroom lecture (more carefully, some faculty members thought). Possibly no convictions were changed as a result of Brown's great debate, but the arguments had rarely been stated so sharply or received so much attention. Thompson, who never explained his purpose in soliciting signatures for an imaginary petition on behalf of a nonexistent committee, was wearily willing to let the whole matter drop. "I have had a horrible week," he said, rubbing his tired-looking face. Later he added, "I hope the students carry on the debate from now on."

Aftermath and significance

WRITING ASSIGNMENTS

1. The debate between Thompson and Mackesey centered on these two opposing ideas: football should not receive so much emphasis vs. football helps prepare college students for the whole of life. Which do you agree with? Write a defense of the position you favor. In your argument be sure you first explain the background of the argument, giving the reader an introduction to the general subject. Then be sure you get specific in the body of your argument. Exactly what evidence shows football receives too much emphasis? What harm does this do? Or, on the other hand, in what specific ways does football help students? What parts of life does it prepare them for?

2. This article is a news story from a national magazine; it tries to narrate what happened without taking sides or favoring one of the viewpoints in the conflict. Write a news article in which you tell what happened in a situation that involved a conflict (real or imaginary). Do not take sides; do not give your opinion. Here are some examples of situations that involve a conflict: an auto accident, a court trial, a debate, a political argument or campaign, a sports event of any kind, a riot, a strike, etc.

3. Everybody has some pet peeve; that is, something he would like to have abolished. Write an essay that argues that something, your pet peeve, should be done away with, abolished. Again, be sure you show specific reasons why it is harmful, unnecessary or just plain irritating.

Concerning A Rumor In August

ELLIOTT R. DANZIG

PAUL W. THAYER

LILA R. GALANTER

The story below is set in anxious times: two days after the end of the visitation of Hurricane Diane in the night of August 17-18, 1955. The Delaware River had gone twenty feet above its normal level, pouring six feet deep through the riverfront streets of Port Jervis, New York, driving all the lowland dwellers there from their homes. A state of emergency had been declared, the running of the town had been turned over to Civil Defense, volunteer firemen had come from miles around to pump out inundated cellars, and the receding waters were smearing mud across gardens and lawns, through the houses and over the furniture. It was not an altogether placid Saturday night.

[1] At about 10:30 o'clock on Saturday night, August 20, 1955 a stranger ran into a restaurant in Sparrowbush and told the owner (who is also a volunteer fireman) that the Wallenpaupack Dam had broken. The stranger added that firemen in a community up the river were evacuating everyone. The restaurant owner's telephone was out of commission because of the flood. He went with three other men to the highway outside and began to stop cars to warn them of the impending danger.

[2] The second car he stopped was, fortuitously, that of the Sparrowbush Fire Captain, who went to the firehouse and radioed to the fire base in Port Jervis. When he announced, "Emergency— Stand by!" the air was cleared. All radios in the firehouse, in fire headquarters, and and on the fire trucks were held open for the message. He then reported that he had been stopped on the road by firemen (one of whom was the restaurant owner)

and had been told that the Wallenpaupack Dam had gone out.

[3] In Port Jervis, the Fire Chief was in a fire truck in the flooded part of town pumping out a cellar when he heard this broadcast. He notified the radio operator at his own headquarters to ask for a repeat of the message and for identification of the sender. The Sparrowbush Fire Captain repeated the message and identified himself. The Port Jervis Fire Chief immediately told his radio operator to check with the Dam directly through the Middletown (N.Y.) fire base, which had a more powerful radio transmitter than the short-wave link between Sparrowbush and Port Jervis.

[4] The Port Jervis chief fire radio operator heard the original broadcast from Sparrowbush on a monitor set in the meantime and rushed to fire headquarters. When he arrived, he received a telephone call from a Port Jervis resi-

dent stating that one or more fire trucks which had received the Sparrowbush message were driving through town, sounding their sirens, and shouting to get out because the Dam had broken. He decided independently to broadcast to the fire trucks that he thought the report was false and that headquarters was checking on it. He also issued specific instructions to the errant fire trucks mentioned above: "You have been given no orders to do what you are doing. Cut it the hell out and get back to the firehouse." This was at about 11:15 p.m.

[5] By this time, the rumor had gained considerable momentum. Cars were in the streets, and people were clamoring for everyone to get out of town. Residents were waking their neighbors, and groups of people were descending on City Hall, firehouses, and other centers of communication in the city. Across the Delaware, in Matamoras (cut off from its usual traffic with Port Jervis by the flooded highway between) a carful of people who apparently had heard the rumor on the radio came through the main street shouting for everyone to get out. Someone who heard them ran to the firehouse and blew the fire siren before anyone there knew what was happening. To at least some of the people in Matamoras the siren meant impending flood, largely because officials had made an announcement to the effect during the flood which had just passed. A mass evacuation then took place in Matamoras, and the siren was heard in the river-front section of Port Jervis. People who heard its scream joined others who had heard the Port Jervis fire trucks in telephoning the local (Erie) railroad station asking whether or not the report about the Dam was true.

[6] One of the two people on duty at the railroad station helped to spread the rumor by stating that it was true as far as he knew. The other (at another phone in another part of the station) referred the calls to the Police. This employee called the Police himself (as soon as he could get a line through) and received the report that the Police "had no knowledge of the Dam having broken and thought it was a rumor." The railroad man then conveyed this rather ambiguous message to all subsequent callers.

[7] Other worried citizens mobbed the Civil Defense office asking for verification of the rumor and asking further what they should do. The people were generally aware of the approximate location of Wallenpaupack, but there was a good deal of disagreement among them as to how long it would take for waters to reach them if the Dam actually had broken.

[8] The clamor of the people outside its doors was not a complete surprise to Civil Defense headquarters. The rumor had already been picked up there by a chance telephone call. Mrs. A, a Civil Defense official, had rung up a friend to talk about another matter. The friend said, "I can't talk to you because there is a sound truck outside telling us to evacuate because the Dam has broken. I'm packing to leave."

[9] Mrs. A had rung off that conversation and had gone to the shortwave radio in the room next to her office. There she met the chief radio operator and his assistant. The operators had just received a shortwave message from Police headquarters asking them to verify the report that "the Wallenpaupack Dam has broken."

[10] Before this happened, the operators were in contact with a Port Jervis radio "ham" who had established a relay channel through which he could radio Wallenpaupack Dam authorities. From Wednesday to Saturday the "ham" had periodically radioed the latest news on

the condition of the Dam to Civil Defense headquarters. But now he couldn't get through to the Dam. Instead, he radioed the U. S. Army a request to activate the Army's emergency shortwave radio network. "We're not sure," he said. "It may be only a rumor." He then telephoned Civil Defense and told them to try to reach the Dam through their own channels as he himself had been unsuccessful.

[11]   Mrs. A asked the people outside Civil Defense headquarters to wait for verification of the rumor. She told them the report was being checked at that moment. She felt considerable compunction about this because she knew that if the report were true she was cutting down the time there would be to escape. But she looked at the map and estimated that the water would take two hours to reach Port Jervis.

[12]   At this point, one radio operator received a telephone call from Police headquarters saying that the Police had got through to the Dam. The rumor was definitely false.

[13]   Eighty-five minutes had passed since the stranger ran into the restaurant in Sparrowbush. In that interval, between 2,500 and 3,000 of Port Jervis's inhabitants had fled.

[14]   Some had rushed directly from their beds into their automobiles wearing only their nightclothes and carrying nothing. Others had paused long enough to put a few personal belongings into small suitcases. Still others had gathered up families and sometimes neighbors, together packing their cars with food, blankets, and other necessities for camping in the open. All headed for high ground north and northwest of the town.

[15]   People rarely left town alone. One exception was a bartender who got the rumor from his wife by telephone; he handed his apron to his assistant and hurried out without a word of explanation or even a goodby. A town councilman fled with his wife, leaving behind a helpless elderly couple who roomed in their house. A woman who had been feuding with a neighbor for many years ran first to warn that neighbor and helped her to escape, forgetting all about her own mother who lived in the same street.

[16]   The frightened yelling that punctuated the exodus startled the wife of the Port Jervis Civil Defense director, who was sound asleep at home after working day and night during the flood emergency. She wakened her husband. He dressed and drove to Civil Defense headquarters, there to find that the tumult had passed.

[17]   The Port Jervis Fire Chief, who had taken the first act to stem the rumor and so discourage the people from leaving home, was first to act to try to bring them back. It was actually he who received the first denial the town got from the Dam itself. It came in response to his inquiry through the Middletown fire radio. At the time this reassurance arrived he was still out on one of the fire trucks, still pumping water and mud from flooded cellars. Upon hearing the message that the rumor was false, he directed his radio operator to tell the people that the rumor was false.

[18]   The radio operator went into the street and broadcast the denial to the crowd in front of fire headquarters. Then he went back to the shortwave radio, called all the fire trucks, ordered them to turn up their loud speakers, and used the truck radios as a public address system. He continued to broadcast this denial until 12:20 a.m. at which time the populous seemed to have calmed down fairly well.

[19]   The Fire Chief himself took advantage of the quiescing period to head

out of town to stop a convoy of fire equipment that was coming into Port Jervis from nearby towns and counties to assist in the flood cleanup. There was a tremendous jam of fleeing cars on the highways, in some cases two abreast on a two lane road, the Chief had been informed, and he wanted to stop the incoming fire truck convoy before it became hopelessly entangled.

[20] WDLC, the radio station affiliated with the Port Jervis newspaper, *The Union Gazette,* had signed off for the night at 11 o'clock just before the rumor first came from Sparrowbush. Since many of the townspeople were thought to know and trust certain of the announcers, the Police Chief conveyed the denial of the rumor to them and suggested WDLC go back on the air. WDLC did resume broadcasting at 12:10 a.m., alternating record and organ music with a message carefully edited to eliminate all references to the Dam, to water, or to flood, lest someone might tune in only long enough to hear the word "Dam" and run.

[21] "Ladies and Gentlemen," the announcers said, "It is only a rumor. It is NOT true. There is no need for anyone to be up in the mountains and high places. It would be best if you returned home and did not spread the rumor."

[22] This message was repeated at intervals, the intervening time being filled by music, until 1:15 a.m. when the station broadcast a recorded four minute one way conversation with the Dam superintendent who said that everything in his charge was now in fine shape. In this same message he gave, without identifying it, the only logical explanation of the rumor's origin that anyone heard before or since. He reported that the gates of the Dam had been opened for a few minutes at 9:30 p.m. to relieve pressure from the impounded water. One hour later the rumor was loose.

WRITING ASSIGNMENTS

1. This article attempts to explain step by step the actions of a great many people during a time of great confusion. You are to write a similar narrative, that is, an article presenting the sequence of actions of some public event. Describe a crisis at the beach or at a public park, a traffic jam or accident on a road or freeway, a parade or celebration, a rooting section at a sporting event, a fire, a fight, a riot, etc. Select the important things that people did, put them in a clear order, fully explain each action. You may possibly show how various people reacted, or why they did what they did. You may assign blame or praise, although it is not necessary.

2. Analyze the actions of the central figures in the panic at Port Jervis. Show what each did that was helpful or harmful, intelligent or confused. Suggest if you can why they did it or what they should have done instead.

3. Try to imagine what would happen if a crisis struck your town or neighborhood. What would you do, what do you think certain others would do, what public organizations would there be available to help? First, decide on what imaginary disaster it might be and then explain what you think would happen or possibly what *should* happen if all would be handled intelligently.

The Jet That Crashed Before Take-off

BEIRNE LAY, JR.

[1]   Jet fighter Number 313 taxied onto the end of the runway, cleared for take-off. The Pilot, a young major, fastened his safety belt, set his brakes, and ran up 100 per cent rpm on his engine—a huge, long corncob that made up nearly all of his airplane. Then he released his toe brakes. The wheels rolled the first inch. And in that first inch, the Pilot of Number 313 was doomed. In effect, he was already dead.

[2]   A mile and a half of smooth, white concrete runway narrowed into the distance in front of the nose of the gleaming, javelin-sleek, swept-wing fighter—8,000 feet of it, more than ample for the 6,700-foot take-off distance calculated in the flight plan.

[3]   The weather was good, a clear bright morning with a hot sun beating down on the shimmering California desert. Surface winds were nearly dead calm. The J-79 engine was in perfect condition and turning up normal thrust. No mechanical defect lurked anywhere within the complex innards of the aircraft. The Pilot was highly experienced and could point to a spotless safety record and superior past performance. The mission, like every mission in the Air Force, had been minutely planned: gross weight at take-off figured to the pound; runway temperature, surface-wind velocity, and every other factor to insure the mathematical certainty that the wheels of Number 313 would unstick from the runway after a roll of 6,700 feet. No one connected with the planning or preparation for the mission was guilty of a fatal blunder.

[4]   Only one thing was wrong. A series of minor errors, already irrevocably committed, not one of which was fatal in itself, when added together spelled out a stark fact: Number 313 could not possibly get off the 8,000-foot runway safely.

[5]   She needed 8,100 feet, instead of 6,700 feet.

[6]   Why?

[7]   How could this happen in a precision organization like the United States Air Force, where hundreds of heavily loaded jet aircraft take off every day without incident? The Air Force emphasizes "flying safety" second only to accomplishment of its primary mission and has achieved a consistently lower accident rate each year since World War II.

[8]   Part of the answer is that each "routine" take-off is not really routine. Rather, it is a kind of triumph, endlessly repeated, over an un-

14

seen enemy always lying in wait to prove that an accident is "no accident." It is a triumph, illustrated in reverse, so to speak, by the case of
Number 313, which highlights one of the new facts of life in the jet age:
a jet take-off is more critical than the familiar take-off in a propeller-
driven aircraft. Far more so.

Difficulty of jet take-offs

[9] Perhaps the simplest way to visualize the situation that confronted Number 313 is to think of the Pilot's safety margin—that 1,300-
foot surplus between his estimated 6,700-foot take-off distance and the
8,000-foot runway—as money in the bank. As long as he had any or all
of those 1,300 feet, he was in the black. But a series of petty thefts could
conceivably put him in the red. Number 313 was the victim of four such
thefts, plus two other contributing factors.

Important figure

The causes

[10] Theft number one: As the fighter was taxiing out, the control
tower reported practically a dead calm, a zero wind, as forecast in the
flight plan. However, by the time Number 313 actually started her take-
off, she had a four-knot tailwind. This was so small a change that the
tower operator either did not notice it or did not consider it important
enough to relay it to the Pilot. Certainly this was no drastic windshift.
But it cost the Pilot 310 feet of added take-off distance required. Unknown to him, it brought his bank balance down to 990 feet. Still plenty
of margin.

 # 1 wind-shift

Down from 1300 ft.

[11] Theft number two: Take-off had been planned for 11:15 a.m.,
at which time the runway temperature was forecast to be, and actually
was 97 degrees. But Number 313 had taxied out half an hour late because of a valid delay while the crew chief double-checked a malfunc-
tioning fire-warning light and replaced a bulb. During this delay and
later, while the fighter was taxiing for over a mile from the parking ramp
to the end of the runway, the temperature rose slightly to 101 degrees.
A prolonged delay, say of an hour, would have automatically necessi-
tated a revised flight plan, but the Pilot followed common procedure,
in view of the shorter delay, when he followed his original flight plan.
This unforeseen and seemingly negligible rise of four degrees of temperature robbed him of another 190 feet, since hotter air adds to the
take-off roll of a jet in two ways. The engine develops less thrust, and
the wings need a higher take-off speed in the thinner air. As he released
his toe brakes, the Pilot did not know that his bank balance was now
down to 800 feet.

 # 2 Temperature change during delay

More loss

[12] Theft number three: The Pilot was executing his first take-off
from an unfamiliar air base, having arrived the previous day as a tran-
sient. Therefore he was unaware of an optical illusion that confronted
him as he stared down the runway at the desert floor, rising gradually
from the far end of the runway toward a distant mountain range. To
his eyes, the runway appeared to slope slightly downhill in contrast with
the rising ground beyond. Actually, there was an imperceptible uphill
grade, placing the far end of the runway 260 feet higher than where he
sat, and requiring a take-off roll—under existing conditions of a tailwind
and high temperature—of an additional 550 feet. Now, unknown to the
pilot, his bank balance had shrunk to 250 feet. It was still enough, but

 # 3 Optical illusion

State of his "bankroll"

it was getting close to bankruptcy.

[13] <u>Theft number four:</u> Lack of sleep for the pilot, as a result of an unexpected change in the weather during the previous night, became a pertinent factor. Confident he would be weathered in for a couple of days until a cold front passed, he had left the base on the evening before to enjoy a night on the town with a clear conscience.

4
Lack of
sleep

[14] His family and his girl lived not far from the air base, and their convivial reunion lasted into the small hours. He was awakened after three and a half hours of sleep by a call from the base notifying him of a break in the weather. Since he was under orders to return to his home base as soon as possible, there was nothing for it but to bolt a cup of black coffee, hustle on out to the base, and start wheeling and dealing.

[15] You don't just leap into the cockpit of a supersonic jet fighter and take off, unless you are an interceptor pilot on twenty-four-hour alert duty. This was an extended navigational mission requiring careful planning, preflight inspections, and attention to the check lists. And there is where the lack of sufficient rest led to the final withdrawal from the already slim bank account of Number 313.

[16] The Pilot arrived to find that the Assistant Operations Officer, an old pal, had lent a hand and figured the weight of fuel in the main tanks and the auxiliary wing-tip tanks, based on servicing performed the night before. It had been a cold night—an important factor. In arriving at the correct weight, it is necessary to apply a correction for temperature. This his friend had done, but inadvertently he had applied the correction the wrong way, subtracting it instead of adding it. A gallon of fuel will weigh more when it is cold and dense than when it is warm and expanded—just a fraction of a pound more, but it adds up when you're dealing with thousands of pounds of fuel.

Produced
negligence
in catching
an error

[17] The Pilot checked over his friend's figures. Partly because of confidence, based on past experience, in the other man's accuracy and conscientiousness, and partly because lack of rest had affected his alertness, the Pilot failed to spot his friend's slip-up. Thus, when the wheels of Number 313 rolled that first inch, the aircraft weighed slightly more than the Pilot thought she did. Under any other circumstances, it might not have been a costly error, but it was enough in this case to add a disastrous 350 feet to the distance Number 313 must travel before she could become airborne, thereby chipping away the remaining 250 feet still left in the bank—and then some.

In the red

[18] <u>Now the Pilot was in the red.</u> By one hundred feet. Number 313 was bankrupt and prepared to drag down with her a million-dollar fighter and the life of an invaluable combat pilot.

[19] Only two hopes of reprieve for this Pilot still lived. <u>First,</u> if it became apparent in the final stage of take-off that he'd never make it, he could <u>jettison his tip tanks</u> and lighten his load by approximately one ton of the extra fuel. <u>Secondly,</u> at a given point down the runway, he would have an opportunity of recognizing that he had not reached a predicted airspeed. Then he could yank the throttles back and <u>abort the take-off in time for a safe stop.</u> But this second safeguard had already

2 more
hopes

been taken out of his hands through an error of omission, committed by someone now far removed from the scene.

[20] The runway, originally, had been 7,600 feet long. Recently, 400 feet had been added to the end from which Number 313 took off. But the runway markers—large signs placed at 1,000-foot intervals alongside the runway to enable the pilot to see at a glance during take-off how much runway he still has left—were in their original locations. The fact that they were scheduled to be moved back 400 feet the next day was just twenty-fours hours too late.

[21] Black smoke pouring from her tail pipe, Number 313 rolled forward, gathering momentum slowly, the thunder of her departure ricocheting off the buildings along the flight line. When the Pilot passed the first 1,000-foot marker, he was really 1,400 feet down the runway. The same misinformation was waiting to mislead him at the 2,000-foot and the 3,000-foot markers, depriving him of his last chance to judge whether or not his take-off was proceeding according to plan.

Reason second failed

[22] He reached his maximum refusal speed of 106 knots at the 4,000-foot marker. Had his airspeed been appreciably below the briefed speed at this juncture, here is where he could—and undoubtedly would—have refused to take-off. But he saw that his airspeed was indicating within two knots of the desired speed. He continued. What he didn't know, because of the hidden extra 400 feet he had covered, was that he should have been going eight knots faster at the critical moment of decision.

[23] Now the end of that once endless-looking ribbon of white concrete began to unreel alarmingly fast. It was too late to stop. The Pilot pressed the release button to jettison his tip tanks. Nothing happened. Malfunction in the circuit. Consuming precious seconds, he resorted to hand operation of the manual release. The tanks dropped clear.

Reason first failed

[24] But Number 313 was still solidly on the runway, still below the minimum take-off speed of her stubby, razor-blade wings as the last foot of the concrete blurred in under the nose. Reacting out of automatic desperation, the Pilot pulled back on the controls. Number 313 staggered a few feet into the air. Instantly he retracted the landing gear, fighting to reduce the drag and gain that two or three knots of airspeed that might still spell the difference. Quivering right at her stalling speed, the heavy fighter squashed back onto the rough, rising terrain beyond the runway, plowing ahead at 140 knots. Seconds later came the explosion.

[25] For Number 313, time and distance had run out. And for her Pilot, in that master ledger where no mistakes in the ultimate arithmetic of cause and effect are permitted to occur, the account was now forever closed.

WRITING ASSIGNMENTS

1. In telling the story of the crash of the jet, Mr. Lay emphasizes *why* it happened. Write a similar story of a failure of some kind; it may be an accident, a defeat in sports, a misunderstanding between friends, a problem in school, an error at work, etc. At each step of the sequence of events be sure you stress what caused that step or how it contributed to the final result.

2. Present instructions on how to successfully complete some task or action. Be sure to provide enough detail to make each step of the sequence clear.

3. Why do people want to fly? What reasons can you determine for the lure of this hazardous occupation or hobby?

The Civil War

JAMES STREET

[1]   It's been almost a hundred years since the first shot was fired at Fort Sumter, and we Americans cannot even agree on a name for our Civil War between the States, much less on what caused it or exactly what happened.

[2]   It was a lapse into national schizophrenia, a madness that cost a young country of 31,000,000 people more than 600,000 dead—a toll of American lives considerably larger than we suffered in World Wars I and II combined.

[3]   It was a family feud that left the South prostrate and the North so bewildered that, in freeing her black brothers from slavery, she put her white brothers in political and economic bondage, thereby breeding a bitterness that flares to this day in books, football games, political elections, barroom brawls and letters-to-the-editor columns.

[4]   It made a martyred demigod of Abraham Lincoln, a melancholy Samaritan who shelved the Constitution long enough to save the Union, and a scapegoat of Jefferson Davis, a stiff-necked Constitutionist and legalist who led his people into total war and total desolation. It made an idol of Gen. R. E. Lee, the vanquished who opposed slavery, and a presidential failure of Gen. U. S. Grant, the victor whose wife owned slaves.

[5]   It gave us *Dixie*, the South's fight song written by a Yankee, and *The Battle Hymn of the Republic*, the North's anthem based on a Southern plantation chant; ironclads and torpedoes, Scarlett O'Hara and Little Eva, our first attempt at air power through observation balloons, and our first income tax.

[6]   It revolutionized the science and art of mass slaughter from tactics to

ships to arms, taught us how to wage wars through conscription and to finance them by popular bond issues. It made Negroes free men but not citizens, then sired the Fourteenth Amendment that gave them citizenship. It gave us the Ku Klux Klan and changed the handy carpetbag from a traveling kit into a symbol of ignominy. It brought a scourge of graft, scandals and suicides, split American Protestanism, made a flock of millionaires and sent brothers and cousins against one another in 2261 battles, including one in New York, one in Idaho and 519 in Virginia.

[7]   It created more myths than the King Arthur legends, from Lincoln's Bixby letter and Barbara Frietchie to General Forrest's "Git thar fust, etc.," none of them true.

[8]   It made us think we were the best fighters in the world, indicating we confused ferocity with ability. It gave us new words and sayings that have become commonplace:

[9]   "That government of the people, by the people, etc." — "War is hell" — "Like Grant took Richmond" — "Unconditional surrender" — "Hold the fort" — "Damn the torpedoes" and "Damyankees."

[10]   It proved that Cotton is not King and that a good big man can whip a good little man—although it took 359,-528 Union lives to prove it, including 313 dead from sunstroke.

[11]   There is no telling how many Southerners were killed. The figure totals 258,000, but many of the South's skimpy records were lost in pyres that burned for four years over thousands and thousands of miles, and left the land so barren that, as the saying goes, even the crows had to carry their own food when they flew over it.

[12]   Mr. Winston Churchill said that it was the last great war between gentlemen. Perhaps Mr. Churchill was thinking of Petersburg, where a Maine regiment of 900 lost almost 700 dead in seven minutes. No machine guns, no grenades; just gentlemen killing gentlemen. Or Antietam, where the 3rd North Carolina had casualties of 90 per cent, or Gettysburg, where the 1st Minnesota had casualties of 82 per cent while Company F of the 6th North Carolina was suffering 100 per cent casualties (thus sustaining that state's boast that she furnished more privates and fewer generals to the Confederacy than any of her sisters).

[13]   Could Mr. Churchill have been thinking of Franklin, Tennessee, where Hood's Southerners lost 6000 men, two major generals, nine brigadiers and 45 regimental commanders in one futile charge after another? Or Virginia in May and June of 1864, when Grant's casualties totaled almost the size of Lee's army that inflicted the losses?

[14]   A gentlemen's war indeed! A holiday for butchers, as testified by a generation of men whose wooden legs echoed on the sidewalks of a thousand towns, whose canes tapped a way for sightless eyes. Some orators have called it our nation's most glorious hour. Maybe so. But it was also our dirtiest, and surely our most stupid.

[15]   The Civil War has been blamed on slavery, States' rights, the protective tariff, free soil, Yankee mendacity, Southern treason, the dictates of God and the Revelation of St. John. For many years historians accepted it as a dog-eat-dog carnage between Northern capitalism and Southern agrarianism. More and more, however, they believe that a moral issue was paramount, and the moral issue was slavery.

[16]   Secession has been a hairsplitting issue since New England threatened to leave the Union in 1814. It was not a sectional doctrine. In 1857, New England again considered secession, and

as late as January, 1861, Mayor Fernando Wood of New York proposed that his city secede from the United States.

[17] Alexander Stephens, vice-president of the Confederacy, was a militant antisecessionist and Jefferson Davis himself grew lukewarm toward the premise that any state has a right to go into business for herself.

[18] Then why? Because two opposing but comparatively small pressure groups were determined to have their way: the Northern high-tariff industrialists who wanted to buy in an open market and sell in a closed market, and the Southern cotton nabobs who wanted to buy and sell in a free market.

[19] The Abolitionists, zealous and vocal, didn't cut much ice at first, but when the North needed a shot in the arm the battle cry of freedom was raised, and the struggle became a crusade to liberate the Negro.

[20] "Mine eyes have seen the glory of the coming of the Lord —"

[21] The South, bled white and suffering from the moral and economic cancer of slavery, didn't have a chance.

[22] The Democratic Party broke into splinters in a squabble between Northern apologists for slavery and Southern firebrands for that "peculiar institution," as human bondage was called.

[23] Abraham Lincoln was elected president by a minority vote on a catch-all platform of protective tariff, Federal aid to railroads, free soil in the West and the slogan "Vote Yourself a Farm." On the slavery issue he shifted between the *status quo* and his premise that ". . . this government cannot endure, permanently half slave and half free . . ."

[24] However, Mr. Lincoln was a Unionist first, last and always. His position seems clear in his statement to Editor Horace Greeley in 1862, with the war underway.

[25] "If I could save the Union without freeing any slave, I would do it; and if I could save it by freeing all the slaves, I would do it; and if I could save it by freeing some and leaving others alone, I would also do that."

[26] These were the words of the Great Emancipator, a politician who grew into a statesman, a humanitarian who gave his life that his country might not commit suicide; the noblest of his era, whose words now sound sweet on Southern tongues and to most Southern ears.

[27] But in 1860, the South, more militant than wise, didn't trust Mr. Lincoln or the coalition that put him in power—the Republicans, the Protectionists, the Free-Soilers, the Know-Nothings and the Abolitionists.

[28] That was that.

[29] Sure, the Democrats still controlled Congress and the Dred Scott decision had favored the South, although many other slavery decrees had gone against her. Sure, secession would block the South from further expansion and, if successful, might make Dixie into a cotton patch for England's mills.

[30] However, the South was convinced that the North was inching her to the end of a limb and soon would cut it off.

[31] The country was in the paralyzed interval preceding Lincoln's inauguration, and South Carolina pulled out first. Mississippi, Georgia, Alabama, Florida, Louisiana and Texas joined her. At Montgomery, Alabama, they organized The Confederate States of America with Jefferson Davis as president. Mr. Davis (his family called him Jeffy) didn't want the job. He was a West Point graduate, a hero of the Mexican War, wounded once, and had served as Secretary of War. He wanted to be a soldier.

[32] Some Northerners were all for letting their sisters go in peace and good

riddance. Longer heads, however, began to see the true picture: every Gulf state was in secession and between them and the North were the buffer states of Delaware, Maryland, Virginia, North Carolina, Kentucky, Tennessee, Missouri and Arkansas. How could the Union attack without crossing these states? And yet, if the Confederacy were left alive it could make the Gulf of Mexico into a Southern mill pond.

[33]   Cuba and Mexico might be annexed into an agricultural empire that could trade raw materials for Europe's finished products. Abraham Lincoln was thinking of the Union, but Northern businessmen were shuddering at the thought of Europe's free-market goods at their back door, of losing the Southern market to England.

[34]   Meanwhile, first South Carolina and then the Confederacy was dickering for evacuation of Fort Sumter in Charleston harbor. South Carolina was fuming because the Union secretly had transferred the tiny garrison of untenable Fort Moultrie to Sumter. No one thought the Confederacy would tolerate a "foreign" garrison at the mouth of Charleston harbor. Here was the dynamite keg.

[35]   Mr. Lincoln became president in March, 1861, and his first official speech stressed peace and restoration of the Union. Slavery in the states where it then existed would not be disturbed, he said. But Federal forts and custom houses must be held.

[36]   Three Confederate commissioners arrived promptly in Washington to negotiate a treaty recognizing the independence of the Southern States and arranging payment for Federal property already seized and for Fort Sumter that must be evacuated.

[37]   President Lincoln did not receive them, but William Seward, his Secretary of State, dickered with them through a go-between. There was a lot of double-talk and the South was given the impression that Sumter soon would be evacuated because supplies were running out. This was not Abraham Lincoln's policy, but his cabinet, heavy with political appointees, figured it was going to run things. It learned better.

[38]   A "peaceful" supply ship was ordered to Sumter and Lincoln informed South Carolina that the fort would be defended. South Carolina notified the Confederacy and the spark glowed. Now here was a matter of national pride and politics, called face-saving by Orientals and prestige by Occidentals. Each side had put a chip on its shoulder, but the South had a tremendous advantage. The Confederacy was a going concern and the North must shoot or give up the gun.

[39]   Incredibly enough, it was the South that shot first. President Davis instructed Gen. P. G. T. Beauregard to reduce Sumter, and at dawn on April 12, 1861, the Confederate batteries opened fire. The dynamite keg blew up.

[40]   President Lincoln, acting as Commander in Chief of the United States Army, declared the Confederacy in rebellion. The secessionists were enraged at first, then amused. Rebels? It never had occurred to them. Rebels were hanged.

[41]   A rebellion is illegal unless it becomes a successful revolution. Rebels, in the broad sense, want change. The South wanted the "good old days"; the North wanted change. Lincoln, however, adroitly put the brand of rebellion on the South and it stuck because the United States had better propaganda weapons than the Confederacy and because it is the winners who write the records.

[42]   Next President Lincoln called for 75,000 volunteers to put down the "rebellion." Congress was not in session and he took the fateful step without call-

ing an extraordinary session. He didn't trust Congress and, besides, he was a man in a hurry. The onus of the first shot was on the South. So was the stigma of rebellion. Mr. Lincoln was playing his blue chips.

[43] Then the South moved. Virginia, the nation's foundation stone, spoke out that she would furnish no troops to the United States and, furthermore, no Yankees would cross her hills to get to her sisters. Quickly, she, North Carolina, Tennessee and Arkansas joined the Confederacy and told Mr. Lincoln to fish or cut bait.

[44] He fished. Delaware was safe. She was Yankee. Politically and militarily, Lincoln moved fast enough to save Maryland, Kentucky and Missouri for the Union, although they were split wide open. But, for that matter, so was much of the South, Virginia so badly that West Virginia seceded from her mother state and joined the Union. And there was enough Union sentiment in Arkansas for that slimly populated state to furnish 8289 white soldiers to the United States.

[45] The Confederate capital was moved to Richmond, Virginia. The stage was set, so let's look at the props.

[46] The loyal states' population was 21,955,513, including 429,501 slaves. The seceding states' population was 8,970,678, including 3,521,111 slaves and 260,000 free Negroes. For a while, the slaves were assets. They helped keep things going while the white men fought; a revolt, with the masters away, could have crushed the South to a pulp. But eventually the slaves became liabilities; as the invasion progressed, thousands of them joined the Union armies and others marauded the countryside.

[47] The United States mustered in about 1,550,000 soldiers, including many new immigrants, some who came over for homes and others to take advantage of liberal bounties for enlistment.

[48] The Confederacy mustered in about 800,000 from her white population of approximately 5,100,000, or roughly every seventh white person. This meant that just about every male old enough to chunk a rock got a lick at the Yanks. She had few immigrants in her armies, mostly because she had no way to get them in and no inducements to offer except an intangible thing called glory and a very tangible thing called death. However, more than one hundred of her important officers were foreigners; knights-errant who chose to lead the Southern armies because of the hell-for-leather fighters in their ranks.

[49] Much of the North's political and military leadership came from the Midwest and spoke the same language. The South's civil leadership was from the Gulf states and her military leadership from the Seaboard. They did not always see alike, for the Gulf Southerner lived in a conservative, new-rich culture that fostered Southern nationalism and the Seaboard Southerner looked to his state.

[50] The surprise of the Civil War is not that the South was defeated, but that she fought so long against such odds. She didn't have industry enough to support herself in peace, much less in war, and soon was using thorns for pins, pokeberry juice for ink, scraping smokehouse floors for salt, and saving urine for gunpowder.

[51] She assumed England would fight the Union blockade to get cotton for her mills. But many British mills already were idle due to overproduction and their warehouses were full of raw cotton. Instead of begging for Southern cotton, England soon was shipping cotton to the North. British nabobs sympathized with the South and dropped a few tokens into the kitty, but the British workingman hated slavery and there were more laborers than lords.

[52] European cheerleaders stood on

the side lines and whooped it up for little David while doing business with Goliath, but when it came to blood and death the South was alone.

[53] Then how did she last so long? For several reasons: she knew what she wanted from the very beginning, while the North couldn't quite make up its mind; she had interior lines for military communications, while the North had to conquer an area almost as large as Europe; she started off with superior military leadership, while the North had to develop its generals.

[54] Abraham Lincoln was the Atlas who held his country on his stooped shoulders until it found its strength. In the beginning, he was surrounded by political leeches and military dolts. Sophisticated Easterners called him an ignoramus, a Kentucky-born hillbilly, a hick lawyer from Illinois; Edwin Stanton, later his Secretary of War, called him a baboon.

[55] Lincoln didn't understand the intricacies of drawing-room diplomacy or the constitutional and economic problems of his country. At first he didn't understand the predatory interests that tried to use him. But he caught on quick and started slugging.

[56] He suspended the writ of habeas corpus, a right vested in Congress, and started throwing men in jail, even on suspicion of disloyalty. Constitutional? Of course not, but a man on the end of a rope doesn't get anywhere by yelling, "You can't hang me. It ain't legal."

[57] He assumed dictatorial prerogatives under contention the South was in rebellion, and carried his foreign policy in his hip pocket. He clamped a "legal" blockade on the Confederacy to keep out European ships, thus tacitly recognizing the *de facto* government of his enemies. He granted them certain belligerent rights, including sanctuary for prisoners instead of death. Once the North

reached for a rope to hang some "rebel" prisoners, but the South reached for two ropes, and nothing happened. All this simply meant that, by Northern reasoning, Johnny Reb was a lawful outlaw. Mr. Lincoln made up his rules as he went along. Mr. Davis tried to play a new game under the old rules.

[58] The North thought the average Southern soldier was a planter's son, a haughty slaver who had never read a book or thought seriously about things cultural. Dear, dear.

[59] For Johnny Reb was a poor boy from a little farm. He didn't think highly of the big planters either, but listened to them at first because they were so elegant and used such pretty words. However, he didn't aim to take much lip from the aristocrats, and none at all from the Yankees.

[60] The South thought the average Northern soldier was a rascal with a blue nose and yellow belly, threatening the sacred hearth of an English-Scotch-Irish people whose hearths were their altars.

[61] Really there was little difference between the boy from Georgia and the boy from Indiana, except one raised cotton and the other raised hay.

[62] Together they raised hell.

[63] Bull Run is a creek in Virginia, northeast of Manassas Junction where an east-west and a north-south railroad came together. Federal strategy was to cut this railroad, separate the Shenandoah Valley from Tidewater Virginia and march on down to Richmond.

[64] The Union had been successful in skirmishes along the Ohio River and over in West Virginia and so, in July, 1861, a Northern army came boiling down from Washington as though on a lark. Congressmen and their ladies followed in buggies to see the fun. There were flowers and songs, champagne and stirring speeches from the men who

wanted votes from the boys who carried muskets.

[65] The Confederates hit them at Bull Run and, after a fair-to-middling fracas, the Union army threw down its guns and melted away in a rout.

[66] Over near a farmhouse stood a stern man with a heavy black beard. He was Gen. Thomas J. Jackson, a praying man who didn't smoke or drink or cuss. He stood there like a stone wall, and they so named him.

[67] The North recoiled in panic and dismay from the First Battle of Manassas and the South herself couldn't quite believe it. She had scored a smashing victory the first time she'd gone into battle, and then she couldn't make up her mind what to do.

[68] Strategists have debated this hour ever since, some contending that had the Confeds pushed on they could have captured Washington and ended the war. In the next breath they argue that capture of Richmond would not have ended the war. Something doesn't add up.

[69] Anyway, the South did not invade and Johnny Reb found that Yankee champagne and some rebel red-eye to wash it down, sat in the shade alongside Bull Run, and waited until his head cleared from his celebration, and then wrote his little Lindy Lou.

[70] The Yanks were whipped and soon he'd be home to chop out the cotton and maybe get in a little fishing before picking time. He never got home and old Aunt Lou died a spinster, cursing Yankees for her loneliness and pouring her bitterness into the young, eager ears of the second and third generations, including me; my first memorized poem was:

> Under the sod and the dew,
>   Waiting the Judgment Day:—
> Under the one, the Blue;
>   Under the other, the Gray.

[71] The Federals recovered from the shock of Manassas and began galloping off in all directions. The military was riddled with politics, deadwood and stupidity. President Lincoln instructed Gen. George B. McClellan to organize an army and take Richmond. Little Mac was a good organizer and made a good speech. And if his ego could have been changed into powder it would have blown Dixie plum' the other side of Pago Pago.

[72] Little Mac collected 115,000 men and moved them by boat to the Peninsula of Virginia, down where the nation got started at Jamestown and where Pocahontas had thrown her arms around Capt. John Smith. It was the spring of 1862; somebody forgot to tell Little Mac that it rains in Virginia in the spring and that Southern mud is glue. His army floundered, and between him and Richmond were 65,000 Confederates under Gen. Joe Johnston. So he inched along in the mire. Little Mac was a cautious man.

[73] Let's leave him stuck in the mud and take a look at the whole picture and see in a few paragraphs what it took Washington a long, long time to see: that the Confederacy was a scorpion with a hundred legs and steel jaws. A freak? So was the Confederacy.

[74] The head was in Virginia and the body curved south and west along the railroads and rivers. Its stinger poked into the Mississippi River and fed the body from that end.

[75] A few long thinkers insisted right off that the only way to kill the scorpion was to paralyze it by nipping its legs and then working it over from its stinger to its head. In other words, begin at the tail and take the rivers and the railroads. These thinkers included Miss Anna Carroll, a Maryland pamphleteer, a propagandist and amateur strategist. Her advice was delayed in the

hip-hip-hooray of Washington's bedlam.

[76] Out there in the West, as the East called the Mississippi Valley, was Capt. Ulysses Simpson Grant, who had got nowhere in the Army or out of it. His real name was Hiram Ulysses. The Simpson came from Grandma Simpson in a name mix-up. The world had given U. S. Grant a hard time, due partly to tough luck and partly to liquor. At Georgetown, Ohio, where he was reared, the village wits called him Useless Grant.

[77] He was made a colonel because he was a West Point man and a Mexican War veteran. Besides, the regiment liked him and refused to serve under his predecessor. Soon they had to make him a general because he was willing to fight, although his uniform never fit. He loved horses and sometimes smoked a cigar if his nerves were jangling.

[78] Those closest to William Tecumseh Sherman, another Ohioan, called him "Cump." He, too, was a West Point and Mexican War man, but hadn't amounted to much either except as superintendent of a Louisiana college that now is Louisiana State University. He tried to run St. Louis' streetcar system and didn't quite make it, and was at a pretty low ebb when the Civil War began.

[79] They made him a colonel and he was at Manassas and then was transferred to the West. The newspapers didn't like him because he accused them of printing information that helped the enemy. A story was started that he was losing his mind. Oh, brother.

[80] Grant and Sherman got together in Tennessee.

[81] Back in Virginia, McClellan made a lunge at Richmond and the Confeds whiplashed him. Joe Johnston was wounded and Mr. Davis turned the Army of Northern Virginia over to his personal military adviser—Gen. Robert Edward Lee, called R. E. Lee and Marse Robert, but seldom Robert E.

[82] Lee and Jackson got together in Virginia.

[83] The Union Army, the Army of the Potomac, was thrashed soundly at the side door to Richmond and McClellan was relieved of command. He had given his name to a good Army saddle, thereby earning the gratitude of callused hoss soldiers.

[84] Gen. John Pope took over. He was all spit and polish and even more cautious than McClellan. Wisely he abandoned the Peninsula campaign. Unwisely he moved back around to Manassas and bragged what he was going to do to the Rebels. Lee licked his chops.

[85] Marse Robert had sent Stonewall Jackson over to the Shenandoah Valley in western Virginia to do a little house cleaning and General Jackson dusted the Yanks out while Lee kept Pope off balance. Then Jackson forcemarched his corps completely around the Army of the Potomac without Pope's knowledge and the Confederates squeezed him in the wringer and left him limp.

[86] Pope went out and McClellan came back, and the South invaded Maryland.

[87] This is where Barbara Frietchie came in at Frederick.

Dame Frietchie to Stonewall Jackson:

"Shoot, if you must, this old gray head,
But spare your country's flag," she said.
Jackson to his men:
"Who touches a hair on yon gray head
Dies like a dog! March on!" he said.

[88] McClellan met them around Antietam Creek (or Sharpsburg, if you are a Southerner) and fought them to a standstill. Here was a new McClellan, a wizard who maneuvered as if he knew Lee's plans.

[89] He did. He had a copy of Lee's Special Orders No. 191, found at Frederick wrapped around three cigars. Some

Confederate commander (D. H. Hill, perhaps?) lost his copy instead of swallowing it as they do in the movies, and it showed up as a cigar wrapper. Private B. W. Mitchell of the 27th Indiana Volunteers found it and had sense enough to realize it was valuable, thus proving he was wiser than some of the big brass. Private Mitchell was wounded at Antietam and died about four years later. His destitute widow did not even get a pension.

[90]   Lee loafed back to Virginia and McClellan hibernated. Lincoln tried to nudge him into action, but McClellan just sat; perhaps waiting for three more cigars.

[91]   Gen. A. E. Burnside took over. The press, President and public were screaming for a fight. Well, he'd give them one. Recklessly he lunged at Fredericksburg, Virginia. Calmly the entrenched Confederates cut him to bloody bits. Twelve thousand Union casualties bore testimony to his failure. General Burnside wept. He gave us a fashion of short side whiskers called sideburns.

[92]   Fighting Joe Hooker tried his hand and moved an army of 130,000 to Chancellorsville. The South had 60,000 and Lee divided these, running Jackson around Hooker's right flank while he feigned a frontal attack. Hooker never knew what hit him and again the Army of the Potomac was in confusion and defeat.

[93]   But Stonewall Jackson was killed.

[94]   The war's first half was over in Virginia and the ponderous Union armies had been outclassed by the swift-moving Confederates.

[95]   Lee's army needed shoes and there were shoes in Pennsylvania and in the fat towns along the turnpikes to Baltimore and Washington. There was Chambersburg and York and Lancaster, and the village of Gettysburg in a fringe

of hills. The time had come to give the North a dose of its own cure and the Army of Northern Virginia swung into Maryland and rolled north.

[96]   Jim Longstreet opposed the move. He wanted Lee to divide his army again, take two divisions to Tennessee, reorganize the Confederates down there, raise the siege of Vicksburg and invade through Ohio. Lee disagreed. He was invincible, so it seemed.

[97]   However, a few ominous portents were in the Southern skies. The Union naval blockade was as tight as a wet piece of rawhide and the Confederacy had pulled her belt to the third notch. President Lincoln had issued his Emancipation Proclamation, a political and military document that freed slaves in certain sections if arms could enforce it, and Northern soldiers were indoctrinated with a crusade for freedom.

[98]   The South had begun conscription in 1862, then repealed the provision that a man could hire a substitute to do his fighting, but left in the clause that exempted owners of twenty slaves or more. Some folks mumbled, "It's a rich man's war and a poor man's fight," and the Confederate states started bickering among themselves. They believed that States' rights included the right to act independently at the hour President Davis needed unity.

[99]   The North began drafting manpower in 1863 under a system even more vicious than the South's; it caused riots, but it got men. All this boded destruction of the Confederacy unless she could win quickly. And so did the most important fact of all: the Union had suffered casualties that would have dissipated most armies and yet they kept coming, three men rising where one fell. The South, herself dazed, was handing out much more punishment than she was taking, but she had to give more and take less to balance the ratio of resources.

[100] Some Eastern newspapers misspelled Donelson, a fort in West Tennessee. They spelled it "Donaldson." All it did was control the Cumberland River to Nashville and the Memphis & Charleston Railroad, two arteries that helped feed the scorpion's head up in Virginia.

[101] Gen. U. S. Grant plodded down through Kentucky and Tennessee. He had gunboats and he fought like an elephant instead of a fox. A Confederate army dug in at Donelson and, after a beating, suggested that Grant talk terms.

[102] His reply was blunt: "No terms except an unconditional and immediate surrender can be accepted. I propose to move immediately upon your works."

[103] Nathan Bedford Forrest swore the Confederate equivalent of "Nuts" and got his cavalry out, but about 15,000 Confeds were surrendered. The North's mouth popped open.

[104] The papers didn't know much about Grant and pulled their stories out of thin air. Somebody said he was smoking a cigar when he received the surrender and the folks almost swamped him with cigars. He became an inveterate smoker and eased up on his drinking. One of his generals was Lew Wallace, who later wrote *Ben Hur*.

[105] Gen. Albert Sidney Johnston, the Confederate commander in the West, consolidated his scattered forces and hit Grant at Shiloh Church, down on the Tennessee River.

[106] Sherman was with Grant by then and together they pulled a resounding victory out of seeming defeat. Johnston was killed.

[107] Shiloh was the greatest battle fought on the American continent up to that time. The North lost more than 13,000 men, the South more than 10,000 and it convinced the skeptics that a rivers-and-railroads strategy was the only way to win the Civil War.

[108] Three weeks after Shiloh, a Union fleet under Adm. David Farragut, a Tennessee mountaineer, captured New Orleans in a daring exploit that stunned the South. Then Memphis fell to a flotilla of river boats. By June of 1862 the scorpion was feeding itself through its stinger that poked into the Mississippi River at Vicksburg.

[109] Its legs had been cut off in Kentucky, Missouri, Arkansas and much of Tennessee and Louisiana. Its stinger must be pulled at Vicksburg, where river and railroad brought supplies to the Confederacy from as far away as Texas.

[110] There were five campaigns against Vicksburg, defended at the end by Gen. John Pemberton, a Pennsylvanian. There came the homemade Confederate ram *Arkansas*, single-handedly to scatter two Union fleets and scare off an army. There came Sherman to smash his legions against the bluffs while Grant was isolated back in North Mississippi.

[111] In desperation, Grant worked an army south of Vicksburg, cut entirely free from his line of supplies and wheeled north, lashing Confederate armies on both sides. The brilliant maneuver was Jacksonian in concept and execution. Grant learned he could be a fox as well as an elephant.

[112] Vicksburg fell like a ripe plum. That was July of 1863, at the same time Lee was recoiling from Gettysburg and George Meade's Union heroes.

[113] Gettysburg is the great storied battle of the war; more than 50,000 casualties between July 1, when it started, and July 4, when Lee limped away and Meade was too exhausted to follow him.

[114] That was the South's high tide and now it must ebb.

[115] Mississippi was ground into cinders and Tennessee was cut wide open along her railroads and rivers, down to Chattanooga where the Federals were hurt badly at Chickamauga in fighting that was bloodier than Gettysburg.

[116] Grant was called East to take Richmond and began grinding away, pouring men against the Army of Northern Virginia only to watch them melt away before Lee's shifting tactics.

[117] Sherman was given all the troops and supplies he needed and fought slowly down to Atlanta, the last deep South railroad center. That city was burned, Georgia was devastated and Sherman cut up into South Carolina; waste and misery in his path as he followed Joe Johnston's long retreat.

[118] It was all over, only there was no referee to stop the fight. The South kept going down, each time getting up more painfully than before. Her fatal weakness now was obvious: The Confederate States of America never were united states, only a nation stillborn.

[119] Lee's men were ghosts and Johnston's men were skeletons. Desertions were rampant and Sherman was moving north toward Richmond's back door. Grant made one more lunge and overran Lee's thin line. Marse Robert tried to get to the mountains to keep fighting, but Grant cornered him at Appomattox, eighty miles from Richmond. The Army of Northern Virginia passed into a few accurate history books, a hundred biased ones and a slew of historical novels.

[120] Johnston capitulated to Sherman near Durham, N. C. One by one the scattered Southern forces gave in while some of the leaders chose exile to surrender.

[121] The Northern generals gave liberal terms. Congress did not follow suit and Reconstruction was started.

[122] Abraham Lincoln was assassinated on April 14, 1865, by John Wilkes Booth of Maryland, an egomaniac. On April 26, Booth himself was trapped in a burning barn at Port Royal, Virginia, and shot to death by Sgt. Boston Corbitt. Later, while doorkeeper for the Kansas legislature, Corbitt went berserk and emptied two revolvers at the legislators, missing them all.

[123] Mrs. Lincoln's mind wandered, and Maj. Henry Rathbone, whose duty it was to protect the President and who failed that tragic night, went stark mad and killed his wife and himself.

[124] Annie Surratt tried to get to Pres. Andrew Johnson to plead for the life of her mother, Mrs. Mary Surratt, whose conviction for the Lincoln conspiracy looked tainted. Her way was blocked by Preston King, a New York politician, and Sen. James Lane of Kansas. Within a year King loaded his pockets with lead and stepped off a New York ferry, and Lane shot himself.

[125] The last great war between gentlemen started off in the stars and ended in the gutter.

[126] Eventually, the carpetbaggers were run out of the South, or absorbed, and then came native sons seeking favors by waving the Stars and Bars and singing *Dixie*. An old Confederate veteran (he was my grandpa-in-law) heard a stump orator rhapsodizing the paths of glory Johnnie Reb had trod in the Civil War. The old man called out, "Wait a minute, brother. What was *civil* about it?"

WRITING ASSIGNMENTS

1. The story of the greatest internal conflict in our history is here briefly told. In it Mr. Street begins with an interpretation of the issues, the causes of the conflict. He then discusses the strengths and weaknesses of the two sides and proceeds to narrate the sequence of significant events. He then reveals the outcome of the conflict and the reasons for it. He ends with a brief picture of the after-effects of the conflict. Following his same pattern, write the story of a conflict—a conflict that involves either individuals or groups or nations.

2. We often hear that the Civil War has never really ended. Can you describe current evidences of the fact that in some ways this may be true?

3. Who do you think is the most interesting and significant hero of the Civil War? Using what knowledge you possess or, if your instructor wishes, doing some research first, defend your answer.

Too Early Spring

STEPHEN VINCENT BENET

[1] I'm writing this down because I don't ever want to forget the way it was. It doesn't seem as if I could, now, but they all tell you things change. And I guess they're right. Older people must have forgotten or they couldn't be the way they are. And that goes for even the best ones, like Dad and Mr. Grant. They try to understand but they don't seem to know how. And the others make you feel dirty or else they make you feel like a goof. Till, pretty soon, you begin to forget yourself—you begin to think, "Well, maybe they're right and it was that way." And that's the end of everything. So I've got to write this down. Because they smashed it forever—but it wasn't the way they said it.

[2] Mr. Grant always says in comp. class, "Begin at the beginning." Only I don't know quite where the beginning was. We had a good summer at Big Lake but it was just the same summer. I worked pretty hard at the practice basket I rigged up in the barn, and I learned how to do the back jackknife. I'll never dive like Kerry but you want to be as all-round as you can. And, when I took my measurements, at the end of the summer, I was 5 ft. 9¾ and I'd gained 12 lbs. 6 oz. That wasn't bad for going on sixteen and the old chest expansion was O.K. You don't want to get too heavy, because basketball's a fast game, but the year before when I got my height, and I was so skinny, I got tired. But this year, Kerry helped me practice, a couple of times, and he seemed to think I had a good chance for the team. So I felt pretty set up—they'd never had a Sophomore on it

before. And Kerry's a natural athlete, so that means a lot from him. He's a pretty good brother, too. Most Juniors at State wouldn't bother with a fellow in High.

[3]   It sounds as if I were trying to run away from what I have to write down, but I'm not. I want to remember that summer, too, because it's the last happy one I'll ever have. Oh, when I'm an old man—thirty or forty—things may be all right again. But that's a long time to wait and it won't be the same.

[4]   And yet, that summer was different, too, in a way. So it must have started then, though I didn't know it. I went around with the gang as usual and we had a good time. But, every now, and then, it would strike me we were acting like awful kids. They thought I was getting the big head, but I wasn't. It just wasn't much fun—even going to the cave. It was like going on shooting marbles when you're in High.

[5]   I had sense enough not to try to tag after Kerry and his crowd. You can't do that. But when they all got out on the lake in canoes, warm evenings, and somebody brought a phonograph along, I used to go down to the Point, all by myself, and listen and listen. Maybe they'd be talking or maybe they'd be singing, but it all sounded mysterious across the water. I wasn't trying to hear what they said, you know. That's the kind of thing Tot Pickens does. I'd just listen, with my arms around my knees—and somehow it would hurt me to listen—and yet I'd rather do that than be with the gang.

[6]   I was sitting under the four pines, one night, right down by the edge of the water. There was a big moon and they were singing. It's funny how you can be unhappy and nobody knows it but yourself.

[7]   I was thinking about Sheila Coe. She's Kerry's girl. They fight but they get along. She's awfully pretty and she can swim like a fool. Once Kerry sent me over with her tennis racket and we had quite a conversation. She was fine. And she didn't pull any of this big sister stuff, either, the way some girls will with a fellow's kid brother.

[8]   And when the canoe came along, by the edge of the lake, I thought for a moment it was her. I thought maybe she was looking for Kerry and maybe she'd stop and maybe she'd feel like talking to me again. I don't know why I thought that—I didn't have any reason. Then I saw it was just the Sharon kid, with a new kind of bob that made her look grown-up, and I felt sore. She didn't have any business out on the lake at her age. She was just a Sophomore in High, the same as me.

[9]   I chunked a stone in the water and it splashed right by the canoe, but she didn't squeal. She just said, "Fish," and chuckled. It struck me it was a kid's trick, trying to scare a kid.

[10]   "Hello, Helen," I said. "Where did you swipe the gunboat?"

[11]   "They don't know I've got it," she said. "Oh, hello, Chuck Peters. How's Big Lake?"

[12]   "All right," I said. "How was camp?"

[13]   "It was peachy," she said. "We had a peachy counselor, Miss Morgan. She was on the Wellesley field-hockey team."

[14]   "Well," I said, "we missed your society." Of course we hadn't, because they're across the lake and don't swim at our raft. But you ought to be polite.

[15]   "Thanks," she said. "Did you do the special reading for English? I thought it was dumb."

[16]   "It's always dumb," I said. "What canoe is that?"

[17]   "It's the old one," she said. "I'm not supposed to have it out at night. But you won't tell anybody, will you?"

[18]   "Be your age," I said. I felt gen-

erous. "I'll paddle a while if you want," I said.

[19] "All right," she said, so she brought it in and I got aboard. She went back in the bow and I took the paddle. I'm not strong on carting kids around, as a rule. But it was better than sitting there by myself.

[20] "Where do you want to go?" I said.

[21] "Oh, back towards the house," she said in a shy kind of voice. "I ought to, really. I just wanted to hear the singing."

[22] "K.O.," I said. I didn't paddle fast, just let her slip. There was a lot of moon on the water. We kept around the edge so they wouldn't notice us. The singing sounded as if it came from a different country, a long way off.

[23] She was a sensible kid, she didn't ask fool questions or giggle about nothing at all. Even when we went by Petters' Cove. That's where the lads from the bungalow colony go and it's pretty well populated on a warm night. You can hear them talking in low voices and now and then a laugh. Once Tot Pickens and a gang went over there with a flashlight, and a big Bohunk chased them for half a mile.

[24] I felt funny, going by there with her. But I said, "Well, it's certainly Old Home Week"—in an offhand tone, because, after all, you've got to be sophisticated. And she said, "People are funny," in just the right sort of way. I took quite a shine to her after that and we talked. The Sharons have only been in town three years and somehow I'd never really noticed her before. Mrs. Sharon's awfully good-looking but she and Mr. Sharon fight. That's hard on a kid. And she was a quiet kid. She had a small kind of face and her eyes were sort of like a kitten's. You could see she got a great kick out of pretending to be grown-up—and yet it wasn't all pretending. A

couple of times, I felt just as if I were talking to Sheila Coe. Only more comfortable, because, after all, we were the same age.

[25] Do you know, after we put the canoe up, I walked all the way back home, around the lake? And most of the way, I ran, I felt swell, too. I felt as if I could run forever and not stop. It was like finding something. I hadn't imagined anybody could ever feel the way I did about some things. And here was another person, even if it was a girl.

[26] Kerry's door was open when I went by and he stuck his head out and grinned.

[27] "Well, kid," he said. "Stepping out?"

[28] "Sure. With Greta Garbo," I said, and grinned back to show I didn't mean it. I felt sort of lightheaded, with the run and everything.

[29] "Look here, kid—" he said, as if he was going to say something. Then he stopped. But there was a funny look on his face.

[30] And yet I didn't see her again till we were both back in High. Mr. Sharon's uncle died, back East, and they closed the cottage suddenly. But all the rest of the time at Big Lake, I kept remembering that night and her little face. If I'd seen her in daylight first, it might have been different. No, it wouldn't have been.

[31] All the same, I wasn't even thinking of her when we bumped into each other, the first day of school. It was raining and she had on a green slicker and her hair was curly under her hat. We grinned and said hello and had to run. But something happened to us, I guess.

[32] I'll say this now—it wasn't like Tot Pickens and Mabel Palmer. It wasn't like Junior David and Betty Page—though they've been going together ever since kindergarten. It wasn't like any of

those things. We didn't get sticky and sloppy. It wasn't like going with a girl.

[33] Gosh, there'd be days and days when we'd hardly see each other, except in class. I had basketball practice almost every afternoon and sometimes evenings and she was taking music lessons four times a week. But you don't have to be always twos-ing with a person, if you feel that way about them. You seem to know the way they're thinking and feeling, the way you know yourself.

[34] Now let me describe her. She had that little face and the eyes like a kitten's. When it rained, her hair curled all over the back of her neck. She wasn't a tall girl but she wasn't chunky—just light and well made and quick. She was awfully alive without being nervous—she never bit her finger-nails or chewed the end of her pencil, but she'd answer quicker than anyone in the class. Nearly everybody liked her, but she wasn't best friends with any particular girl, the mushy way they get. The teachers all thought a lot of her, even Miss Eagles. Well, I had to spoil that.

[35] If we'd been like Tot and Mabel, we could have had a lot more time together, I guess. But Helen isn't a liar and I'm not a snake. It wasn't easy, going over to her house, because Mr. and Mrs. Sharon would be polite to each other in front of you and yet there'd be something wrong. And she'd have to be fair to both of them and they were always pulling at her. But we'd look at each other across the table and then it would be all right.

[36] I don't know when it was that we knew we'd get married to each other, some time. We just started talking about it, one day, as if we always had. We thought maybe when we were eighteen. That was two years but we knew we had to be educated. You don't get as good a job, if you aren't. Or that's what people say.

[37] We weren't mushy either, like some people. We got to kissing each other good-by sometimes, because that's what you do when you're in love. It was cool, the way she kissed you, it was like leaves. But lots of the times we wouldn't even talk about getting married, we'd just play checkers or go over the old Latin, or once in a while go to the movies with the gang. It was really a wonderful winter. I played every game after the first one and she'd sit in the gallery and watch and I'd know she was there. You could see her little green hat or her yellow hair. Those are the class colors, green and gold.

[38] And it's a queer thing, but everybody seemed to be pleased. That's what I can't get over. They liked to see us together. The grown people, I mean. Oh, of course, we got kidded too. And old Mrs. Withers would ask me about "my little sweetheart," in that awful damp voice of hers. But, mostly, they were all right. Even Mother was all right, though she didn't like Mrs. Sharon. I did hear her say to Father, once, "Really, George, how long is this going to last? Sometimes I feel as if I just couldn't stand it."

[39] Then Father chuckled and said to her, "Now, Mary last year you were worried about him because he didn't take any interest in girls at all."

[40] "Well," she said, "he still doesn't. Oh, Helen's a nice child—no credit to Eva Sharon—and thank heaven she doesn't giggle. Well, Charles is mature for *his* age too. But he acts so solemn about her. It isn't natural."

[41] "Oh, let Charlie alone," said Father. "The boy's all right. He's just got a one-track mind."

[42] But it wasn't so nice for us after the spring came.

[43] In our part of the state, it comes pretty late, as a rule. But it was early this year. The little kids were out with

scooters when usually they'd still be having snowfights and, all of a sudden, the radiators in the classrooms smelt dry. You'd got used to that smell for months —and then, there was a day when you hated it again and everybody kept asking to open the windows. The monitors had a tough time, that first week—they always do when spring starts—but this year it was worse than ever because it came when you didn't expect it.

[44]   Usually, basketball's over by the time spring really breaks, but this year it hit us while we still had three games to play. And it certainly played hell with us as a team. After Bladesburg nearly licked us, Mr. Grant called off all practice until the day before the St. Matthew's game. He knew we were stale —and they've been state champions two years. They'd have walked all over us, the way we were going.

[45]   The first thing I did- was telephone Helen. Because that meant there were six extra afternoons we could have, if she could get rid of her music lesson any way. Well, she said, wasn't it wonderful, her music teacher had a cold? And that seemed just like Fate.

[46]   Well, that was a great week and we were so happy. We went to the movies five times and once Mrs. Sharon let us take her little car. She knew I didn't have a driving license but of course I've driven ever since I was thirteen and she said it was all right. She was funny—sometimes she'd be awfully kind and friendly to you and sometimes she'd be like a piece of dry ice. She was that way with Mr. Sharon too. But it was a wonderful ride. We got stuff out of the kitchen—the cook's awfully sold on Helen—and drove way out in the country. And we found an old house, with the windows gone, on top of a hill, and parked the car and took the stuff up to the house and ate it there. There weren't any chairs or tables but we pretended there were.

[47]   We pretended it was our house, after we were married. I'll never forget that. She'd even brought paper napkins and paper plates and she set two places on the floor.

[48]   "Well, Charles," she said, sitting opposite me with her feet tucked under, "I don't suppose you remember the days we were both in school."

[49]   "Sure," I said—she was always much quicker pretending things than I was—"I remember them all right. That was before Tot Pickens got to be President." And we both laughed.

[50]   "It seems very distant in the past to me—we've been married so long," she said, as if she really believed it. She looked at me.

[51]   "Would you mind turning off the radio, dear?" she said. "This modern music always gets on my nerves."

[52]   "Have we got a radio?" I said.

[53]   "Of course, Chuck."

[54]   "With television?"

[55]   "Of course, Chuck."

[56]   "Gee, I'm glad," I said. I went and turned it off.

[57]   "Of course, if you *want* to listen to the late market reports—" she said just like Mrs. Sharon.

[58]   "Nope," I said. "The market— uh—closed firm today. Up twenty-six points."

[59]   "That's quite a long way up, isn't it?"

[60]   "Well, the country's perfectly sound at heart, in spite of this damfool Congress," I said, like Father.

[61]   She lowered her eyes a minute, just like her mother, and pushed away her plate.

[62]   "I'm not very hungry tonight," she said. "You won't mind if I go upstairs?"

[63]   "Aw, don't be like that," I said. It was too much like her mother.

[64]   "I was just seeing if I could," she said. "But I never will, Chuck."

[65] "I'll never tell you you're nervous, either," I said. "I—oh, gosh!"

[66] She grinned and it was all right. "Mr. Ashland and I have never had a serious dispute in our wedded lives," she said—and everybody knows who runs *that* family. "We just talk things over calmly and reach a satisfactory conclusion, usually mine."

[67] "Say, what kind of a house have we got?"

[68] "It's a lovely house," she said. "We've got radios in every room and lots of servants. We've got a regular movie projector and a library full of good classics and there's always something in the icebox. I've got a shoe closet."

[69] "A what?"

[70] "A shoe closet. All my shoes are on tipped shelves, like Mother's. And all my dresses are on those padded hangers. And I say to the maid, 'Elsie, Madam will wear the new French model today.'"

[71] "What are my clothes on?" I said. "Christmas trees?"

[72] "Well," she said. "You've got lots of clothes and dogs. You smell of pipes and the open and something called Harrisburg tweed."

[73] "I do not," I said. "I wish I had a dog. It's a long time since Jack."

[74] "Oh, Chuck, I'm sorry," she said.

[75] "Oh, that's all right," I said. "He was getting old and his ear was always bothering him. But he was a good pooch. Go ahead."

[76] "Well," she said, "of course we give parties—"

[77] "Cut the parties," I said.

[78] "Chuck! They're grand ones!"

[79] "I'm a home body," I said. "Give me—er—my wife and my little family and—say, how many kids have we got, anyway?"

[80] She counted on her fingers. "Seven."

[81] "Good Lord," I said.

[82] "Well, I always wanted seven. You can make it three, if you like."

[83] "Oh, seven's all right, I suppose," I said. "But don't they get awfully in the way?"

[84] "No," she said. "We have governesses and tutors and send them to boarding school."

[85] "O.K.," I said. "But it's a strain on the old man's pocketbook, just the same."

[86] "Chuck, will you ever talk like that? Chuck, this is when we're rich." Then suddenly, she looked sad. "Oh, Chuck, do you suppose we ever will?" she said.

[87] "Why, sure," I said.

[88] "I wouldn't mind if it was only a dump," she said. "I could cook for you. I keep asking Hilda how she makes things."

[89] I felt awfully funny. I felt as if I were going to cry.

[90] "We'll do it," I said. "Don't you worry."

[91] "Oh, Chuck, you're a comfort," she said.

[92] I held her for a while. It was like holding something awfully precious. It wasn't mushy or that way. I know what that's like too.

[93] "It takes so long to get old," she said. "I wish I could grow up tomorrow. I wish we both could."

[94] "Don't you worry," I said. "It's going to be all right."

[95] We didn't say much going back in the car, but we were happy enough. I thought we passed Miss Eagles at the turn. That worried me a little because of the driving license. But, after all, Mrs. Sharon had said we could take the car.

[96] We wanted to go back again, after that, but it was too far to walk and that was the only time we had the car. Mrs. Sharon was awfully nice about it but she said, thinking it over, maybe we'd better wait till I got a license. Well, Father didn't want me to get one till I

was seventeen but I thought he might come around. I didn't want to do anything that would get Helen in a jam with her family. That shows how careful I was of her. Or thought I was.

[97] All the same, we decided we'd do something to celebrate if the team won the St. Matthew's game. We thought it would be fun if we could get a steak and cook supper out somewhere—something like that. Of course we could have done it easily enough with a gang, but we didn't want a gang. We wanted to be alone together, the way we'd been at the house. That was all we wanted. I don't see what's wrong about that. We even took paper plates, so as not to litter things up.

[98] Boy, that was a game! We beat them 36-34 and it took an extra period and I thought it would never end. That two-goal lead they had looked as big as the Rocky Mountains all the first half. And they gave me the full school cheer with nine Peters when we tied them up. You don't forget things like that.

[99] Afterwards, Mr. Grant had a kind of spread for the team at his house and a lot of people came in. Kerry had driven down from State to see the game and that made me feel pretty swell. And what made me feel better yet was his taking me aside and saying, "Listen, kid. I don't want you to get the swelled head, but you did a good job. Well, just remember this. Don't let anybody kid you out of going to State. You'll like it up there." And Mr. Grant heard him and laughed and said, "Well, Peters, I'm not proselytizing. But your brother might think about some of the Eastern colleges." It was all like the kind of dream you have when you can do anything. It was wonderful.

[100] Only Helen wasn't there because the only girls were older girls. I'd seen her for a minute. I wanted to tell her about that big St. Matthew's forward

—and—oh, everything. Well, you like to talk things over with your girl.

[101] Father and Mother were swell but they had to go on to some big shindy at the country club. And Kerry was going there with Sheila Coe. But Mr. Grant said he'd run me back to the house in his car and he did. He's a great guy. He made jokes about my being the infant phenomenon of basketball, and they were good jokes too. I didn't mind them. But, all the same, when I'd said good night to him and gone into the house, I felt sort of let down.

[102] I knew I'd be tired the next day but I didn't feel sleepy yet. I was too excited. I wanted to talk to somebody. I wandered around downstairs and wondered if Ida was still up. Well, she wasn't, but she'd left half a chocolate cake, covered over, on the kitchen table, and a note on top of it, "Congratulations to Mister Charles Peters." Well, that was awfully nice of her and I ate some. Then I turned the radio on and got the time signal—eleven—and some snappy music. But still I didn't feel like hitting the hay.

[103] So I thought I'd call up Helen and then I thought—probably she's asleep and Hilda or Mrs. Sharon will answer the phone and be sore. And then I thought—well, anyhow, I could go over and walk around the block and look at her house. I'd get some fresh air out of it, anyway, and it would be a little like seeing her.

[104] So I did—and it was a swell night—cool and a lot of stars—and I felt like a king, walking over. All the lower part of the Sharon house was dark but a window upstairs was lit. I knew it was her window. I went around back of the driveway and whistled once—the whistle we made up. I never expected her to hear.

[105] But she did, and there she was at the window, smiling. She made mo-

tions that she'd come down to the side door.

[106]   Honestly, it took my breath away when I saw her. She had on a kind of yellow thing over her night clothes and she looked so pretty. Her feet were so pretty in those slippers. You almost expected her to be carrying one of those animals that kids like—she looked young enough. I know I oughtn't to have gone into the house. But we didn't think anything about it—we were just glad to see each other. We hadn't had any sort of chance to talk over the game.

[107]   We sat in front of the fire in the living room and she went out to the kitchen and got us cookies and milk. I wasn't really hungry, but it was like that time at the house, eating with her. Mr. and Mrs. Sharon were at the country club, too, so we weren't disturbing them or anything. We turned off the lights because there was plenty of light from the fire and Mr. Sharon's one of those people who can't stand having extra lights burning. Dad's that way about saving string.

[108]   It was quiet and lovely and the firelight made shadows on the ceiling. We talked a lot and then we just sat, each of us knowing the other was there. And the room got quieter and quieter and I'd told her about the game and I didn't feel excited or jumpy any more— just rested and happy. And then I knew by her breathing that she was asleep and I put my arm around her for just a minute. Because it was wonderful to hear that quiet breathing and know it was hers. I was going to wake her in a minute. I didn't realize how tired I was myself.

[109]   And then we were back in that house in the country and it was our home and we ought to have been happy. But something was wrong because there still wasn't any glass in the windows and a wind kept blowing through them and we

tried to shut the doors but they wouldn't shut. It drove Helen distracted and we were both running through the house, trying to shut the doors, and we were cold and afraid. Then the sun rose outside the windows, burning and yellow and so big it covered the sky. And with the sun was a horrible, weeping voice. It was Mrs. Sharon's saying, "Oh, my God, oh, my God."

[110]   I didn't know what had happened, for a minute, when I woke. And then I did and it was awful. Mrs. Sharon was saying, "Oh, Helen—I trusted you . . ." and looking as if she were going to faint. And Mr. Sharon looked at her for a minute and his face was horrible and he said, "Bred in the bone," and she looked as if he'd hit her. Then he said to Helen—

[111]   I don't want to think of what they said. I don't want to think of any of the things they said. Mr. Sharon is a bad man. And she is a bad woman, even if she is Helen's mother. All the same, I could stand the things he said better than hers.

[112]   I don't want to think of any of it. And it is all spoiled now. Everything is spoiled. Miss Eagles saw us going to that house in the country and she said horrible things. They made Helen sick and she hasn't been back at school. There isn't any way I can see her. And if I could, it would be spoiled. We'd be thinking about the things they said.

[113]   I don't know how many of the people know, at school. But Tot Pickens passed me a note. And, that afternoon, I caught him behind his house. I'd have broken his nose if they hadn't pulled me off. I meant to. Mother cried when she heard about it and Dad took me into his room and talked to me. He said you can't lick the whole town. But I will anybody like Tot Pickens. Dad and Mother have been all right. But they say things about Helen and that's almost worse. They're

for me because I'm their son. But they don't understand.

[114] I thought I could talk to Kerry but I can't. He was nice but he looked at me such a funny way. I don't know—sort of impressed. It wasn't the way I wanted him to look. But he's been decent. He comes down almost every weekend and we play catch in the yard.

[115] You see, I just go to school and back now. They want me to go with the gang, the way I did, but I can't do that. Not after Tot. Of course my marks are a lot better because I've got more time to study now. But it's lucky I haven't got Miss Eagles though Dad made her apologize. I couldn't recite to her.

[116] I think Mr. Grant knows because he asked me to his house once and we had a conversation. Not about that, though I was terribly afraid he would. He showed me a lot of his old college things and the gold football he wears on his watch chain. He's got a lot of interesting things.

[117] Then we got talking, somehow, about history and things like that and how times had changed. Why, there were kings and queens who got married younger than Helen and me. Only now we lived longer and had a lot more to learn. So it couldn't happen now. "It's civilization," he said. "And all civilization's against nature. But I suppose we've got to have it. Only sometimes it isn't easy." Well, somehow or other, that made me feel less lonely. Before I'd been feeling that I was the only person on earth who'd ever felt that way.

[118] I'm going to Colorado, this summer, to a ranch, and next year, I'll go East to school. Mr. Grant says he thinks I can make the basketball team, if I work hard enough, though it isn't as big a game in the East as it is with us. Well, I'd like to show them something. It would be some satisfaction. He says not to be too fresh at first, but I won't be that.

[119] It's a boys' school and there aren't even women teachers. And, maybe, afterwards, I could be a professional basketball player or something, where you don't have to see women at all. Kerry says I'll get over that; but I won't. They all sound like Mrs. Sharon to me now, when they laugh.

[120] They're going to send Helen to a convent—I found out that. Maybe they'll let me see her before she goes. But, if we do, it will be all wrong and in front of people and everybody pretending. I sort of wish they don't—though I want to, terribly. When her mother took her upstairs that night—she wasn't the same Helen. She looked at me as if she was afraid of me. And no matter what they do for us now, they can't fix that.

WRITING ASSIGNMENTS

1. Explain what you think the author's purpose was in writing this story, what comment on life and people he seemed to be making. Refer to specific actions and characters in the story to support your ideas. Decide how successful you believe he was in fulfilling his purpose. Show why.

2. Describe a situation involving yourself or someone else in which the different ways that youth and adults look at things caused a conflict. Explain the reasons for the conflict, show what actions resulted, what conclusion was reached. Determine who you think was right or wrong.

3. Present your impressions of the characters in the story and show how the kind of person each character was helped to produce the unfortunate outcome.

PART 2

Reading the

DESCRIPTION

INTRODUCTION

A description—it must be pointed out immediately—does *not* tell you what something looks like, sounds like, feels like (in both meanings of the word feel), smells like, tastes like, or acts like. It does *not* tell you what something *is*. Rather, it tells you what one particular human being *thinks* something looks like, (etc.), what one particular human being *thinks* something *is*. This recognition of someone's doing the describing can be a valuable help in improving your reading (and, for that matter, your writing) of descriptions.

Asking Why

For, probably, in no other kind of writing is it as easy to lose sight of the forest because of the trees, to notice only the individual details and not the whole, to forget that someone's mind is at work here, that someone has selected these details for a purpose. No matter how objective and specific a description may be, it still presents someone's *interpretation* of a part of the real world, not the real world itself. And no matter how vividly you may remember some of the details, you have not really read the material until you have determined what that interpretation is.

By reminding yourself that some writer is behind the description, you will stay alert for the interpretation he is making.

Another way to explain what is meant by the writer's interpretation is to say that he selects the details to leave you the reader with a dominant impression of the subject. As he reacted to the real subject, so he wants you to react to his description of that subject.

These reactions to something—whether we call them interpretations or impressions—are what give descriptions their unifying force and meaning. Without them, the details are like rebels without a cause, wandering and aimless. So it is important to pin down further, and more specifically, the kind of reactions involved.

Asking What

There are basically two different kinds of reactions—and thus two kinds of statements—that have to be made clear here.

1. The first leads the writer to shape the material, to seek a unity in it, to fit it all into one pattern. What the writer is doing is finding some characteristic, some trait or quality—or possibly, of course, several—that sums up what his subject *is*. This *central characteristic* is what we might call the essence of the subject—that is, what it really means to the writer. All the details of his description are then used to illustrate, to make vivid to you, what this essential quality is. If the subject is a person, this central quality is usually some dominant trait of personality or character, something that is the key to all, or at least most, of the person's various acts, beliefs, and feelings. If the subject is a place, this central quality might be its dominant atmosphere, the "feel" of the place, which would be similar to the personality of a person. Or it might be what the place seems to stand for, what it might represent in a country or a society. In this case, this one place is really an illustration of some central quality in some larger geographic or social unit.

We might use advertising as an example. An advertisement about a new automobile doesn't merely present eight or ten specific but unconnected facts about that car; it has a point. It tries to use those specific facts to point out that this car is the fastest, the safest, the easiest to drive, or the most sophisticated. Or, since advertisers often do not know when to stop, it probably claims that the car is all of these at once. One of the new compact cars, for example, is described as the *biggest* of the small cars.

2. In addition to this kind of interpretive reaction, the writer may be transferring to the reader a reaction of approval or disapproval. This kind of reaction is a *judgment:* of good or bad, like or dislike, love or hate. Thus, a writer might be saying, "Kokomo is the quietest town in the USA" (first kind of reaction). But he might also be saying "That's why I love it" *or* "That's why I hate it" (second kind of reaction). Generally, then, this second kind of reaction —this *judgment*—is created because of the *central characteristic* the author has discovered as part of the first kind of reaction.

Both reactions may then be part of the central, controlling statement made by a single piece of description. But they may also be found separately. The first kind—the characterization—particularly, may often be found alone, with no additional judgment of good or bad, like or dislike.

Finally, you should have gathered by now that the usual subject of a description is a person or a place. Sometimes it is a non-human or non-living thing—a horse, say, on the one hand; an automobile, on the other. In any case, the subject is something from the real, physical world. In trying to convey the sense —the "feel"—of this real, physical world, the writer gathers his specific details around some controlling attitude or idea, some unifying interpretation. For it is really only when we place a part of the physical world in this kind of interpretive pattern that it can have any meaning for us.

IN READING THIS SECTION—

1. Be sure you determine the two kinds of reactions and statements: the *central characteristic* and the *judgment.*

2. Notice if both kinds of reactions and statements are made in all of the selections.

My Average Uncle

ROBERT P. TRISTRAM COFFIN

[1] He stood out splendidly above all my uncles because he did not stand out at all. That was his distinction. He was the averagest man I ever knew.

[2] You would never pick him out in a crowd. He became just another man the minute he was in one. So many more pounds of man. Good solid pounds, but just pounds. You would never remember his hair or his chin, or the shape of his ears. If he said something, you would agree with it, and an hour later, you would be sure you had said it yourself.

[3] Sometimes I think men like that get along about the best. They are the easiest on their houses, their wives, and their children. They are easiest on the world. They slide along without having to do anything about it as small boys do on their breeches after they have slid on them enough to wear them down smooth. The world is all so much pine needles under them.

[4] Uncle Amos was easy on his wives and children. He had three of them, in all. Wives, I mean. I never did get the count of his children straight, there were too many assortments of them. Three wives. It seemed surprising to me at the time. With all the trouble I had, myself, having to stand on my head and work my legs, or bung stones at cherrybirds, to keep the attention of just one girl for a month. I often won-

dered how Uncle Amos, who never stood on his head or whittled out even a butter-pat, could attract so many women as he did. With hair a little thin on his head, and legs that could not possibly do more than three and a half miles an hour on the road, there he was, with three families behind him. Of course, he had the families spaced. The wives of Uncle Amos did not come all at once. They were drawn out. One batch of children grew pretty well up by the time the next batch hove in sight, waddling and falling on their faces—to save their hands—as waddling children do.

[5] I knew my *Bible,* especially the marital parts, in which I took deep interest. I had read the *Bible* through many times under the eye of one particular aunt. I knew a lot about matrimony from that. But Uncle Amos had me puzzled. He had broken no commandments. All his marriages were open and above-board. He wasn't like the patriarchs who didn't always wait for one wife to go before another came. Yet Uncle Amos's status and his children's status were rather complicated.

[6] The women must have been drawn to him because he was so much like what an average fair husband would seem to a woman to be.

[7] This man made no flourishes to attract anybody. He never drove a fast

43

horse. He never wore trousers with checks any larger than an inch square—which, for the time, was conservative. His house never got afire and burned down just after the fire insurance had run out. Not one of his boys and girls ever got drowned or run over by the steam-cars. The few that died growing up died of diphtheria or scarlet fever, which were what children died of then, the usual ways.

[8]   Uncle Amos never had a fight.

[9]   Uncle Amos never lost a pocket-book. At least not one with much money in it.

[10]   Uncle Amos never went even as far as Boston.

[11]   But there he was, never making much money, but with all the comforts of home around him, eating his stewed eels, sitting in his galluses out in the orchard in the cool of the evening, with a plump baby to climb up in his lap, whenever he felt like having a baby on his lap and had his old trousers on and didn't care much what happened to him. There he was, shingling his house only when it got to leaking so it put the kitchen fire out. Drinking a little ale now and then, when he came by it easy. No big hayfields to worry about. No wife that craved more than one new dress a year, and that one she generally ran up herself on her sewing machine. One best pair of trousers to his name, which the moths got into, but not so deep but what they could be healed up with a needle. Not many books to excite him and keep him awake nights, or put ideas into his head and make him uneasy. No itch ever spreading out upon him to go out and take the world by its horns. There he was, in clover!

[12]   Amos was a Republican. But then, most everybody around was. It was an average condition. Uncle Amos didn't have much to do except carry a torch-light when the Republican Presidents got elected, as they did regularly. And if Uncle Amos got grease on him, it never was very much grease, and his current wife took it out of him with her hot iron. Politics passed him by. Great events passed him by. And big taxes.

[13]   But we nephews did not pass him by. We were strangely drawn to him. Especially when some of our specialist uncles wore us down with their cranki-ness and difference. I spent some of the quietest Sundays of my life in Uncle Amos's yard, lying under apple trees and listening to bees and not listening to Uncle Amos who was bumbling away at something he did not expect me to listen to at all. And caterpillars came suddenly down on fine wires shining like gold, and hit Uncle Amos on his bald spot, and he brushed them off and went on bumbling. The heat was a burden, and the apple blossoms fell to pieces and drifted down on me, and I could see the roof of the world over the black twigs they came from. These were my solidest hours of pure being. I did not have to do anything to live up to this quiet, friendly man. He did not expect me to stand on my head and show off, or go after his pipe, or keep the flies from lighting on his bald spot. And he always had lemon drops somewhere deep in his roomy pockets, fore or aft, and he liked to give them to me.

[14]   The only trouble Uncle Amos had in his life was after he had got through with it. When they came to bury him, they could not fix it so he could lie next to all his three women. He had liked them all equally well. But there was not enough of Uncle Amos to go round. So they put him on the end of the row.

[15]   Uncle Amos did not mind, I am sure. I am sure he sleeps average well.

WRITING ASSIGNMENTS

1. Write a character sketch, such as Mr. Coffin has done, of your favorite person of one kind or another. As he had done, first find one central quality or trait that you will use to define just what that person's distinction is. Then, to explain that quality, and thus the person, use concrete examples of the person's appearances, habits, actions, conversations. Be as specific as possible and select details that prove your opinions and ideas.

2. In Paragraph 13 Coffin describes one scene with his Uncle Amos that meant a great deal to him. Write a similar description of a memorable moment in your life, stressing, as Coffin does, actual things that you saw, did, said, felt that produced the significance of that scene.

3. Which is it better to be, average or outstanding? Or to put it another way, what kind of goals would you set for yourself to produce the best life?

New York

GAY TALESE

[1] New York is a city of things unnoticed. It is a city with cats sleeping under parked cars, two stone armadillos crawling up St. Patrick's Cathedral, and thousands of ants creeping on top of the Empire State Building. The ants probably were carried up there by wind or birds, but nobody is sure; nobody in New York knows any more about the ants than they do about the panhandler who takes taxis to the Bowery; or the dapper man who picks trash out of Sixth Avenue trash cans; or the medium in the West Seventies who claims, "I am clairvoyant, clairaudient and clairsensuous."

[2] New York is a city for eccentrics and a center for odd bits of information. New Yorkers blink twenty-eight times a minute, but forty when tense. Most popcorn chewers at Yankee Stadium stop chewing momentarily just before the pitch. Gum chewers on Macy's escalators stop chewing momentarily just before they get off—to concentrate on the last step. Coins, paper clips, ballpoint pens, and little girls' pocketbooks are found by workmen when they clean the sea lion's pool at the Bronx Zoo.

[3] A Park Avenue doorman has parts of three bullets in his head—there since World War I. Several young gypsy daughters, influenced by television and literacy, are running away from home because they don't want to grow up and

become fortunetellers. Each month a hundred pounds of hair is delivered to Louis Feder on 545 Fifth Avenue, where blond hairpieces are made from German women's hair; brunette hairpieces from Italian women's hair; but no hairpieces from American women's hair which, says Mr. Feder, is weak from too-frequent rinses and permanents.

[4] Some of New York's best-informed men are elevator operators, who rarely talk, but always listen—like doormen. Sardi's doormen listen to the comments made by Broadway's first-nighters walking by after the last act. They listen closely. They listen carefully. Within ten minutes they can tell you which shows will flop and which will be hits.

[5] On Broadway each evening a big, dark, 1943 Rolls-Royce pulls into Forty-Sixth Street—and out hop two little ladies armed with Bibles and signs reading, "The Damned Shall Perish." These ladies proceed to stand on the corner screaming at the multitudes of Broadway sinners, sometimes until 3 A.M., when their chauffeur in the Rolls picks them up, and drives them back to Westchester.

[6] By this time Fifth Avenue is deserted by all but a few strolling insomniacs, some cruising cab drivers, and a group of sophisticated females who stand in store windows all night and day wearing cold, perfect smiles. Like sentries they line Fifth Avenue—these window mannequins who gaze onto the quiet street with tilted heads and pointed toes and long rubber fingers reaching for cigarettes that aren't there.

[7] At 5 A.M. Manhattan is a town of tired trumpet players and homeward-bound bartenders. Pigeons control Park Avenue and strut unchallenged in the middle of the street. This is Manhattan's mellowest hour. Most *night* people are out of sight—but the *day* people have not yet appeared. Truck drivers and cabs are alert, yet they do not disturb the

mood. They do not disturb the abandoned Rockefeller Center, or the motionless night watchmen in the Fulton Fish Market, or the gas-station attendant sleeping next to Sloppy Louie's with the radio on.

[8] At 5 A.M. the Broadway regulars either have gone home or to all-night coffee shops where, under the glaring light, you see their whiskers and wear. And on Fifty-First Street a radio press car is parked at the curb with a photographer who has nothing to do. So he just sits there for a few nights, looks through the windshield, and soon becomes a keen observer of life after midnight.

[9] "At 1 A.M.," he says, "Broadway is filled with wise guys and with kids coming out of the Astor Hotel in white dinner jackets—kids who drive to dances in their fathers' cars. You also see cleaning ladies going home, always wearing kerchiefs. By 2 A.M. some of the drinkers are getting out of hand, and this is the hour for bar fights. At 3 A.M. the last show is over in the night clubs, and most of the tourists and out-of-town buyers are back in hotels. And small-time comedians are criticizing big-time comedians in Hanson's Drugstore. At 4 A.M. after the bars close, you see the drunks come out—and also the pimps and prostitutes who take advantage of drunks. At 5 A.M., though, it is mostly quiet. New York is an entirely different city at 5 A.M."

[10] At 6 A.M. the early workers begin to push up from the subways. The traffic begins to move down Broadway like a river. And Mrs. Mary Woody jumps out of bed, dashes to her office and phones dozens of sleepy New Yorkers to say in a cheerful voice, rarely appreciated: "Good morning. Time to get up." For twenty years, as an operator of Western Union's Wake-Up Service, Mrs. Woody has gotten millions out of bed.

[11] By 7 A.M. a floridly robust little man, looking very Parisian in a blue beret

and turtle-neck sweater, moves in a hurried step along Park Avenue visiting his wealthy lady friends—making certain that each is given a brisk, before-breakfast rubdown. The uniformed doormen greet him warmly and call him either "Biz" or "Mac" because he is Bis Mackey, a ladies' masseur extraordinaire. He never reveals the names of his customers, but most of them are middle-aged and rich. He visits each of them in their apartments, and has special keys to their bedrooms; he is often the first man they see in the morning, and they lie in bed waiting for him.

[12] The doormen that Biz passes each morning are generally an obliging, endlessly articulate group of sidewalk diplomats who list among their friends some of Manhattan's most powerful men, most beautiful women and snootiest poodles. More often than not, the doormen are big, slightly Gothic in design, and the possessors of eyes sharp enough to spot big tippers a block away in the year's thickest fog. Some East Side doormen are as proud as grandees, and their uniforms, heavily festooned, seem to come from the same tailor who outfitted Marshal Tito.

[13] Shortly after 7:30 each morning hundreds of people are lined along Forty-Second Street waiting for the 8 A.M. opening of the ten movie houses that stand almost shoulder-to-shoulder between Times Square and Eighth Avenue. Who are these people who go to the movies at 8 A.M.? They are the city's insomniacs, night watchmen, and people who can't go home, do not want to go home, or have no home. They are derelicts, homosexuals, cops, hacks, truck drivers, cleaning ladies and restaurant men who have worked all night. They are also alcoholics who are waiting at 8 A.M. to pay forty cents for a soft seat and to sleep in the dark, smoky theatre. And yet, aside from being smoky, each

of Times Square's theatres has a special quality, or lack of quality, about it. At the Victory Theatre one finds horror films, while at the Times Square Theatre they feature only cowboy films. There are first-run films for forty cents at the Lyric, while at the Selwyn there are always second-run films for thirty cents. But if you go to the Apollo Theatre you will see, in addition to foreign films, people in the lobby talking with their hands. These are deaf-and-dumb movie fans who patronize the Apollo because they read the subtitles. The Apollo probably has the biggest deaf-and-dumb movie audience in the world.

[14] New York is a city of 38,000 cab drivers, 10,000 bus drivers, but only one chauffeur who has a chauffeur. The wealthy chauffeur can be seen driving up Fifth Avenue each morning, and his name is Roosevelt Zanders. He earns $100,000 a year, is a gentleman of impeccable taste and, although he owns a $23,000 Rolls-Royce, does not scorn his friends who own Bentleys. For $150 a day, Mr. Zanders will drive anyone anywhere in his big, silver Rolls. Diplomats patronize him, models pose next to him, and each day he receives cables from around the world urging that he be waiting at Idlewild, on the docks, or outside the Plaza Hotel. Sometimes at night, however, he is too tired to drive any more. So Bob Clarke, his chauffeur, takes over and Mr. Zanders relaxes in the back.

[15] New York is a town of 3,000 bootblacks whose brushes and rhythmic rag snaps can be heard up and down Manhattan from midmorning to midnight. They dodge cops, survive rainstorms, and thrive in the Empire State Building as well as on the Staten Island Ferry. They usually wear dirty shoes.

[16] New York is a city of headless men who sit obscurely in subway booths all day and night selling tokens to people in a hurry. Each weekday more than

4,500,000 riders pass these money-changers who seem to have neither heads, faces, nor personalities—only fingers. Except when giving directions, their vocabulary consists largely of three words: "How many, please?"

[17]   Each afternoon in New York a rather seedy saxophone player, his cheeks blown out like a spinnaker, stands on the sidewalk playing *Danny Boy* in such a sad, sensitive way that he soon has half the neighborhood peeking out of windows tossing nickels, dimes and quarters at his feet. Some of the coins roll under parked cars, but most of them are caught in his outstretched hand. The saxophone player is a street musician named Joe Gabler; for the past thirty years he has serenaded every block in New York and has sometimes been tossed as much as $100 a day in coins. He is also hit with buckets of water, empty beer cans and eggs, and chased by wild dogs. He is believed to be the last of New York's ancient street musicians.

[18]   New York is a town of nineteen midget wrestlers. They all can squeeze into the Hotel Holland's elevator, six can sleep in one bed, eight can be comfortably transported to Madison Square Garden in the chauffeur-driven Cadillac reserved for the midget wrestlers.

[19]   In New York from dawn to dusk to dawn, day after day, you can hear the steady rumble of tires against the concrete span of George Washington Bridge. The bridge is never completely still. It trembles with traffic. It moves in the wind. Its great veins of steel swell when hot and contract when cold; its span often is ten feet closer to the Hudson River in summer than in winter. It is an almost restless structure of graceful beauty which, like an irresistible seductress, withholds secrets from the romantics who gaze upon it, the escapists who jump off it, the chubby girl who lumbers across its 3,500-foot span trying to re-

duce, and the 100,000 motorists who each day cross it, smash into it, short-change it, get jammed up on it.

[20]   When street traffic dwindles and most people are sleeping in New York, some neighborhoods begin to crawl with cats. They move quickly through the shadows of buildings; night watchmen, policemen, garbage collectors and other nocturnal wanderers see them—but never for very long. There are 200,000 stray cats in New York. A majority of them hang around the fish market, or in Greenwich Village, and in the East and West Side neighborhoods where garbage cans abound. No part of the city is without its strays, however, and all-night garage attendants in such busy neighborhoods as Fifty-Fourth Street have counted as many as twenty of them around the Ziegfeld Theatre early in the morning. Troops of cats patrol the water-front piers at night searching for rats. Subway trackwalkers have discovered cats living in the darkness. They seem never to get hit by trains, though some are occasionally liquidated by the third rail. About twenty-five cats live seventy-five feet below the west end of Grand Central Terminal, are fed by the underground workers, and never wander up into the daylight.

[21]   New York is a city in which large, cliff-dwelling hawks cling to skyscrapers and occasionally zoom to snatch a pigeon over Central Park, or Wall Street, or the Hudson River. Bird-watchers have seen these peregrine falcons circling lazily over the city. They have seen them perched atop tall buildings, even around Times Square. About twelve of these hawks patrol the city, sometimes with a wingspan of thirty-five inches. They have buzzed women on the roof of the St. Regis Hotel, have attacked repairmen on smokestacks, and, in August, 1947, two hawks jumped women residents in the recreation yard

of the Home of the New York Guild for the Jewish Blind. Maintenance men at the Riverside Church have seen hawks dining on pigeons in the bell tower. The hawks remain there for only a little while. And then they fly out to the river, leaving pigeons' heads for the Riverside maintenance men to clean up. When the hawks return, they fly in quietly—*unnoticed*, like the cats, the headless men, the ants, the ladies' masseur, the doorman with three bullets in his head, and most of the other offbeat wonders in this town without time.

WRITING ASSIGNMENTS

1. Describe a city or a section of a city. In doing this, first, as Mr. Talese did, choose one or two significant qualities you want to stress about the place, qualities which capture the spirit, the "feel" of the place. Then choose examples, to illustrate those qualities. These examples, again like Mr. Talese's, should be specific stories of things that happen, specific descriptions of people or places.

2. Where would you rather live, in a small, country town or in a big city? In defending your answer to this question, itemize those things you feel one has to offer and those drawbacks the other is stuck with. Again, get as specific as you can by referring to individual places, events, people.

3. Describe the different kinds of people you find at some public event or vacation spot. For each type of person explain his qualities or traits by showing what they actually *do* at this event or vacation spot.

Miami—Florida's Gold Coast

BUDD SCHULBERG

[1] Florida's first recorded tourist was a certain Mr. Ponce de Leon, who checked in from Puerto Rico (another resort he had recently captured) in 1513. He was in search—so legend has it—of a marvelous water that could restore his vanished youth. Though he cruised down the entire east coast of what he called "Florida Island" he was never to find his magic fountain.

[2] Present-day visitors to the same golden shores think old Ponce found it all right. Trouble was, he didn't recognize it when it was there all around him. The Fountain of Youth, they'll tell you, is simply the magic combination of Florida

sunshine and Gulf Stream waters. Every winter one of the largest human migrations of all time draws Americans south from the damp cold of the Atlantic Seaboard and the freezing Middle West into the subtropical comfort of the fabulous Southeast Florida coast.

[3] Millions of vacationers, moving toward the sun in private Pullmans, yachts, planes, luxury trains, chauffeur-driven limousines, excursion-rate coaches, or as part of an armada of private cars and busses, pour into a hundred-mile stretch of beach from Jupiter Island, at Hobe Sound at the north, to Miami Beach, near the southern tip of the mainland. This is the Gold Coast, where—in true "nothing's-too-good-for-the-tourist" spirit—even the Gulf Stream obligingly curves in closer to shore than at any other section of the coastline, bringing the big fish within casting range of the beaches, bringing ideal swimming, evening breezes that rustle the palm leaves and fan the warm evenings, and a climate that often measures up to the extravagant claims of the travel folders.

[4] Yet, for all its uniformity of sunlight, sand and sparkling water, the Gold Coast is a study in contrast—the very rich withdrawing to their secluded estates on Jupiter Island or settling down for a season of stylized gaiety behind the great walls of their Palm Beach mansions; the sporting rich nosing their great yachts into the serene waters of Lake Worth or Bahia Mar at Fort Lauderdale, or arriving at Delray or Gulf Stream with their polo ponies; the new rich from Broadway and Hollywood basking in their Boca Raton and Miami Beach cabanas; the swarm of middle-income vacationers crowding the second-class hotels and mushrooming motor courts (many of them as ornate in their own way as the towering monuments to spendthrift ease that form the incredible coast line of Miami Beach); the plebeians

who fill the fishing camps or park their trailers along deserted beaches—for between the famous resorts there are still miles of deserted water front where you can surf cast for pompano, camp out and indulge the illusion that you have established your own tropical (and peaceful) beachhead.

[5] On the south is the hurdy-gurdy of Miami, to the north the genteel and exclusive well-being of the Palm Beach Bath and Tennis Club; but at any number of perhaps unglamorous yet appealing spots around Hillsboro Inlet and Port Everglades you will find devoted fishermen, oblivious of sixty-dollar-a-day hotel rooms, twenty-dollar swimming shorts, sixty-dollar-a-day charter boats and elaborately tiled Florentine swimming pools, simply enjoying the dazzling reflections on the blue-green water as they wait for the strike of grouper, king mackerel, snook, amberjack, tarpon or any of the hundreds of other varieties of pan and sporting fish that make this one of the world's great fishing grounds. But while there's everything here from blues and channel bass to sailfish and marlin, and while the charter-boat business from Stuart to Miami has become a multimillion-dollar proposition, fishing is still a minor thread in the Gold Coast pattern.

[6] The average Gold Coaster, from blue-blooded members of the Palm Beach Everglades Club to the first-generation-American Horatio Algers at Hollywood Beach or Miami, is an indolent vacationer who rises for a late breakfast under a sun umbrella in his patio or in his cabana by the pool, idles the time away at cards or gossip, enjoys a sun bath, a brief dip, a massage, maybe tries his luck at the track or in the Gulf Stream, retires for a late afternoon siesta, reappears for cocktails glowing with health and expensively attired in fashionable or flashy evening resort style, dines elaborately, and goes out for an alcoholic

evening of night clubbing or private partying that may last until the sun begins to rise out of the sea. That's the general idea, by and large, whether your name is in the social register or just in the telephone book, whether you're paying a hundred dollars a day for a suite or a mere hundred a week for a room in one of the new glorified motels built around a luxurious swimming pool. Physical ease, indulgent comfort, tropical splendor—these qualities rather than strenuous play make the Palm Beach — Miami Beach axis the Riviera of the New World—the most popular, most lucrative and most celebrated watering place since man first began to grumble about cold weather and to move toward the equator to escape the ice age nipping at his ankles.

[7] Reclining on beach chairs by the edge of the hotel pool with tall rum drinks in their freshly manicured and sun-lacquered hands, a middle-aged couple surveyed the cream-puff clouds in the powder-blue sky, the royal palms, the twinkling surface of the sea, the tanned, well-cared-for bodies of their fellow guests. I heard the lady sigh, "Look, Leo, like a picture—it's so beautiful!"

[8] Leo's head, shiny with sun oil, moved lazily in little nods of contentment. At his feet the Miami *Herald* headlined the latest cold wave in the North. The tone of his voice seemed to combine layer on layer of culture and sun-tan lotion. "Who else but God could make something so perfect?"

[9] I am not one to question pious sentiments, but Miami Beach—indeed the entire Gold Coast—is actually one of the more spectacular collaborations between God and His supreme creation. God made the sun to shine (average year-round temperature 75°) six days out of seven; God saw to it that this region was free of the pollens that plague hay-fever

victims (severe cases clear up in twenty-four hours); God produced sand and water and fish in abundance. But there God called a halt. There He leaned back and folded His Great Hands as if to say, "All right, children, I gave you a start—now let's see what you can do."

[10] Man took over, a mere half century ago, with a sustained burst of energy, imagination, cussed disregard for physical obstacles and concentration on the main chance that has come to be recognized and hailed as American enterprise.

[11] Thus did Miami Beach become the Manhattan of the Gold Coast, the vacation Mecca (in terms of numbers attracted and dollars spent) of the entire world.

[12] Driving along hotel-happy Collins Avenue or along Fifth Avenue-like Lincoln Road it seems almost impossible to conceive of Miami Beach less than forty years ago as a desolate sand bar cut off from the mainland and surrounded by swampy mangrove islands.

[13] A visionary horticulturist by the name of Collins thought it might be developed into tropical farm land, but no ordinary person would have offered a nickel for it. Along came Carl Fisher, an irrepressible millionaire from Indianapolis. Fisher liked to move fast. He had graduated from bicycle racing as a boy to rivaling Barney Oldfield in the early racing-car days: he spark-plugged the Prest-O-Lite Company into a multimillion profit, then decided to play God to Miami Beach. In lieu of supernatural powers he used great gobs of money; for an extended period he spent $50,000 a day. He declared let there be islands, and the picturesque islands of the present-day water-front villas rose out of Biscayne Bay; let there be canals, and miles of Venetianlike waterways appeared, to provide what is now a popular and rewarding $2 sight-seeing tour; let

there be travel between the mainland and the islands, and soon spanning the Bay were the great causeways that annually channel some two million visitors into sunny and money-happy Miami Beach; let there be magnificent playground hotels, and lo, year by year, the despised sand bar of 1910 became the foundation for the greatest concentration of luxury hotels on earth. In 1930 there were 61 enormous hotels along the eight-mile beach. By 1935 there were forty more; by 1940 over 260; a hundred more have gone up since the war, and even as this is being written ten more are rising into the sky with fairy-tale rapidity, each one a million-dollar deal, each seemingly larger and more beglamoured than the last, a fantastic total of 370, each with its palm-bordered, De Mille[1]-inspired swimming pool, its *moderne* sun deck, its shaded patios for alfresco dining, its svelte cocktail lounge, its lavish dancing pavilion with its own Broadway stars, its own streamlined shopping arcade—even, in more relaxed days, its own bookie, who was glad to shell out $50,000 for the season's concession.

[1] The late director of movie "spectacles."

Miami

EDMUND WILSON

[1] *Miami:* I have never been here before and am astounded and appalled by this place. It is not that it is particularly different from other American seaside resorts, from Asbury Park to Coronado Beach, but that here both the cheap and the expensive aspects have been developed on a scale that I have never elsewhere seen equalled. You have acres of nougat-like shops, mountain ranges of vanilla ice-cream hotels. Miami Beach goes on for miles, with its monotonous lines of palms, its thousands of hotels and houses which seem to have had imposed on them, by the exigency of a city-planning board, a blanched and insipid uniformity. It even makes one feel more kindly toward Southern California, with its elements of lunatic fantasy. What draws people down to this vacuum? How do they amuse themselves here?

[2] These vacationists look soft and vapid. You rarely see a really pretty girl, and the men do not give the impression of doing much fishing or swimming. You find them at the movies in the evening. The American ideal of luxury is in Miami carried to lengths that I have never encountered before. At my hotel, I had the annoyance of removing encasements of cellophane from the toilet seat and the drinking tumbler.

[3] In the movie-house, the seats are the kind that swing noiselessly back and forth to let people get in and out, and their cushions melt beneath one like a featherbed. A subdued indirect lighting,

like the sweet creamy liquid of an ice-cream soda, bathes a dove-gray and shrimp-pink interior, the walls of which are ornamented with large cameo-like white seashells framing naked mythological figures that seem to have been badly imitated from the bas-reliefs of Paul Manship in Rockefeller Center, and with branching white plaster exfoliations that remind one of the legs and defensive antennae of the crayfish in the Miami aquarium.

[4]   The film—*Oh, You Beautiful Doll* —was a technicolor that covered the whole surface of a high and overpowering screen with a routine sentimental romance, trumped up to manufacture glamor from the career of an American song-writer whose songs were widely sung in my college days. They were commonplace enough then, and today they are simply sickly. These attempts on the part of Hollywood to exploit the immediate past—in which the fashions of the eighties and nineties are sometimes confused with those of the twenties—show the precipitous decline of the movies as purveyors of entertainment, since the producers, after wrecking such contemporary talent as their salaries have tempted to Hollywood, have now been obliged to fall back on the favorites, first, second or third rate, of the day before yesterday and yesterday, when it was possible for a producer or an actor, a composer or a dancer, to perfect an art of his own and create for himself a reputation. Yet this product has its steady customers: one finds oneself among them here. Comfortably padded in the muffled atmosphere that seems to smell of scented face-powder— one cannot tell whether the theater has been perfumed or the women are all using the same cosmetics—this inert and featureless drove that have been drifting through the bleached sunny streets now sit watching stereotyped characters that

are made to appear impressive by being photographed in very bright colors and gigantically magnified.

[5]   The three shorts that follow the first showing of the film all happen to deal with animals: a hunting number, an animated cartoon that gets some not ill-deserved laughs, and a picture about racing whippets. The commentator seems slightly embarrassed at the spectacle of the uniformed attendants who have a full-time job grooming the whippets. "You may think they work as hard as the dogs," he propounds, with his microphone emphasis that gropes through time and space and can never drive any nails. "Well, they work a lot *harder!*" The truth is that so many Americans, specialized in operating machines or in transacting long-distance business, have deteriorated as animal organisms, that we now have a special pleasure in watching almost any agile animal. What the audience gets out of these animal shorts is the same thing that I have been getting out of looking out the window at the birds and contrasting them with the Miami vacationers.

[6]   This is all the kind of thing, I realize, that strikes foreigners who visit this country, but that I have long ago arranged my life in such a way as to avoid or ignore, so that I am likely to be shocked by and to discount the uncomplimentary reports of visitors. Miami is a rude revelation: I had not really known this was going on. I read uneasily of President Truman's recent arrival in Florida for one of a long series of sunlit holidays. This is the place where he seems most at home.

[7]   It is only when I get to the airfield that my national self-respect picks up. It is a feat to have conceived, to have built and to navigate these passenger planes. We humans have contrived our wings by deliberate calculations, out of

inorganic materials, instead of growing them out of our bodies, and this does leave us less hardy than the buzzard, less graceful than the white egret; but we have, after all, by our planes, in other ways surpassed the birds and there had been moments in Miami when I was doubtful of that before I took off for Haiti. And those disparate rhythms of flight that I found so delightful to watch, Walt Disney, in his film *Snow White,* where deer and rabbits and other animals are shown running together at different speeds and gaits, has rendered them for the first time in plastic art. The multiplied drawings of the studio that turns out the Disney cartoons are as anonymous as the hundreds of parts that go to make up a plane. I couldn't myself have invented the simplest of these mechanisms or processes; but the current prestige of the United States is partly derived from these, and I cannot help feeling a pride in them.

WRITING ASSIGNMENTS

1. These two articles illustrate a complimentary and then a critical interpretation of the same place. Choose a comparable resort, vacation or entertainment spot and describe it in one of these two ways—using judgments and carefully chosen details to make it seem very appealing or very appalling. In other words, why I like or why I hate _____.

2. An interesting experiment would be to describe a single place in both a complimentary *and* a critical way. Take each approach in a separate paragraph or two (don't try to combine them in one unified statement) and change your judgments and the details that you emphasize so that the reader gets a different impression of the place from each of your descriptions.

3. Would *you* like to vacation in Miami? If so, what would you look forward to; what are its attractions for you? If not, what would keep you away? What is unappealing about it?

The Innocence of Marilyn Monroe

DAVID SYLVESTER

[1] Think of the names Gish, Pickford, Garbo, Dietrich, Harlow, Stanwyck, Bergman, Hayworth. They evoke something more than a face, a voice, a shape, expressions on the face, inflexions of the voice, movements of the shape: they evoke a personality so clearly defined as to embody a mode of feeling, an attitude towards the world, a personality issuing from the fertilization of natural endowments by a collective wish or ideal current at that time the star was born. It is a personality confirmed by film after film—even by films in which the star may play a character that is out of character, so certain do we feel that this can only be a disguise. For its attributes belong as much to her, and she to them, as love to Venus or wisdom to Minerva.[1] Her personality becomes more tangible than flesh and blood, delivering her from the ravages of time, and making her ageless as a goddess, in that her magic does not die with her beauty but endures as long as what she stands for casts its spell. Conversely, if the ideal she embodies loses its hold, the magic will be drained from her long before her beauty (though she may then be reborn, as Joan Crawford was, on abandoning musical comedy for raging passion, the

same in body but renewed in spirit—one might even say, renewed in body, and the same only in name). So much more potent, indeed, is the myth of a star than her physical reality, that she is real even for those who have never seen her on the screen, so real they no longer know whether they have ever seen her.

[2] It is her possession of—or rather her possession by—a clear-cut personality, as limited as it is vivid, that differentiates the star as a species from the actress. From time to time, however, a star appears who is not possessed by a really distinct personality. Generally, as in the case of Anne Baxter, this is because she falls between being a star and being an actress. But lately Hollywood has bred a star who is as surely a star as she is surely not an actress, yet failed to find an ideal she could embody. It has created an ideal Ava Gardner, an ideal Judy Holliday an ideal Audrey Hepburn, an ideal Grace Kelly, had done so by the time they had starred in a single film. Yet with the brightest star of the cinemascopic era, filmdom's pink-and-white hope in the struggle with TV, Hollywood in this regard has so far failed: there is still no ideal Marilyn Monroe.

[3] In her first starring part, in *Niagara*, Marilyn played a petulant and

[1] Roman goddesses, of love and wisdom, respectively.

adulterous wife who is murdered by a jealous husband. Then, in *Don't Bother to Knock*, she played a psychotic waif with tendencies towards murder and suicide who ends up in an asylum. In *Gentlemen Prefer Blondes*, she turned to comedy and played a gold-digger. In *How to Marry a Millionaire*, she was a gold-digger again, but a myopic and vague one, a dumb blonde in glasses. In *River of No Return*, she relinquished comedy and played a part in which she was first a good-bad girl in a saloon, and then a babe in the woods. In *There's No Business Like Show Business*, she has returned to comedy and is a go-getter again. But is clear that Hollywood has not found Marilyn a unifying formula.

[4] There was no trouble finding a unifying formula so long as Marilyn was playing minor roles. In *All About Eve, Let's Make it Legal, Love Nest, Monkey Business*, among others, she was the dumb-blonde temptress for whom husbands never quite leave home. It was simply a question of exploiting her outrageous sex-appeal. Yet she was far from being just another Hollywood cutie writ large. The sex-appeal was already qualified by attributes which have come to the surface in her starring roles—namely, her evident awareness that there is something rather comical about being provocative, which she shares with Mae West,[2] and, what is the absolute antithesis of Mae West, her apparent innocence of the mechanism by which she is being provocative, in short, her artlessness. In Howard Hawks's comment, "She automatically makes any move, any gesture, insufferably suggestive," the keyword is surely "automatically." As a temptress, Marilyn was at the opposite extreme from a Mae West, a Hayworth, or a Stanwyck: she was a temptress-in-

spite-of-herself. One felt that, if husbands really had left home she would have been embarrassed and confused.

[5] It might be supposed that here was a personality already sufficiently individuated for its apotheosis to present no difficulties. In fact, elevation to stardom disintegrated it. The personal attributes have endured, but have been manifest in a fragmentary way. Instead of each new role's confirming the validity of the last and giving the accumulated personality an added force and complexity, each role has to some extent denied the last.

[6] Two reasons suggest themselves for Hollywood's inability to consolidate the Monroe doctrine at stellar level. The first is that the kind of character she was in her supporting parts was necessarily not a central but an attendant figure, "one that will do/To swell a progress, start a scene or two." A star must get her man, or lose him tragically, but for the early Marilyn there were only men to tempt, there was no man to get. The second reason relates to a contradiction between Miss Monroe's looks and her talents. A very clever comedienne, she has yet to act convincingly in a straight part. Yet it is natural that Hollywood should want to give dramatic roles to anyone so outstandingly beautiful. As a consequence they have split her screen personality.

[7] The essential rift in Marilyn's personality is between the go-getter of her comedy parts and the waif of her straight parts. She first starred in comedy as Lorelei, of *Gentlemen Prefer Blondes*, and Lorelei has remained the prototype of this side of Marilyn. For the thing about her as a go-getter is that she shares Lorelei's peculiar mixture of business instinct and wide-eyed innocence, of calculation and demureness, of the pursuit of gold and the pursuit of tone. Apart from "diamonds," Lorelei's

[2] Hollywood's famous symbol of frank, open sex, whose favorite saying was "Come up and see me some time."

favorite word is "refined," and the importance for Marilyn of being refined can be gathered from her version of the couplet about girls who wear glasses. "Men aren't attentive/To girls who wear glasses," she solemnly recites, in *How To Marry a Millionaire*.[3]

[8] Actually, Marilyn partakes far more of Lorelei's distaste for coarseness than of her taste for gold. In *How To Marry a Millionaire*, she doesn't: after finding herself a man-about-town she goes and marries someone less laden with money than with money-troubles. When it comes to the point, diamonds count for less than love. But what kind of love?

[9] It isn't as if the husband she chooses is rich in good looks or brains. Grable and Bacall, her co-stars, get married to highly romantic young men; not so Monroe, for all that she tops the billing. She may get the lion's share of the publicity, but her share of the beefcake is roughly equivalent to that which would have gone to Joan Davis[4] when a trio of girls shared an apartment a generation ago. In *Gentlemen Prefer Blondes*, it is Jane Russell who gets the romantic young man, while Marilyn gets the zany. True, the zany is a millionaire. But it isn't just his millions that she likes: she actually quite likes him. And this is where Marilyn's Lorelei shows her dissimilarity to Anita Loos's Lorelei. In the novel,[5] Lorelei starts off with a rich sugar-daddy who bores her and a romantic lover on the side, and ends up with a rich husband who bores her and another romantic lover on the side. In the movie, Lorelei starts off with a poor little rich man as her fiancé, ends up

with the same poor little rich man as her husband, and never has a lover at all.

[10] Even when, in *There's No Business Like Show Business*, she falls in love with a good-looker like Donald O'Connor, Marilyn betrays no signs of romantic passion. His ardour, like that of the others, only makes her feel affectionate and protective, and, by the way, quite faithful. Sexual passion is not for her—except when she makes love to sofas, pillars or microphones in her song-numbers. But when she turns from fetishes to flesh, nothing happens. Marilyn may have become an international symbol for sex but, after all, a dollar-sign is an international symbol for money, and you still can't spend a dollar-sign. Marilyn never lets herself go with a man because, however often she may get engaged, she never feels *engagée*.[6]

[11] Her refusal to be committed can even take in marriage and children. In a film of her antestellar days, *We're Not Married*, Marilyn was a wife whose time was so much taken up with winning beauty contests that her husband had to stay at home to do the cooking and the housework and take care of baby. This is one of the two movies in which Marilyn has appeared as a married woman. The other is *Niagara*, in which Marilyn for once felt seriously sexy (towards her lover, so leaving room in her relations with her husband for the usual pattern). But as she earnestly wiggled and jiggled her way across the screen, audiences went on laughing—and this time it wasn't with her, it was at her.

[12] Marilyn cannot help but make a joke of sex. And the beauty of the joke is that she never sees it. She is only bewildered by the effect she has. She is quite surprised to find how much Donald O'Connor wants to kiss her, and,

---

[3] The original version goes: "Men don't make passes/At girls who wear glasses."

[4] A comic whose appeal was not sex.

[5] *Gentlemen Prefer Blondes* was originally a popular novel of the 20's, written by Anita Loos.

[6] Committed.

having been allowed to do so once, how much he wants to go on kissing her. In the same way, the "real" Marilyn was reported to have been "bewildered," when, as she was walking to work on her first day with Twentieth Century Fox, seventeen cars stopped to offer her a lift. Marilyn is an innocent.

[13] Marilyn's innocence, indeed, is the unifying factor in her divided personality. In her comedy parts, it engenders absurdity in her suitors and even in herself. In her straight parts, it makes her a waif—the poor mixed-up girl of *Don't Bother to Knock* whose anguished efforts to get a man only brings him closer to another woman and herself to the madhouse; or the good little bad girl of *River of No Return* who has to be rescued from the influence of a bad man by a fatherly (if virile) good man together with his small boy, to whom she becomes less a mother than an elder sister.

[14] If innocence is the constant factor in Marilyn's variable screen personality, it appears only rarely in her pin-up personality, which tends to perpetuate that of the girl who posed for the calendar-picture with nothing but the radio on. And this suggests the origins of that innocence. It derives above all from her voice, a voice that cannot sound its r's, has to speak with great care to make any articulate sound at all, is in fact the grave, deliberate, little voice of a child. The innocence can also be found in her face, but only so long as it is seen by the cine-camera, is not hardened and stylised by the still camera, which tends to iron out the softness of the cheeks, the drop of the chin, the surprise in the eyes, the impreciseness of the features, everything that makes it the wondering, translucent face of a child. And so we see that Marilyn is simply the little girl who is aware of her charms, knows that if she flaunts them she can make men look at her in a funny way, and likes it when they do, though she only has a vague idea why they should.

WRITING ASSIGNMENTS

1. Discuss a recent role (or roles) of Miss Monroe by applying some of Mr. Sylvester's terms and interpretations. For example, was she serious or comic? What kind of person did she play? Was her innocence apparent? Was her sexiness? In what ways? (Refer to specific situations.) Were any other personality traits apparent, or even dominant?

2. Present your interpretation of some other famous show business personality. What is the dominant trait (or traits) of his or her public personality? Is there any mixture, as in the case of Miss Monroe? What evidence in this personality's public appearance or roles can you supply to support your interpretation?

3. Most real people do not have the clearcut, unified personality of a screen star. Quite often they present contradictory, conflicting aspects of personality. Explain the type of conflicting personality Mr. Sylvester discussed, as it applies to a personal ac-

quaintance of yours. Select two opposing traits (such as aggressive and mild, selfish and thoughtful, conceited and humble) and show how they appear at different times or even at the same time in the life of this person.

Marlon Brando: The Gilded Image

JERRY TALLMER

[1]   As a recruit in the army I was thrown together in friendship ⌐ with a fellow named Eddie Szemplenski; half a year later at another base I became buddies with a soldier named John J. Wodarski. Edward Szemplenski was a hulking, rough-looking drugstore cowboy from Hamtramck, Michigan, the place the men who make the automobiles come from. I had hardly heard of it before I met him; before long, I was to hear enough from him to fill a couple of novels. Johnny Wodarski was a shorter, chestier, far more handsome laughing boy from Paterson, New Jersey, a famous hard-boiled town that in those days meant nothing more to me than that it was across the river from my own New York. Wodarski had a white-gold shock of hair which inevitably gained for him, wherever he went, the nickname Whitey. There was a typically scrappy St. Louis Cardinal third baseman of that era named Whitey Kurowski. I always associated the two of them.

[2]   Whether either of those enlisted men is now alive—whether they even survived the combat for which we were preparing—I do not know. I hope so, and rather suppose so, for each was a young man of strength, stamina, adaptability, intelligence (not education), and each was far more than generously endowed with a ferocious appetite for life. Also with the loud indelicate snort of life, which they were given to expressing and acting on, irreverently, coarsely, sometimes brutally, wherever and whenever the G.I. strait jacket offered a gaping seam.

[3]   Yet they were not brutes. If Johnny Wodarski could love the ladies and leave them and even gladly boast about them, I also once saw him go in against a larger man than he (a snotty Ivy League washout named Aten) just to teach him the impropriety of some very sustained and nasty anti-Semitic talk directed at Whitey's comrade Isadore Lieber-

Personal reminiscence as background to Brando's performance

man. Whitey emerged not unmarked, but Whitey taught him. It was like a scene from a lot of the movies of the same period, only it happened to be for real. And if Eddie Szemplenski could cut a rampaging track through every bar and whorehouse and Polish dance hall of East St. Louis, Illinois, with me like a wide-eyed kid brother on his heels, there were also those dozens of other times when, back in the barracks or in the mess hall or on guard, we would talk all through the night about America, Germany, Poland, Roosevelt; about the Negroes, the Catholics, the Jews; about rich and poor; about factories, unions, colleges, movies, sports; about Hamtramck and New York; about non-coms, officers, airplanes, radios; about ack-ack; about bombs; about death; about the world after the war.

[4]   And then one fine day the war was over and without announcement there came walking in on me, from stage-right, fresh from the bowling alley, the sweat still drying on his neck and forearms, the most living breathing Szemplenski-Wodarski that I'd laid eyes on since the Army had separated me from the originals: a phenomenon, a sheer, fabulous, heartstopping phenomenon. He had their brow, their jaw, their mouth, their shoulders; his stance was theirs, his walk, his temper, his pride; certainly his crassness, and that snorting hoot; certainly also his unabashed and thrusting masculinity. He even had their thickness of speech, Eddie Szemplenski's anyway, and from his lips there seemed to issue every word and attitude they had ever mumbled or proclaimed. He even had their name, or next thing to it . . . he had the name of Stanley Kowalski, and though I had been going to theatre, or been taken there, more or less regularly since the age of ten, I had never before in all my days seen anything on any stage (or any screen) that equaled this. There he was, down there in the dark, fifty feet away from me, with that poor sick crazy woman planting herself in his house and bathroom—and I knew him! I knew everything about him. Hadn't I lived with him, even closer than that deranged invader, in some ways even closer than her sister Stella who was his wife, during the four entire years immediately preceding? How he must detest that Blanche Dubois . . . and be bugged by her. Like an inside straight, a come-hither smile on Water Street, a gnawing itch. I knew him and I understood.

His first view of Brando's greatness

[5]   Since then I have had professional reason to see a great deal of theatre. Only once or twice, before or since, have I seen anything on Broadway to match the brilliance and verisimilitude and freedom of Marlon Brando as Stanley Kowalski in *A Streetcar Named Desire*.

His great qualities

[6]   The other day I asked for a think-back evaluation of that original (i.e., pre-movie) Brando performance from an up-and-coming New York director whose productions (off Broadway) have seemed to me to have shown unusual awareness of what theatre is all about. He is roughly Brando's age, and my own.

[7]   "Marlon Brando," he replied, "was the greatest new actor this country has produced, or will produce, in my lifetime. What he did in *Streetcar*, and in *On the Waterfront*, has changed everything that's followed. Liberated it. Liberated us. But the only person it hasn't liberated

is Marlon Brando. He's done to himself just what Stanley did to Blanche Dubois; it's weird, it's almost mystical."

[8]   I said: "Uh-huh, but let's stay on the subject of *Streetcar*."

[9]   He thought a minute. "In *Streetcar*," he said, "Marlon Brando broke the box of the American theatre and threw away every restriction we'd been nursing for as long as we'd *had* a theatre. He came to it with a sort of, I dunno, gigantic super-naiveté: the naiveté of <u>absolute self-reliance</u>. Let's see if I can phrase this. There's plenty of self-assurance in the theatre, whatever the actuality underneath. But self-reliance is something else; something of a higher order completely. Carried to extremes, of course, it means something terrible. It means . . . what was his name? that fellow in New Jersey . . . Unruh, Howard Unruh . . . it means walking down the street with a .22 in your hand and blasting everybody in sight because you don't need *any* of them. But Brando needed Tennessee Williams and Elia Kazan and Stanley Kowalski, and Stanley needed his Stella, so it wasn't dreadful then but . . . a miracle. A miracle still relating to other people and still under control."

A director on
Brando's
qualities

[10]   I said: "Like *Waterfront?*"

[11]   "Like *Waterfront*," the director said, and as he said it I was visited with perhaps my ten-thousandth mental flashback of how the kid that Brando played in Waterfront still had, no matter how punchy, <u>this urgent need to relate to the girl, the crooked brother, the priest, the Lee J. Cobb mobster, and even the pigeons on the roof.</u> Even to that Hoboken scenery, and the river—there was something working back and forth between him and those roofs and those streets and that river which to this day I can't forget and won't forget, and neither will any of you who ever saw it. Relatedness? <u>Nobody in any Hollywood movie ever related more to the texture of the place and situation of his movie.</u>

A key
factor

[12]   "And then," said the director, "it all stopped. Just as with Howard Unruh. Or bit by bit it all stopped, movie by movie, headline by headline, kook by kook, gossip item by gossip item, until at last it had absolutely all stopped and there was nothing left but the boy with the .22 and the universe his oyster and a lot of dead people everywhere. Only not a boy any more. And no more of that free-flowing self-reliance. Just some kind of unbelievable self-indulgence, and the hell with everyone else in the world, on or off the movie screen. Or the stage. I will be kind enough not even to mention the American stage."

Director
on the
change in
Brando

[13]   Now the director stopped to stare bleakly into his coffee. "Grandiosity," he said. "It's as if he were <u>permitting nothing but his grandiosity to really move him.</u> You seen his latest mishigass, *Orpheus Descending?*" (He meant the movie version of the Williams drama, retitled by Hollywood *The Fugitive Kind*.) "It's like something that at last is absolutely entirely frozen, like a huge giant frozen custard of self-indulgence. The face! the lips! the walk! the pose! the slow gargle that has nothing to do with New Orleans or the South or fugitives or rebels or anything else in reality or otherwise. The absolute enforced subservience of the camera, and the drama, and Magnani, and Lumet [director Sidney Lumet] and even the props and lights and music. Everything subservient to this one

The ruin of
Brando's
talent

enormous baroque self-image. If it were only that, an actual self-image. But it isn't even that. It's an image of an image of an image. It is nothing laid on nothing laid on nothing, and the outright murder of a play that wasn't the best in the world to begin with, but had its points.

[14] "It's tragic," he said, "it's very sad." He did not say these last three words with the quotation marks of irony that many of us now so often put around them. "What greater tragedy is there in life than to stop growing? And Brando hasn't grown an inch in almost ten years. I don't think he ever grew as an actor, after the first few successes. If he'd only been pushed, had pushed himself, into things where he'd have had to reach, to strain. Well, he wasn't. He didn't. And it's our loss, believe me, more than his, because he was the beacon and the standard. I don't have to tell you all the junk that's come down on us merely in imitation of Marlon Brando. Or in imitation of this empty set of mirror images, one facing the other into eternity. But just think what might have been, for him, for every other actor, had he chosen to go right on breaking boxes."

. . .

What happened to Brando

[15] The decline and fall of the artistry of Marlon Brando is a classic case straight out of what is by now almost the cliché American myth on the fate of the creative personality in our society. One thinks immediately of Nathanael West's *The Day of the Locust*, of *The Big Knife* and Clifford Odets himself, of *The Last Tycoon* and Scott Fitzgerald himself, of Budd Schulberg's several cotton-pickin' inquests into the Fitzgerald corpus, and of a whole minor tide of variations on the theme which each season floods onto our national bookshelves, magazine stands, movie screens, 21-inch picture tubes. The myth runs as follows: As the career goes up, and the fame, the man and his integrity must go down.

First statement of the author's point

The point: ruined by success

[16] Often enough it is true enough—so sickeningly often that some not only buy the myth but start to live up to it, to conform to it, even before their careers stagger aloft on anything firmer than the bamboo stilts of press-agentry. Where it is always truest of all is when some young talent manifests itself among us like a sunburst a few years too soon for its own good—not that it knows its own good or can properly be blamed for its God-granted abilities—and this is what happened to Marlon Brando.

. . .

[17] I'll tell you where I first became aware that the paralysis had set in (I learn slow). It was about a third of the way through *Viva Zapata!* (an ingenious Kazan production, stolen from the imagery of Eisenstein, André Malraux, many others) when it gradually began to dawn on me that Zapata was none other than the motorcycle boy of *The Wild One* with a Leo Carrillo accent and a whole country on his hands. What he had most essentially was the same wounded psyche, the same morbid grudge against one-to-one human intercourse.... Then I realized he was also the even blacker-browed paraplegic brooder of *The Men* (whose blackness had at the time seemed only appropriate for the role) and that the cinema (or belly-button and beer-foam) version of Stanley Kowalski had also now transferred operations to the Rio Grande. The movie version of *Streetcar* had bothered me so much, with its Stanley

Example of loss of truth in his acting

so constantly thrust down your craw in huge and violent close-up, its poetic intentions so ruthlessly disintegrated, that I had simply entered that state of shock which for some years may cause the suspension of all coherent counter-intelligence. If I had viewed the Broadway play and the printed text through some sort of private distorting glass, the motion picture had taken it and turned it around and magnified Stanley into a ghoulish cross between Gargantua, Bluebeard and Huey Long. What price Johnny Wodarski now? What price Eddie Szemplenski, or any other such American I had ever encountered outside of the sorriest brands of whodunits and comic books? But Kazan had also staged the play. It was what they call confusing.

[18]   And then we began to get all those other films, one following the next, and then at last, as I say, it finally penetrated: what we were watching on our screens was <u>no longer an actor but a Hollywood Star.</u>

An important change and contrast

[19]   Then things became still further confused, because it was a little difficult to fit into that new cosmology the nutty private kicks which Brando seemed bent on savoring, whatever the cost, as the cryptic, whispering, certainly unstellar Napoleon that was next unfurled to us in *Desirée*—until I learned from the usual disreputable and public sources that Brando had hated being assigned to the picture and had done his excellent best to foul it up. It was yet more difficult to comprehend his oddball, pre-beatnik Mark Antony in *Julius Caesar*, all fits and starts and unique irrational inflections, until I presently caught up with other examples of the incapacities of director John Houseman to steer an actor beyond his ego. And it was altogether impossible to fit in, and still is, an intervening performance so superb that it may well constitute one of the two or three high points of all movie acting since the invention of the talkies.

More examples of his self-indulgence

Transition

[20]   I suppose it is easier, especially for Method actors, to study up on living American longshoremen than on dead Mexican revolutionaries or French emperors or Roman avengers of assassinated colossi. Nevertheless there is a kind of glory which endures even for "easier" portrayals if they are of the calibre of those introduced into the American commercial film by Marlon Brando and his colleagues (Kazan, Rod Steiger, Lee Cobb, Karl Malden, Eva Marie Saint) of *On the Waterfront.*

One great movie he did

[21]   What they pumped into Hollywood movies was <u>the priceless, the unbelievable fresh air of spontaneity.</u> Everything else grew from this spontaneity as love might grow in a summer garden. The story outline (by Schulberg) was, at best, an expedient tidying-up of a heap of dockside mud so mountainous that every schoolboy from the Bronx to Walla Walla, Washington, knew it could never even be dented by either a Congressional investigating committee (as in the film) or (as in the film) a quick spot of happy-ending Pier 6 brawl. This mattered not to Brando's betrayed, corrupted, cauliflower-cortexed young protagonist: he gave birth to himself within these multiple rings of betrayal (not least the scenario's) as if <u>something new and clean and questing had just set foot into the world.</u> It gave him those rarest of all qualities in the flat kingdom of celluloid: <u>tenderness, vulnerability, possibility.</u> Once again I

The value of the film

What Brando's great performance captured

knew his prototype: an Irish boy from a longshore family who lived two doors from where I lived for ten recent years, and the prospective lightweight champion of the world until the mob started to make him take his dives. To this day he is a hero to all the kids on those blocks; to this day, as you pass him on the sidewalk, you can see on his clobbered features the vulnerable and desolating glance of a man looking for something he knows not how he lost. The tenderness I can't testify to; or against. Brando imparted that to him on his own; nor can I ever recall seeing toughness and tenderness so organically fused in any American film, though a certain kind of Hollywood picture (Gable, Tracy, Cagney, *et al.*) has been trying to do it for as long as pictures have been made.

An example of the realism of the film

[22]   It is what in turn imparted to the love affair between Brando and Eva Marie Saint the truest sense of reality that we may know outside reality itself, and not often there. Do you remember where Brando, on the walk from the church, picks up the girl's glove and idly shoves as much of it as he can onto his own big fingers and hand? Do you remember how the beginning of love aches through, and how ten seconds later, by the fence, momentarily rebuffed, he conveys with a single negligent grinning shrug at least fifty-seven varieties of *C'mon, what's to be scared of?* Somebody once told me, or I once read, that this happened by accident: the actress dropped her glove by accident, and Brando picked it up as a fellow, that fellow in the movie (and he, Brando himself) would do, and put it on his hand that way, and kept on walking and talking the girl along, and she talking him along, until they crossed over to the fence and the river and the shrug; and Kazan kept it in. Things like that occur fairly frequently amid the errata of the legitimate stage, but you will just have to believe it when I tell you that they never happen in the ordinary prefabricated American film. More power to the Brando, the Kazan, of this bold pure isolated venture of nearly a decade

Transition

Back to his decline

ago, a venture which neither was ever to repeat. Since then, for Brando, Brando the serious actor, everything has been downhill. The machine rolls only in reverse. Brando had become a commodity, even to himself.

Examples of the ruin of his talent; conceited and phony

[23]   It rolls through the comedy phase, when he tries *(Teahouse)* to turn himself into a David Wayne: an elephant sent to mime the flea, and an elephant who with his every particle should have known better than to make the effort. It rolls through the musical phase, when he tries *(Guys and Dolls)* to turn himself into a breezy Robert Alda: the elephant doing the racetrack tout. Versatility is an admirable acquisition for the actor, but the goal here was not versatility; it was Box Office. And that goal, one admits, was attained. The only thing somehow misplaced was Brando.

[24]   It rolls then through his famous die-hard insistence in making a sympathetic character of the Nazi in *The Young Lions* . . . for when a person becomes a Movie Star how can he afford to grant the masses any opportunity not to love him? (Some movie stars fortunately know better.) If the final product we saw on screen was not merely not sympathetic but completely numb and inexplicable, a golden boy from outer space— well, so much for the masses, and for us, and for the human brain, and

even, if anyone cares, for Irwin Shaw. For who *does* care? The masses are dimwits and they'll forget. Who cares if the *Orpheus Descending* of Tennessee Williams exudes from the screen as nothing more than a heavily shadowed camera study of the hips, nipples, cheek-planes, firebrand eyes of the inarticulate monolith (shot always upward from the floor) that is its ostensible protagonist and spokesman for freedom, grace and understanding?

[25]   It rolls on through *One-Eyed Jacks* (should it turn out a masterpiece then come and shoot me). It will probably roll on through all eternity, unimpeded by yours truly. There will be movie after movie, epic after epic, and then one fine day somebody will dare to inquire: "When is Marlon Brando going to do another *play?*" and the myth will be complete. Just like poor Charlie Castle of *The Big Knife*, who was always talking about the return to Broadway and never quite pulling it off, just like all the dozens and dozens of others in fact or fiction who have sought out the Great American Myth and hurled themselves ardently into its maw, Marlon Brando is not going to come back. It is too late. *La commèdia è finita.*

Success has ruined him for good

WRITING ASSIGNMENTS

1. Mr. Tallmer claims that as Marlon Brando has become more of a star, a celebrity, he has become less interested in creating serious, honest, meaningful characters on the screen—characters that illustrate something about the truth of human beings. If you agree, criticize one of Brando's recent performances in terms of Tallmer's complaint. If you disagree, discuss the value and effectiveness of one of Brando's recent performances.

2. Who do you feel is the best actor (or actress) in the field today? Defend your choice by explaining the kind of acting he does, the kind of characters he plays, what in life he seems to represent. Be sure to refer to specific movies, plays or television dramas.

3. Mr. Tallmer's article is, indirectly at least, concerned with the general problem of the star, the "Big Name" who does not live up to his promise or, possibly, just never had the talent to begin with. For an attack of your own, select a target from any phase of show business. Show why he, or she, achieved success, and why you feel it is undeserved or no longer deserved.

Disneyland and Las Vegas

JULIAN HALEVY

[1]   This is written in Mexico, my home in recent years. I've just re-turned from a visit to the United States, and am now once more enjoy-ing the taste of unfrozen orange juice and fresh fish, conversations lasting four or five hours in which all sorts of cabbages and kings are discussed, meetings with friends where no one asks if I watched TV last night to see Mickey Rooney do Oedipus Rex[1] on the Benign Cancer-Producing Cigarette *Walpurgisnacht* Spectacular. Now I feel myself once again re-assured of my personal identity and critical faculties to the point where this article, which I have been trying vainly to write from within the revolving U.S. Barrel of Fun, comes to my typewriter as easily as a re-membered dream being noted down for the psychiatrist.

Sarcasm

[2]   Perhaps, as I'd been advised to do, I should have taken a child along when I visited Disneyland, but I'm glad I didn't. For one thing, most of the visitors were grownups, in the sense that President Truman and the Prince of Saudi Arabia are grownup, and I was able to pass more easily, although I never did get over the feeling that I was being watched. Too, I didn't have to temper my revulsion to the place with middle-of-the-road thoughts that anything giving pleasure to a child can't be alto-gether bad. My companion on the expedition was a woman with vitality and good taste, capable of feeling, a good friend of the kind you want beside you when you're in a tight spot. I must report that she was some-what disturbed by the experience: she didn't have a plane reservation in her pocket, as I did. She was going to have to stay in Los Angeles, which is a suburb of Disneyland, and the prospect was frightening.

More sarcasm: an indication of his attitude

[3]   The amusement park advertised throughout the world as Disney-land is a collection of Midway rides, concessions, hot-dog stands and soft drink counters, peep-shows and advertising stunts for big corporations, neatly laid out on several hundred flat acres twenty minutes' drive on a super-highway from downtown Los Angeles or a few minutes flight by direct, scheduled helicopter service from the Los Angeles International Airport.

[1] Oedipus the King, tragic hero of the famous Greek play and myth.

66

[4]   For the convenience of <u>pilgrims</u> who have traveled considerable distances and who don't want to be distracted from the main purpose of their visit, there is a large hotel on the grounds; and, if one can believe the billboards, it's possible to relax there in a luxurious hotel atmosphere, where formal attire is unnecessary, while enjoying an extended visit. There is a limit to how much punishment even the most <u>devout Disney-ite</u> can absorb in one day.

Sarcasm

Sarcasm

[5]   The huge park is laid out in several sections radiating from a center, a city plan also used to good effect in Washington, D.C., and Paris. Each section has a national character or *leitmotif* and an appropriate title: Frontierland, Tomorrowland, Adventureland, Wonderland and so on.

[6]   Frontierland features the Old West: mine train, a ride on a Mississippi-type riverboat around Tom Sawyer's Island, an authentic movie saloon where a moustachioed bartender informed me that "no alcoholic beverages are served in Disneyland," a diorama of the Grand Canyon, shooting galleries, horse cars, cowboys, Indians and stuffed, motorized animals.

[7]   Tomorrowland offers rocket-ship rides to the moon, <u>a plastic House of the Future advertising Monsanto, a 360-degree motion-picture exhibit belonging to General Motors,</u> and a wide variety of jet-plane and spaceship rides. The Wonderland pitch uses gimmicks from Disney movies: Snow White's Castle, Mr. Toad's Scooter Ride, The Seven Dwarfs' Souvenir Shop; Gepetto's Toys.

Commercialism

His summary of Disneyland

[8]   We got off a model train at Adventureland, passed through an Oriental Bazaar, and boarded a river launch that, for fifty cents, took us up country into darkest Disneyland on a seven-minute voyage. The pilot of our crowded little craft pointed out dangers and assuaged our fears over a public-address system which he handled very competently with one hand while brandishing a pistol with the other. He steered, incidentally, with his elbows, which was less foolhardy than it might seem, because the launch was towed on an endless underwater belt. We passed a temple full of sacred jewels, guarded by stuffed crocodiles which attacked us on whirring wheels, a tribe of headhunters brandishing assegais and shrunken heads, and a whole slew of stuffed, mechanized gorillas, cannibals and elephants, all intent on doing us bodily harm. We had some pretty close calls, but the pilot was a crack shot from Central Casting,[2] and he placed noisy bullets between the eyes of anything or anybody that threatened us. Given to sage observations, he remarked over the P. A. system, after coolly despatching a monster crocodile that had poked its rubber snout against the side of the boat, "You can't trust those fellows!"

[9]   As in the Disney movies, <u>the whole world, the universe, and all</u>

[2] Where "extras" for Hollywood films are hired.

Direct
statement
of his
complaint

man's striving for dominion over self and nature, have been reduced to a sickening blend of cheap formulas packaged to sell. Romance, Adventure, Fantasy, Science are ballyhooed and marketed: life is bright-colored, clean, cute, titivating, safe, mediocre, inoffensive to the lowest common denominator and somehow poignantly inhuman. The mythology glorified in TV and Hollywood's B films has been given too solid flesh. By some Gresham's law of bad art driving out good, the whole of Southern California and the nation indivisible is affected. The invitation and challenge of real living is abandoned. It doesn't sell tickets. It's dangerous and offensive. Give 'em mumbo-jumbo. One feels our whole mass culture heading up the dark river to the source—that heart of darkness where Mr. Disney traffics in pastel-trinketed evil for gold and ivory.

Seen as
typical of
our culture

[10] But the overwhelming feeling that one carries away is sadness for the empty lives which accept such tawdry substitutes. On the river boat, I heard a woman exclaim glowingly to her husband, "What imagination they have!" He nodded, and the pathetic gladness that illuminated his face as a papier-maché crocodile sank beneath the muddy surface of the ditch was a grim indictment of the way of life for which this feeble sham represented escape and adventure.

Las Vegas
and
Disneyland
compared

[11] Las Vegas is a very different kind of place from Disneyland, although both seem to me to illustrate a growing need in the United States to escape from reality. Disneyland is total make-believe; I suspect that a lot of the customers leave it with a sense of having been oversold and underestimated, and it would surprise me if many of them keep coming back for another fling at big-game hunting, Disney style. On the other hand, Las Vegas is a habit: every Saturday night, once a month, an annual vacation—it depends on how much money the sucker has to spend and how far away he lives. The satisfactions sold in Las Vegas are subtler and more profound: they touch on the real lives, the real anxieties of the people who trek there from all over the United States and places even more distant. Las Vegas deals in the essence of the American way, narcotics the number-one preoccupation of daily reality and nightly dream: the Almighty Buck.

[12] A Las Vegas promotion man, in a moment of inspiration, conceived a billboard advertisement which got a big play: "Come to Las Vegas! Bring Money!" The ad implied that money, after all, is only a commodity like potatoes; it ridiculed the over-importance of money in our lives, and mischievously, entertainingly, invited us to act out the burlesque.

[13] Las Vegas itself carries out the gospel proclaimed by the billboard.

[14] For the duration of your visit, you wear your brain tilted. You live in a luxury world where the fact of money seems beneath notice; a world of Olympic swimming pools, hanging gardens, waitresses beautiful as movie stars, marble baths and bars a block long, air conditioning, deep carpets, royal buffets and obsequious waiters offering free drinks.

The basic
lure of
Las Vegas

The illusion is created that we are all rich, that money means nothing. It is changed into chips, which are buttons, sort of; losing them on the gaming tables can seem trivial, until the sucker gets back home and converts his losses into real things like groceries and rent.

[15]   Every hotel is designed so that all roads lead through its gambling casino, the heart of the institution. To get to the dining room, the pool, or merely from one's room to the street, one must pass by the brightly-spinning roulette wheels, the glowing green pasture of the crap tables, the corridors of slot machines pleading to be stripped of their jackpots. Shills keep the show looking busy. It seems that everyone is playing the game: to toss a handful of colored buttons on the table is easy; one does it casually, airily; for a moment one has the illusion of omnipotence. Lose, shrug, and pass on: what a wonderful relief from checking prices at the supermarket and trying to balance the check book.

[16]   It certainly appeals to a lot of people. I saw all sorts, in Magnin [3] originals and cotton housedresses, blue jeans and evening clothes. There was a corporation executive and his wife who had brought along their cook and houseman to share the holiday, and all four were gambling. The sight of thousands of people shedding their financial inhibitions and traditional respect for money is somewhat startling, but the most provocative, puzzling aspect of the whole spectacle was that <u>many of the gamblers, certainly a majority of the big plungers, weren't gambling to win</u>. To put it simply, they were throwing their money away.

They don't want to win!

[17]   This requires some explanation. Games of skill, like power, or real games of chance, like traditional craps, are not available in the plush casinos of the great hotels along the Strip. There is an illusion of gambling fostered and tales are told of the Man Who Broke the Bank, but it is impossible for anyone to continue playing for a considerable length of time and win. The odds are fixed for this purpose. The house takes a sizeable percentage on every turn of the card in blackjack, every spin of the roulette wheel, every throw of the dice. Incidentally, the traditional odds of craps, which favor the house only very slightly, have been altered in Las Vegas so as to increase the house percentage, and house rules prevent gamblers from playing the house side and enjoying their favored position. The slot machines, of course, are commonly and properly known as one-arm bandits. Yet the wheels keep turning, the cards continue to be flipped, the crap tables are booming, and the same suckers keep getting fleeced.

[18]   A lot of them don't know any better, I suppose. They think they can win, despite the laws of mathematics. But there are businessmen in the crowds; sharp, hard-headed operators who figure their profits in fractions of a cent on the dollar, who buy and sell on tiny variations in the market and maintain systems of accounting far more complex than the simple arithmetic involved in figuring the house percentage in a crap game where "come" bets lose on box cars but players fading the shooter do not win.

[19]   I had a conversation with one of these businessmen that tells something, if only a small part, of the emotional factors motivating this

[3] An expensive department store.

unbusinesslike behavior. It was in the bright, blue desert morning beside the swimming pool, and during an ordinary conversation in which we chatted about our home states and occupations, my acquaintance mentioned that he had dropped about $2,000 on this weekend trip, which brought his losses for the year to about forty grand.

[20] "You can't win," he said, at one point, "but I like to play. I'm the kind of sucker these operators dream about. Why, at home, on a Saturday night I'll drive two hours to get to a game I know is crooked."

[21] On another occasion, this man, who in all other respects impressed me as sane, energetic and far from self-destructive, told me, smiling ruefully, that since the end of World War II he had lost, gambling, $300,000—profits from wartime black market deals that had been salted away in safe-deposit boxes. "It was dirty money, anyway," he said.

[22] What he meant, I think, was not that he had strong conscience pangs about how he had earned the money, but rather that there wasn't any way he could spend it that would give him greater satisfaction than that provided by this form of throwing it away.

[23] As I write, I am reminded of a religious practice in certain remote Mexican villages. When the parishioners are fed up with the way things have been going, they take the holy images from their place beside the altar and throw them in the lake to indicate their dissatisfaction with the ruling powers. It strikes me that there is some parallel beween this primitive getting even and the behavior of the U.S. businessmen; as one of them said in my hearing about his gambling losses, "I guess I like to throw it away."

Use of comparisons to explain why

[24] And while I'm playing with analogies among primitives, I wonder if there isn't some common human denominator linking these pilgrims to Las Vegas with those Indians who, in their potlatch ritual, insist that those individuals who have amassed a certain surplus get rid of it, either by destroying or giving away the excess money and goods.

A contrast

[25] There is another kind of gambling at Las Vegas which contrasts markedly with the phenomenon just described. One has to hunt for it, though. In a few saloons, downtown, there are old-fashioned, frontier-style poker games, the kind of game that went on in Virginia City when Mark Twain and Bret Harte were working on the newspaper there. In these places, the house doesn't participate, merely providing the table and facilities, including a dealer who cuts the pot for a half-dollar now and again. The players are a different breed from the guilt-happy, self-destructive penitents at the Strip hotels. Men, mostly, in contrast to the hotel casinos where there seemed to be as many women players as men, these gamblers were for the most part older, more taciturn, more serious. They dressed—differently from the hotel crowd, who favored fashionable sportswear—in worn, drab suits of a cut popular ten years ago; a very few among them wore unassuming polo shirts and slacks. Calculating odds, sizing up their opponents thoughtfully, drinking coffee (if anything), they made their bets or dropped out with an individually inexpressive style that did not vary with the size of the pots which, in the games I watched, were as low as $5 or as high as $3,000. There was a

Serious gambling downtown

tension in their cryptic speech and deliberate movements, drama that made the alcoholic feverishness of play in the hotels seem, in comparison, pathetic.

[26]   There was one odd character who intrigued me. I watched him for hours, along with several other remarkable gamblers, in a no-limit five-card stud game. He was a short, plumpish, sharp-featured man about fifty, with a loud, arrogant voice and cheap, flamboyant clothes, including a green felt Tyrolean hat with a peacock feather. A cold cigar was gripped between his teeth, and he kept relighting it with a *Flammenwerfer* lighter at tense moments in the betting. During intervals when he was sitting out a hand, a messenger brought him cards from a nearby bingo game and he marked them, watching anxiously as the numbers were posted. His behavior irritated the other players. I'm sure he was deliberately provoking them. When they were angry, their judgment was affected, which gave him an advantage. How effective his strategy was, I do not know; but I was impressed by his style.

[27]   The most consistent winner, though, was a thin, leathery old man who kept a blanket wrapped around his legs. In a coldly dispassionate atmosphere, he was icily detached. I saw him call a $500 bet with a pair of tens and win.

[28]   Whatever else you can say about that old man's line of work, it takes moxie. On the New York block where I grew up, the word meant a kind of spirited courage that we all admired. If life put a chip on its shoulder and flung a challenge, the kid who knocked it off and then danced around with his fists up in a fancy boxing stance had moxie. It's a word I haven't used much lately. In the months since I visited Las Vegas, I've found myself, now and then, remembering that no-limit poker game and the players; if not for them, the town would have been an altogether terrible place.

> He admires
> his
> courage

[29]   I don't really believe that poker-playing is an adequate substitute for the excitement that's missing from the contemporary package of adjusted organization life. It's rather a sign that the longing for it hasn't yet been entirely channeled into fantasy outlets; and perhaps some of the other socially censured activities that are permitted to flourish in the nooks and crannies of the American Way are also symptomatic of the still-glowing spark. There must be some good reason why social delinquency is concentrated in the livest segment of our population, the youth.

> His position
> on the real
> gamblers

[30]   But I'm writing about Disneyland and Las Vegas to make another point: that both these institutions exist for the relief of tension and boredom, as tranquilizers for social anxiety, and that they both provide fantasy experiences in which not-so-secret longings are pseudo-satisfied. Their huge profits and mushrooming growth suggest that as conformity and adjustment become more rigidly imposed on the American scene, the drift to fantasy release will become a flight. So make your reservations early.

> The
> meaning of
> Disneyland
> and
> Las Vegas

WRITING ASSIGNMENTS

1. Why do you think people gamble? Is it the hope of winning, the thrill of throwing money around, the escape from real problems, the skill of playing, the excitement of the contest, or something entirely different?

2. Do you believe Mr. Halevy's attack on Disneyland and Las Vegas is fair or justified? It might be helpful, in answering this question, to explain why you would like to go to either or both places or why you would not.

3. Mr. Halevy's opinion of American life today is not very high. Particularly, he suggests a growing inability to take part in "real living." What is he talking about? Can you find any examples of this deadening tendency in American life today or, more importantly, in your own life?

PART 3

Reading the

EXPLANATION

INTRODUCTION

This introduction is an explanation. I want to make clear to you what something is, what it does, and what you have to do to operate it (in this case, to read it). This time that something is an explanatory piece of writing itself, but no matter what the *something* is, an explanation seeks to "expose" the subject in this same way. That is why this type of writing is often called exposition. It seeks to answer such questions as *what is it? what does it do? why does it do it? how is it done? how does one operate it? how did it develop? and what does it mean to us?*

Asking Why

Explanations, then, are a result of man's constant desire to understand—to know the *how,* the *what,* the *why* of the world in which he lives and the world he has made. Reading explanations probably forms the major part of your reading activity. You read recipes, directions on boxes and bottles, textbooks and encyclopedias, informative articles and books. All of them focus on the world about us and on theories and concepts that are made about that world. Their subject may be a juniper bush (or how to prune it) or world disarmament (or how to achieve it); rock and roll records (and why they sell) or the Roman Empire (and why it fell). Their aim is understanding.

You should have noticed that in the first paragraph of this explanation I said I was going to cover three questions about explanations; I have now discussed the first two (what an explanation is and what it does), and will continue to discuss the second as I move on to the third. For, to explain how to read ex-

planations (my third point), I will have to explain further, and more specifically, what they do and how they do it.

Asking What

As a reader, you must first determine just what it is that is being explained, how wide or narrow a slice of some general subject it is.

This brings us to the most important thing you, the reader of an explanation, must do. That is, determine just *what* this particular explanation consists of. We might call this the *thesis*—the central concept, the central meaning—of the piece. There may be a major idea with several supporting ideas, or possibly several equal and related ideas. In any case the thesis is specific, and your understanding of it must be specific. It's not enough to know that a writer is telling us about space travel; *what* exactly is he telling us? It's not enough to know there are certain difficulties in space travel; *what* are those difficulties and *what* is difficult about them? In the first essay of this section, is history said to be a way of *predicting* the future? In a later article, why *do* auto drivers race with fate?

In determining the specific thesis, you should develop three mental habits. There may be others, too, but three are a beginning. *One* is to look for and recognize summary statements that clearly and directly announce the central ideas. These not only occur at the beginnings and ends of pieces, but are often repeated in some form throughout. The *second* is to look for key conceptual words, words that are emphasized, words that are repeated, words that are carefully defined. These words, and of course their meanings, are often the heart of the material. The *third* habit is to notice the clues of organization of the material. These may be numbers or, most commonly, words. There may be numbers used to show divisions, certain words used to show emphasis (notice the use of "most important" in the first sentence of the previous paragraph), other words used to show transition; that is, movement from one part to another. Some of these latter words are: *on the other hand, therefore, now, next, however, but, also,* and *meanwhile.* There are many more.

As a matter of fact, in no other kind of writing do single words of all kinds assume so much importance. This extra importance, and difficulty too, arises because explanations very often deal with specialized subjects. Explanations are attempts to make these special subjects clear to the general reader. And so you are often faced with the special vocabulary of a particular field—the language of psychology, of physics, of music, of mechanics, of sports. These special terms may be explained by what surrounds them in the piece, but they may also demand that you use the dictionary. Not until you understand the words will you understand the explanation.

Asking How

You must determine what the writer's approach to his specific subject is. What method of explanation is he employing? If you can see *how* the writer is making his statement, you have a better chance of seeing *what* he is saying. Here are some of the alternatives he might use:

1. *Summarizing.* Rather than a direct, original explanation of certain facts, he may merely be summarizing, possibly simplifying, possibly even distorting, some other theory or theories about these facts.

2. *Defining.* He may be explaining the meaning of a special, important word. This word in turn is usually the key to some concept or theory, and the writer often ends up defining this concept as well.

3. *Dividing.* This is what I have been doing here: dividing up explanations into sub-types or sub-divisions and explaining each one of these itemized divisions. But by this itemizing or enumerating I am actually still trying to make clear what the general overall process of explanation is.

4. *Classifying.* The opposite of the last approach is classifying. Here the writer places his whole subject in the pattern of a larger subject. He assigns one item to its rightful place in a general category. He shows how it is in some ways similar to other items in the same category and in some ways different and unique. Thus, racing is seen as a kind of sport, jazz as a kind of music.

5. *Instructing.* He stresses how to operate something.

6. *Explaining a process.* He tells how something works, without telling how to work it.

7. *Analyzing problems.* He sets forth something as a problem that needs definite solutions, usually presenting its causes and its results (probably harmful), and sometimes, although not necessarily, presenting its supposed solution.

8. *Comparing.* He shows how something is similar to or different from something else.

All of these methods or approaches come back to the same basic point of explaining some concept or process. A writer may be using more than one of these approaches at a time to help accomplish his general purpose of explaining.

IN READING THIS SECTION—

1. Be sure to determine just how much of a subject is covered and just what the *thesis* is.

2. Notice *how* the author is explaining it; which of the eight methods he is using.

3. Remember to look for (a) summary statements, (b) key conceptual words, and (c) clues of organization.

What Is History?

CARL L. BECKER

[1] Students often say to me: "I don't know any history; I think it would be a good thing to learn some." What they seem to mean is that they have never had a "course" in history, or have never read Gibbon's *Decline and Fall of the Roman Empire,* or Mr. Rhodes's *History of the United States from the Compromise of 1850,* or other books similar to these. But they are greatly mistaken if they think they "don't know any history." Every man, woman, and child knows some history, enough at least to stumble along in the world.

[2] Suppose, for example, that you had awakened this morning totally unable to remember anything—all your other faculties working properly, but memory entirely gone. You would be in a bad way indeed! You wouldn't know who you were, or where; what you had done yesterday, or what you intended or other people expected you to do today. What could you do in that case? Wander about helplessly, seeing and hearing things, taking them in as altogether new, not at all knowing what they might mean in relation either to the past or the future. You would have to discover your little world all over again, much as you discovered it in childhood; you would have to "re-orient" yourself and get a new running start.

In short, you would be a lost soul because you had ceased to have any knowledge of history, the history of your personal doings and associations in the past.

[3] For history is no more than things said and done in the past. It is as simple as that; and we might as well omit the word "past," since everything said and done is already in the past as soon as it is said or done. Done, but not done *with.* We have to remember many things said and done in order to live our lives intelligently; and so far as we remember things said and done we have a knowledge of history, for that is what historical knowledge is—*memory of things said and done.* Thus everyone has some knowledge of history, and it is quite essential that everyone should have, since it is only by remembering something of the past that we can anticipate something of the future. Please note that I do not say *predict* the future. We cannot predict the future, but we can *anticipate* it—we can look forward to it and in some sense prepare for it. Now if memory of some things said and done is necessary, it seems that memory of more things ought to be better. The more we remember of things said and done (if they be the right things for our purpose), the better we can manage our

78

affairs today, and the more intelligently we can prepare for what is coming to us tomorrow and next year and all our lives.

WRITING ASSIGNMENTS

1. In writing about history, Mr. Becker defines it, discusses its importance and use, and indicates common misconceptions people have about it. Write a similar essay, doing the same thing Becker does, about some other field of human knowledge (such as science, literature, etc.) or some field of human action (such as law, medicine, sports, electronics, etc.).

2. Mr. Becker mentions that the things we remember should be the right things for our purposes. In line with this, what do you think the best subjects or parts of history would be for you today? That is, what "things" (times, nations, events, statements, ideas) would be most useful to you and to what uses would you put them?

3. Describe your favorite course in history, showing what there was about the teacher, the teaching, the specific subject, the approach to the subject, the books, etc., that made it so.

The Individual and the Group

JOHN F. CUBER

[1] The term *group* is the pivotal concept of sociology. Since the word is loosely and variously used in popular language and in the language of other sciences, it is necessary to define somewhat precisely what it means in the technical nomenclature of sociology. Stated tersely, *a group is any number of human beings in reciprocal communication*. It may be well to emphasize certain aspects and implications of this short definition which beginning students, as well as some sociologists themselves, frequently overlook or do not appreciate fully. First, a group refers only to persons *in communication*. Mere physical closeness, if there is no communication, does not make a group. The communication creates the group, not the mere fact of spatial proximity of physical contact. Second, a group may be of any size from two persons to, theoretically and potentially, the entire population of the world. Third, communication need not be face-to-face or by "word of mouth," it may be indirect through writing or at long range through such instruments as the telegraph. Persons need not "know each other personally" in order to be in communication; they merely need to

contact one another via language, oral or written or gestural. Finally, the persons in a group influence each other reciprocally; one-way communication does not form a group. This, of course, does not mean that the various persons in a group influence each other equally.

"Group" Distinguished from Other Human "Plurals"

[2] The concept of the group we are employing will perhaps become more clear when we have distinguished two other kinds of human pluralities—aggregations and categories.

[3] *The category.* A category is a number of persons who are *thought of* together, whether they are in communication or not. Morons are a category. So also are the males 40 to 44 years of age in the population of the United States, or all the women in the United States who have failed in college. None of these are groups, as we have defined the term, because *they are not ordinarily in intercommunication.*

[4] *The aggregation.* An aggregation is a collectivity of persons who are held together in a physical sense by some factor other than intercommunication. The populations of a country or of the world are cases in point. Aggregations may, of course, be groups also, but all aggregations are not groups because the people involved may not be in interaction.

Why Grouping?

[5] Wherever humans are found, they are living in groups. The universality of human grouping has attracted attention, and several false notions have arisen claiming to explain the "reason" for groups. These errors have become so widely diffused that it seems necessary to examine them critically at the outset.

Instinct or Learning?

[6] Perhaps the chief fallacy is the widespread explanation of human groupings in terms of an *inherited* "need" or "urge" or "instinct" for group activity. Evidence for this explanation is lacking. Stated tersely, modern sociology finds that grouping is practically a necessity for most people—a necessity because through their socialization they have acquired, that is, learned, wants which can be satisfied effectively only by group participation. Each person has become so dependent in so many different ways upon other people, that permanent and consistent living outside of groups is virtually unthinkable and impossible. From the birth cry to his burial, the desire of the human being are ministered to by other humans. While at times interaction with other people may not be wholly pleasant, the over–all experience of his life is characterized by association with other people. Having learned, as everyone has, that he needs other people in order to satisfy his wants, there is no alternative. Group living becomes a necessity.

"Common Interest" or Functional Interdependence

[7] A second popular fallacy pertaining to groups is the "common interest" cliché. Men are said to be found everywhere functioning in groups because they have common interests, and through group participation the common interests are satisfied. Undeniably *some* of man's interests are common, but others are individualized or specialized, while some are openly antagonistic. Observe, for example, the larger number of groups found in the modern community which grow out of men's conflicts with one another. Courts, strike mediation boards, and legislative bodies are only a few of the many groups which come into existence because of conflicts among men. Other groups are made possible only by the fact of divergent, but not necessarily

antagonistic, interests. The market-place, stores, banks, and schools, come into being because different members of the society have different needs which can often be satisfied through interaction among persons, whose interests are reciprocal. Thus, the seller and the buyer form a brief group which fulfills the needs of the seller to sell and the buyer to buy. The bank provides a medium through which people who have money to lend for interest may make contact with persons having a desire to borrow money and are willing to pay interest for the privilege. Schools arise because there is a category and perhaps also a group of people (teachers) who have talents which they are willing to sell and which the pupils directly or indirectly buy. The teachers' interests are to sell their services and the students' to buy them. Thus it is readily demonstrated that the common generalization to the effect that groups are based on common interest is an oversimplification, or an exaggeration, of one factor which accounts only for the existence of *some* groups. A great many groups, possibly a majority, are based on divergent interests or antagonistic ones. All the evidence taken together would seem to indicate that groups are a practical manifestation of our interdependency.

[8] In preceding chapters it has been pointed out that a major part of each personality consists of patterns of behavior called *rôles*. A person's rôles are usually numerous in modern society, and vary greatly, as a rule, from one another. Through these rôles a person's participation in groups is carried on. Personality can be conceived as a collection of group-related rôles.

WRITING ASSIGNMENTS

1. Explain why a large number of people take part in a certain activity—anything from watching television to going to college, from taking drives on Sundays (on crowded highways) to going to church on Sundays. As Mr. Cuber has done, explain first exactly what it is they are doing. Then present a mistaken explanation of the reason for their activity, only to demolish it with your own correct explanation.

2. Would you like "to get away from it all," to live—at least for a while—in some isolated spot? Or would you rather remain a part of the group? Supply reasons for your choice.

3. It is obvious that groups are helpful and valuable for humans, but are they not also in some ways restricting, even dangerous and harmful? In what way or ways does a group come in conflict with an individual and possibly restrict or harm him? Be sure to refer to specific situations.

Thinking Machines Are Getting Smarter

ROBERT STROTHER

[1] At the Vanguard Computing Center in Washington, D. C., I watched a young woman present a machine with an extremely complex problem in ballistics involving hundreds of variables. At once lights on a control panel twinkled and winked as the computer checked to see that all equipment was operating properly. Then it set briskly to work. Magnetic tapes spun in their shiny glass-and-steel vacuum cabinets, the high-speed printer muttered. Suddenly the machine stopped and the electric typewriter wrote: "Last entry improperly stated!"

[2] A little embarrassed, the young operator corrected her error, and the machine started again. Four minutes later it gave an answer that had required several million individual calculations.

[3] "This is a wonderful machine," the girl said, "but it makes you shiver sometimes, especially when you give it a wrong figure. Once in a while we give it an incorrect figure on purpose—just to see it sneer at us."

[4] The machine was an IBM electronic computer—one of the new "giant brains" which differ from previous computing and tabulating machines in that they function with the speed of light—

186,000 miles per second. They can read, write and calculate simultaneously; they have tenacious "memories" and they can learn by experience. In the last half dozen years these electronic computers have come into wide use to perform miracles that touch the lives of all of us.

[5] Most commercial and scientific computer systems are huge affairs that fill a good-sized room which must be air-conditioned and dust-free. The largest digital computers cost from $500,000 to $4,000,000 each and yet they are being produced on an assembly-line basis by several companies. An idea of the complexity of the manufacturing job is given by a single statistic: there are 500,000 electrical connections in a giant computer.

[6] Some machines are sold outright, some are rented, and some are available on a job basis, like a washing machine in a laundry center. Several computing service centers where problems are solved for a fee have been established by the leading U. S. producers in principal cities here and in Europe. Some of the more spectacular uses for computers are in national defense. A ballistic missile in flight, for example, must be in exactly the right position at precisely

the right speed when the thrust is cut: An error of one foot per second in speed can cause a one-mile miss at the point of impact.

[7] As it climbs a missile sends radio signals to a computer on the ground, informing it about variations in wind, fuel consumption, center of gravity, temperature, rotation of the earth and a score of other items. The computer figures the effect of these factors and instantly flashes instructions to keep the missile on course. When the great "bird" hits the right speed and is properly trimmed, the computer cuts the motor and the missile coasts at 14,000 miles an hour to its target. No human being could possibly work with the speed and accuracy required by this complex operation.

[8] One of these machines has almost every one of us at its electronic fingertips: Computers at the Social Security Administration in Baltimore keep track of 160 million names and 1,750 billion dollars in wages. Formerly a change in a person's name, or a transposed serial number, caused trouble. Now the computers know some 25 common sources of trouble—and search for them in order of probable occurrence. Correspondence in this, the world's largest bookkeeping job, has been greatly reduced and the same staff can handle three times as many accounts.

[9] One of the routine marvels computers are performing nowadays for business is the operation of the Boston home office of the John Hancock Mutual Life Insurance Company, where a Remington-Rand Univac II under the direction of five operators keeps all the records on two million policy accounts. The computer selects the accounts on which premiums are coming due, and calculates the amounts owed by matching data from magnetic tapes with premium and interest tables in its memory. It wraps up the job by printing out premium notices, ready for mailing, at the rate of 100 per minute.

[10] Once a week it makes out the home office payroll, figuring income tax, bond purchase, health insurance and other deductions as it writes 7,500 checks an hour.

[11] On the anniversary of each policy, the computer calculates cash values, dividends, loan interest due, or interest payable on accumulated dividends, and prints out a statement.

[12] The present computers grew out of the early tabulating, calculating and teletype machines. Combined into one complete system, and speeded up by electronics, the most advanced of them can solve any problem that can be expressed in writing. Here, briefly, is how they work. An operator types information and instructions on a special typewriter that converts letters and numerals into a code of dots on a magnetic tape. The computer then "reads" these signals and sends them to its central "brain" or "memory"—which consists of thousands of pinhead-size iron doughnuts or cores, each linked electrically to all others.

[13] This "memory" temporarily stores partial answers to a long problem until the computer's ingenious circuits call them out at the right moment to complete the answers. It also permanently stores for repeated use such standard data as logarithm tables or withholding-tax figures. The actual calculating is then done on orders from an instruction tape that tells the computer precisely what to do with the stored information.

[14] An involved problem may require thousands of steps, but computers make light work of it by performing 40,000 arithmetical operations per second. Electrons flash through the bewildering maze of up to 500,000 circuits and

deliver the correct answers to a high-speed printer which types it out at speeds up to 900 lines a minute. The printers are versatile, too: they will express the answer in figures, plain language, or a diagram. And to top it all, the computer automatically checks the accuracy of its own answers. In rare cases of error—dust specks are the usual villains—the machine stops and refigures.

[15]   One of the most popular exhibits at the World's Fair in Brussels is a computer that answers questions in any one of ten languages. The questions are about major historical events in any year from 4 B.C. to the present. A visitor calls out, in German for instance, the years 1480 and 1766. The operator enters these years and the language on the keyboard. In less than a second the machine's electric typewriter begins printing, in German: "1480—Leonardo da Vinci invented the parachute. 1766—Mozart composed his first opera at the age of 11."

[16]   When a concordance of the Revised Standard Version of the Bible was needed last year a computer was given the task: to identify and list by location and context the Bible's 800,000 words. The 2,000-page Concordance that resulted contains 350,000 cross references. To prepare the previous Concordance took 30 years. After a few months of preparatory coding, the computer did the job in a few hours.

[17]   A computer demonstrated detective talents while indexing the Dead Sea Scrolls. The Concordance technique was used but in many cases the computer had to guess at letters or entire words missing from the crumbling old documents. It did this by analyzing the words preceding and following each gap. Then it scanned the thousands of index words to find the one that most early fitted the context. To test the accuracy of the method, portions of known text were blocked out and the partial sentences

given the machine. It replaced correctly as many as five consecutive words.

[18]   The giant brain has also been set to work translating the current flood of scientific papers produced in a score of languages. First, every word in a sizable English dictionary is listed on tape under a code number. The Russian, French or German equivalents for each word are given the same number. Then, to translate from Russian to English, for example, a tape with the Russian code numbers is fed into the machine, which matches the numbers and prints out the English. In an early experiment, the computer was asked to translate the English saying "Out of sight, out of mind," into Russian. The result was startling: "Invisible and insane." Newer computers are much more sophisticated, and while human editing to rearrange awkward word sequences is still needed, the computer can make hundreds of rough translations in a day.

[19]   Computers make business forecasts, prepare weather predictions, run refineries. They hunt up legal precedents, help in the diagnosing of diseases, and compose harmonic but uninspired music. They even help design better computers.

[20]   "Computers can be programmed to do almost any mental work a man can spell out," says Dr. Alan Perlis, one of the mathematician-philosophers who have played key roles in extending the scope of computers. "Each generation of human pupils must be taught afresh, but once you've taught any single computer to perform a process, you've taught them all, and forever. After a method for solving a certain problem is successfully worked out, it becomes part of the huge library of machine methods now available to users everywhere."

[21]   Manufacturers have been working to give computers larger and faster memories and greater flexibility; they also have sought to realize the goal expressed

a decade ago by the late John von Neumann, a trail-blazer in computer development. "Computers must be able to modify their behavior on the basis of their experience," he said. One of the scientists tackling this problem is Dr. A. L. Samuel, who has taught an electronic computer to play checkers. This has a serious purpose: to train the machine to learn by experience.

[22]   The first step was to number the 32 checkerboard squares and the 12 men on each side. Then into the computer's brain went a few thousand plays, selected from books written by experts—a half dozen promising moves for every situation. A few instructions were added, and it was ready. The computer politely gives its human opponent the choice of colors then prints out "M1 12 16"—indicating the machine's first move is piece 12 into square 16. Its human opponent replies by punching out the numbers of his play on a card which he gives to the computer.

[23]   The machine now runs over all plays open to it. It "mentally" makes a move, calculates what would be the best response for its opponent, figures its next probable move in that case, then the probable reply to *that*. It carries this procedure forward six steps before printing out the play it has selected. It does all this in seconds and then waits—humming quietly—for its opponent's next move.

[24]   The checker-playing computer knows every move of every game stored in its "memory," and it displays uncanny powers: it will sacrifice a piece to gain a future advantage; and it marks the plays that have led to losing games. When it next encounters the same situation, it selects a different move from its repertoire. The result is that it shows improvement in almost every game, and now easily defeats anyone except a real expert. To watch it print: "EXPECT TO WIN IN FIVE MOVES" gives some observers an uneasy feeling.

[25]   Computer men, thrilled by the powers of the *genie* they have created, like to speculate on the tremendous promise it holds for human advancement. "Computers open up scientific possibilities that were unthinkable before," says Ralph J. Cordiner, Chairman of the Board of General Electric Co. "They will make possible entirely new products and industries. These computer-derived technologies will be a major source of new employment in the coming decades."

[26]   Such leaders as Dr. Simon Ramo of Ramo-Wooldridge believe that the computer, by making vast new areas of knowledge manageable, and by directing operations too fast or too complex and requiring too much speed for a man to handle, will prove to be the most valuable of all the developments of these fast-moving times. No man can foretell what the future holds, but there is no doubt that many of our questions about it will be answered with the speed of light.

WRITING ASSIGNMENTS

1. Explain the process of operation of some machine or device in the same way Mr. Strother has explained the operation of the computer in Paragraphs 12-14. Follow the steps of the process in sequence, showing what the operator and the machine do at each step.

2. Many writers have expressed fears about the over-use of machines, and particularly of thinking machines, to solve man's problems. Do you see any dangers or

problems that these machines might present to man? If so, explain each in detail. If not, to what further uses might thinking machines be put to benefit man?

3. Science fiction writers for years have been using thinking machines in their stories; now the machines are a reality. There are still, however, possible uses and actions of machines that fit a world of fantasy more than they do our world of reality. Can you invent a plot that involves some fantastic use or action of a thinking machine and the way it affects the people involved, and write a brief science fiction "thriller" about it?

Why They Race With Fate

GILBERT MILLSTEIN

[1]   The other night, in a motel room in suburban Speedway, which got its name as the site of the Indianapolis Motor Speedway, a racing-car driver named Edward Julius Sachs examined himself in a mirror with evident affection. Sachs' features combine some arresting suggestions of both Basil Rathbone and Vince Barnett, a comic, and, although he will be only 32 on Wednesday, his forehead is advancing rapidly to the back of his head. With a delicate show of annoyance, he plucked a tiny thread from a lapel of his slubbed, iridescent, bronze-colored jacket, ran a finger inside the collar of a brutally starched shirt and announced jauntily to his two companions, "I'm going out in silk tonight, gentlemen, and after May 30, I'll be going out in silk every night."

[2]   He is a slender man, but he strode through the doorway as though it were slightly too narrow for him. "Not so long ago," he added, "I never knew what comfort was. Anything uncomfortable was just right for me." His nostrils flared

and he patted his chest with his palms. "I'm the cockiest little guy in the world and I know it and I don't mind telling anybody," he confided. "At the same time," he said, running full throttle into the homestretch, "I'm very, *very* concerned about my life."

[3]   Sachs is one of the thirty-three men set to drive in the 500-mile Memorial Day race Saturday. He invariably and worshipfully refers to the two-and-one-half-mile track as "the great Indianapolis Motor Speedway." Most other people call it "The Brickyard," since it was once paved entirely in red brick. Save for a few remaining city blocks of brick in the vicinity of the starting line, it is now all asphalt, to accommodate the increasing speeds of the beautiful, dangerous, handmade machines that race on it once a year. Indeed, they are the sole reason for the speedway's existence. Apart from nine holes of a golf course within the tremendous oval (its infield and grandstands can handle 200,000 spectators), it is used only for the Memo-

rial Day event and for the qualifying trials and practice runs in the month preceding.

[4] As for the cars themselves, they are suitable for nothing else but racing—and only closed-circuit counter-clockwise racing, at that—although the claim is made (and disputed) that they have contributed heavily to advances in automotive engineering. (So quickly do they become obsolescent, that the owner of the car which won the race last year and the year before spoke of it recently as "a museum piece.")

[5] Even motionless, these championship cars—as distinguished from sprint cars and midget racers, which are, to put it simply, smaller and slower—somehow imply speed and mortality to a degree achieved neither by jet airplanes nor missiles. This is a palpably false impression but not an entirely invalid one. The velocity of an Indianapolis car and its capacity to kill are at once limited and dictated by the earth and can still be grasped by the mind more easily than the corresponding characteristics of jet aircraft and missiles. (It is worth noting that most race drivers do not fly planes.)

[6] When Sachs speaks as he does, he articulates for all other racing drivers, few of whom, however, are within, say, 500 miles of being able to talk so fluently. His extroversion and love of publicity are regarded by his fellows with affectionate amusement. But they accept them because they do not doubt his obsessed dedication, which they recognize to be exactly like theirs, and they respect his ability, which exceeds that of most. Silk suits for Sachs are, of course, an offhand symbol of success. (Actually, he has a thriving cocktail lounge in his home town, Center Valley, Pa., not far from Bethlehem.) Poverty and near-poverty are the portion of all but a dozen or so

of the roughly 450 who can properly be called professionals.

[7] Limitless confidence is to be found in every man as well as the conviction that he takes every precaution possible to preserve life and limb. Like a soldier under fire, he believes it is someone else who will be killed. Sachs has calculated that for him, at any rate, there are thirty-nine predetermined moves he must make to negotiate successfully a single lap of the speedway; beyond that, he knows he is helpless before an infinity of mechanical and human aberrations. In his rarely laconic moments, he is apt to lump such an infinity under the heading of "radical behavior."

[8] All kinds of theories, from the familiar psychiatric generalizations about sexual satisfactions and death wishes, to those analogous to the bromide about men climbing mountains ("Because they're there") have been brought forward to explain this race of pathetic heroes chasing each other literally in circles in pursuit of some inexplicable grail.

[9] "It may not be adequate but the only answer I have is, 'Because they love to race,' " Dr. Caryle Bohner, the speedway's medical director, said. "Physically, mentally, emotionally and morally, these drivers are no different than millions of men on the street. Money's no factor. Most of these boys don't make enough money to eat on. I remember, the father of one of them, a very rich man, offered his son a million to quit. He did—for a year. He came back the next season and was killed. As far as fatalities are concerned, it's always the other fella's going to get it. By comparison with other sports, the glory and publicity is negligible."

[10] Bob Stroud, a former racing driver and now the United States Auto Club's supervisor of midget racing for

the Midwest, has likened the drivers, not derogatorily but in a syndromatic sense, to drunkards. "I think most of them intend to make a little money and quit," he said, "but they race so much they can't. They can't get it out of their blood."

[11] "It's something that gradually gets deeper and deeper inside," according to Tony Bettenhausen, the 1958 national champion. Bettenhausen, who has been racing for twenty-one years, is 42, an extremely advanced age for one in his profession, and he has "retired" twice.

[12] "I've always been of the opinion your days are numbered," he added. "Of course, you can go out and hurry it. But I don't think there's any more danger in my particular job than there is for men climbing poles and working on high lines in zero weather, for example. If I had to make my living that way, I'd starve to death. I've been on the under side of race tracks—in accidents —twenty-seven different times and I feel my chances for the kind of money I can make are much better than for these other types of workers." Days after he made these observations, he saw the under side the twenty-eighth time: his car was overturned and wrecked in a qualifying trial, but he walked off with a bloody nose.

[13] "Somewhere in their makeup," Duane Carter, a former U. S. A. C. official who returned to driving this year, has concluded, "the four-wheel vehicle is the only thing that will satisfy their desire for speed." And Sachs himself says —briefly, for a wonder—"I'm a man who has tried pretty much everything in life and found what he wants."

[14] How much of the ascertainable things Sachs wants out of life and has got thus far requires some examination. In terms of universal recognition, he can never hope to match baseball, football or tennis players, who not only get writ-

ten about more but last longer. (The first factor is, possibly, a consequence of the second. It is also well known in racing—and advertising—circles that advertisers are reluctant to sign up drivers for testimonials, the reason being that they are apt to be killed or maimed by the time their preferences for cigarettes, beer or whatever appear in print.)

[15] Financially, Sachs has got a lot for a racing driver. Last year, he drove in eleven championship events—races, with the exception of Indianapolis, of up to 200 miles. He was seventh in point standings and won purses totaling $26,451.

[16] As Midwest champion, he competed in ten races, mostly fifteen-mile sprints, and earned $7,831. In the 500-mile Miglia di Monza in Italy, he was forced out after twenty laps by a mechanical failure, but none the less was awarded sixteenth place and a prize of $1,761, and, on the Eastern circuit, in which he ranked fourth, his purses were $2,201.

[17] Of this $38,244, Sachs kept only 40 per cent, or $15,297.60, since a racing purse is split three ways, with half going to the car owner and the remaining 10 per cent to the mechanic. (He also earned a few thousands more in "appearance money," or guarantees, which go only to a handful, and in a retainer from the owner whose car he drove last year at Indianapolis. Retainers are infrequent.)

[18] Last year's Indianapolis winner, Jimmy Bryan, won a purse of over $105,000 in that race (his share was $42,000), but the average driver does not earn above $4,000 a year from racing and must work at any number of other trades to make out. It is not at all uncommon for a driver—Sachs was no exception in his time—to beat his way from track to track from April through November, paying his own expenses, hitch-

hiking and hoping a car owner will hire him to drive when he gets there.

[19] The owner's cut is felt to be fair, since he pays for the car, its transportation, servicing and repairs (and, quite often, rebuilding) and the five-man crews who maintain it. Sachs' car this year is a new one, commissioned for him by a big, baby-faced, red-complexioned man named Peter Schmidt, a St. Louis, Mo., supermarket operator. The engine alone for the new car cost $11,000 and Schmidt has bought a spare. In the last decade, his hobby has cost him upward of half a million dollars in equipment and expenses.

[20] His motives are completely comprehensible—he wants to win at Indianapolis, and failing that, at least to be in the race, if only by proxy. "I've had yachts and planes and all that," he said recently, "but there's 180,000,000 people in this country and I can say I'm one of the thirty-three fastest." It then occurred to him that he wasn't doing the driving. "I want to get in that race," he finished, "and I want Eddie Sachs all in one piece."

[21] To understate the case, a racing driver's chances of staying all in one piece are much lower than those of other athletes. Of the hundred or so who competed regularly last year, eight have since been killed at one track or another. So have eleven of the thirty-six Indianapolis winners since the event was begun in 1911. It is almost a mathematical certainty that of the thirty-three men who race at Indianapolis in any year—the undoubted élite of all drivers—four will not be alive next Memorial Day.

[22] Sachs himself has been in eleven racing smashups, to say nothing of breaking a leg skiing. The most serious of these occurred two years ago in August, at a midget track, now defunct, across the street from the Indianapolis Speedway. Another driver hit a wall and spun

in front of him. Sachs was catapulted from his car and bounced down the track. His helmet was torn from his head. The left side of his face was ripped away and his left arm broken. (It had been broken before.) The eye was saved but he spent four months in a hospital having his face grafted together again.

[23] The prospect of sudden death or permanent disability, his own or that of any other driver, is one Sachs faces not with bravado but with chilling equanimity and his attitude is typical.

[24] "The very first weeks I was in the racing business," he said, "I saw Jake Pickler and Ducky Pelman die. As the years went on, there were Bob Scott, Joe James, Mike Nazareth, Larry Crockett, Bill Schindler, Bob Sweikert, George Amick. There were plenty of others, but these were the ones I knew well. I feel sorry for all of them and their families, but they're no different than me. We were friends away from the tracks, we worried about each other and tried to point out safety factors to help each other.

[25] "But when they drop that green flag for the start, I don't know who they are, they don't know who I am and I wouldn't give them an inch. And I liked them. And in their deaths, I don't have any direct feeling. I don't grieve for them and I wouldn't want them to grieve for me. It's something I accept. When they were alive, it was something they accepted. As in any profession, there is a percentage of loss." . . .

[26] The very prospect of driving in the Memorial Day race is enough to move Sachs to tears. "When I'm sitting in my car in the pit in that last few minutes before 11 o'clock and that Purdue University band marches down the straightaway, I turn my head and watch it and I hear them play that great Hoosier song, 'Back Home Again in Indiana,' and I know that at the comple-

tion of the song, a voice is going to come over the loudspeakers and say, 'Gentlemen, start your engines,' and a minute later I'm going to roll out.

[27]   "I become all filled up with joy on the inside and I cry so much I can't even put my goggles on for fear I'll get water in them. I cry because I can be part of this great race. Me, Eddie Sachs, just a little guy from Allentown, Pa., who's worked his way to this absolute top of his profession, and three and a half or four hours from now I might even have emerged the victor and have reached the very highest point in my career. Why," he ended, in wonder, "it's right within my grasp."

WRITING ASSIGNMENTS

1. Many recent articles—not this one—have demanded that auto racing be stopped because of the deaths and injuries that occur. Do you believe that some kinds or all kinds of auto racing should be banned, or do you feel that the "sport" is worthy and valuable?

2. This article analyzes the lure that auto racing has for the professional driver. What is its attraction for the racing fan or for the racing amateur? What is its attraction for you?

3. In this article Eddie Sachs describes the attraction his job has for him. Set forth the attractions your planned career has for you and then compare them to what attracts Eddie Sachs. What are their similarities and differences? Which do you think are more valuable and fulfilling?

The Place of Jazz

BARRY ULANOV

What kind of art is jazz?

[1]   The distinction between major and minor art naturally concerns anyone who writes about jazz or any other kind of music. At the same time one must be suspicious of rating systems in any discussion of the arts. Any numerical means of distinguishing one work of art from another is necessarily questionable, for it presupposes a mathematical content that can be set forth with some precision by an accountant-critic who can tote up, mechanically add or subtract, the virtues and vices, achievements and failures, of a work of art. It is important, however, to note certain general

characteristics about jazz, not at all mechanical in nature, which may go some of the way toward indicating its major or minor status.

His purpose

[2] If the art of jazz is only as important as the arts of faïence [1] or petit point, [2] of etched glass or bagpipe music, then we should know it and make our judgments accordingly. If, on the other hand, it has at least some of the significance of that chamber music [3] which composers in the tradition of Haydn and Mozart or Beethoven and Brahms have written for string instruments, or if it is of the order of lyric poetry or landscape or portrait painting, then this we certainly should know and accordingly find our values in jazz at a correspondingly elevated level.

[3] It is not easy to track down those defining characteristics by which we can assign to jazz the importance of a major art or the comparative unimportance of a minor. But certain things are clear. First of all, obviously, jazz is a form of music; any consideration must put it under that general classification. And second, since it is a kind of music, then it is a kind of art. Only the most unreconstructed Philistines, [4] I think, will deny the assertions of the self-evident here.

[4] But what kind of music is jazz? How different is it from other kinds of music? Is there anything about it that at any time moves it, whether boldly or timidly, from the province of music across and into the precincts of any other art? My answer to all of these questions would be that jazz is, in almost all its details, of a piece with the rest of music, that it organizes sounds according to the procedures of Western music. ① It has been, for the most part, a thoroughly conventional kind of diatonic [5] music, made up of combinations of half tones and whole tones, with the same tendencies to the polytonal and the atonal [6] which all our music has had in our time, although certainly jazz has arrived at these notions a great deal later than its more experimental older brothers, and its musicians still, perhaps, feel a little uneasy with them. ② To the extent that any music sometimes sets words or narrates a story, jazz is some of the time literary, some of the time pictorial, some of the time concerned with translations of elements in space into sound, sometimes with translations of events in time into what reads like a contradiction in terms, but isn't: aural pictographs [7]. ③ It is concerned with the same problems of conveying meaning and truth with which all of music is beset: one never knows for sure the precise intention of a serious jazz composer or performer; one never knows with certainty whether it is a purely subjective speculation of the jazzman or a description of an object which should be recognizable to the hearer. ④ The definite and the indefinite both struggle for the jazz musician's attention just as they do for the classical man's; the jazz musician's listeners are left just as the classical musician's are, sometimes satisfied, sometimes bewildered, by

Jazz—similar to other music in many ways

[1] A kind of pottery-making.
[2] A kind of sewing.
[3] Music for small groups of musicians.
[4] Enemies of art, here specifically of jazz.
[5] The basic eight-tone scale of music.
[6] Progressive music that does not observe traditional principles of tone.
[7] A picture representing an idea.

what jazz evokes for them of person or place, mood or atmosphere or
precise meaning.

[5]   There are, of course, among those who listen to jazz, ① all kinds
of people, variously emotional or cerebral, some most fluently associative
in their listening, some more directly musical. ② Jazz elicits from listeners its share of visual images, just as other forms of music do. ③ Jazz
makes its appeal to stock emotional responses, invoking sorrow or joy, the
maudlin or the madcap, the terrified or the delighted, just as other music
does some of the time. ④ And jazz also can draw to itself musically
intuitive listeners, who respond to its sounds with some apparatus which
those who have it will recognize as the musical faculty. To them, technical
distinctions of form are uppermost, and yet there is some unmistakable
content as well, however difficult it may be to make verbal distinctions
of form are uppermost, and yet there is some unmistakable content as
well, however difficult it may be to make verbal distinctions between
the two.

Varieties of responses to jazz—again, like other music

[6]   Perhaps the most significant point about jazz as an art form is
this: at its best what it communicates cannot be communicated in any
other way; to those who know it well there is such a thing as the jazz
experience, one which is entirely different from any other in music. It is
this experience which draws the most intense support from jazz musicians
and jazz fans.

But it is unique too

[7]   By definition the jazz experience cannot be translated altogether
successfully into words. If it could, there would be no need for jazz. All
one can do, really, is select general descriptive headings that permit one
to point to now one set of responses, now another, and the different sorts
of music which summon them forth.

What is the jazz experience?

[8]   Much of jazz is concerned with ① the simple communication
of simple pleasures. Its little masters have presented miniatures of sound,
terse or somewhat more rambling, which declare that this or that kind
of good time has been enjoyed. Not only do they declare that a good time
has been had: they make some attempt to share it. Often the sort of
three- or four- or five-minute ecstasy thus communicated does not rise
above the most elementary physiological level. But some of the time
there is a small poetry of pleasure of which the jazz musician is capable,
which he can not only feel but re-feel, can react to not only once but
several times. As he sorts out his feelings and reactions, he can think his
way through to felicitous reconstructions of experience which many of
us are very glad to have.

One element that jazz communicates

[9]   Occasionally there have been attempts at ② large-scale expression and development of ideas in some complexity over a considerable
range of melody and harmony and rhythm. The starting point for this
sort of work is almost invariably a fairly extended meditation or con-
templation of the life of the jazz musician or of the Negro people in the
United States, or a part of a big town, or life in all the cities of the United
States, even sometimes the more abstract speculation about the nature
of man or God or the relationship between the two. It would be foolish
to assert that any large degree of success has attended these unsystematic

A second element

expatiations upon the obvious. But the systematic and the organic have not altogether eluded the jazz musician. He will not always be confined to an abbreviated discourse and therefore in the larger forms to a kind of fragmentary anthologizing. For there is reality packed away in the music of jazz, a reality to which millions respond with recognition if not always with pleasure. Jazz stirs certain feelings which are apparently universal. As few arts have in our time, it has been accepted internationally; it has evoked in Europe and Asia, in South America and Australia and Africa, essentially the same reaction that it has in its native North America. It obviously expresses something that audiences in the twentieth century want to have expressed for them.

[10] It is not too difficult to point to what jazz does that so delights its millions. ③ It is a big-city music. It reflects, as few other arts in our time do, the massiveness and the matter, the chaos and the conflicts, the frantic pace and the fragmentary nature of life as it is lived by the millions gathered together in the cliff dwellings of the modern metropolis. ⓐ It does more, too, than merely reflect these elements of urban existence. ⓑ it sorts them out, distinguishing certain kinds of individuals from the crowd, and saying something about each of them. ⓒ And with all the poignancy of any of the arts of our time which has sought to chronicle urban life, it describes the loneliness of the big-city dweller. . . .

The reality it reflects: a third element

[11] Jazz musicians do know more than one environment; large numbers of them come from small towns and villages, from the farm and the ranch. But it is usually in a night club, recording studio, ballroom, or hotel that a jazzman finds himself as a jazz musician. In these places jazz is played by professionals, and it is to them that an aspiring jazzman must go, not merely for recognition, but for survival in jazz. And so it is the atmosphere of these places and all that surrounds them that the jazzman soaks up and squeezes out in his playing; it is this environment that he reproduces simply and openly or upon which he makes more extended notes and comment. At his best he is severely conscious of the limitations of this environment and accepts them as necessary. In doing so he performs that conscious act of the will and develops that precise sort of control which together mark the genuine artist in any art form. As that control increases and the jazz musician more and more conforms his will to the limitations of his art, his music becomes more and more an art. For with control and acceptance of limitation comes an apparatus of sign and symbol without which no art of consequence has ever existed. The intimate reflections and secret experiences of the jazz musician can then be communicated with some certainty of understanding. Something of this translation of intimacies has already occurred in jazz: there are large number of people who really do "dig" the arcana of jazz; its *aficionados*[8] really have found something in jazz which cannot be found precisely in the same detail anywhere else. The "something" which is unique to jazz may be as yet nothing more than the passing reflections of typical New Yorkers or Chicagoans, Los Angelenos or Kansas

Basis of its big-city limitations

How this limited environment can be used with profit

[8] Ardent fans.

Its limits and its successes

Citians, or those who travel between these cities and others. Because they are miniature, these reflections do not canvass the sublime, except in the breach; most of the time one knows little of real exaltation in jazz. Still, what is said is said with conviction, and it rings true; a world of vital experience has been put together, piecemeal.

Beginning of Ulanov's final judgment

[12]   The fitting together of small pieces does not make for a major art, although it may be from time to time the secondary function of a major art. If those small pieces are all that a particular group of artists and their audiences have experienced with any great depth of feeling; if this is all they really know about and can talk or dream about, then this must be their expression, their art, no matter how minor. It is to the everlasting credit of jazz that it has made its piecework so compelling to its ardent admirers that for many of them there is no more

Its admirers' judgments

satisfactory expression in the arts, major or minor. The distinction between ecstasy and exaltation could not concern them less. They are content with an iconography⁹ of the subway and the department store, the night club and the radio and the tabloid newspaper. They are more than content, they are thrilled, that the commonplaces of big-city life have been translated with such clarity into a set of sounds and that the work of translation can apparently be expected to go on forever—or at least as

Ulanov's final judgment

long as the cities in which they live go on. Jazz is, then, neither faïence nor petit point, neither etching upon glass nor the music of bagpipes. It is an art that says some of the things that must be said about this society. Ours may be a minor civilization, but to the extent that one of its particular creations, jazz, expresses it with some thoroughness, this creation has a major contribution to make and possesses a universal importance, for our time at the very least.

WRITING ASSIGNMENTS

1. Why do you personally like or dislike jazz? In answering this, can you pin down exactly what it is that affects you, what responses you make? Do you agree or disagree with any of Mr. Ulanov's points? Does Jazz capture for you something real about life? If so, what?

2. Draw a verbal sketch of your favorite musical entertainer or musician. What kind of music is involved, why is this one person outstanding in comparison to others, what have been the stages of his or her career, what audience is affected?

3. There have been many varied stages in the history of jazz, many kinds of jazz, many distinctly different jazz musicians. On the basis of personal knowledge or some further research, describe the history of one particular kind of jazz. Or, instead, compare some of the different schools of jazz. In either case, try to explain what the musicians tried to do, what kind of music resulted, who some of the leading musicians were.

The Science of Dreams

EDWIN DIAMOND

[1] In an unadorned cubicle in the University of Chicago's Abbott Hall, two studious-looking hunters began the chase. They were out to catch a dream —a live, vivid, pulsating dream—before it had been transformed into a pale memory. Their hunting ground was the quiescent mind of a sleeping figure stretched out in the next room. Their weapon was an electroencephalograph machine (EEG) and small disk electrodes attached near the eyes and scalp of their subject.

[2] A deep, nocturnal silence prevailed, marred only by the soft rubbing of a pen as it traced a record of brain waves and eye movements on the EEG's slowly turning drum. Suddenly, a tell-tale track took shape on the moving graph paper—a sure sign that the first act of the dream play was about to begin; then, the sharp rise and fall of a tracing line as the subject's eyes moved back and forth under the eyelids: The plot was unfolding. They sounded a buzzer.

[3] The subject struggled awake, reached for the microphone of the tape recorder near his bed, and began to talk. "We were swimming and doing a lot of things. Everybody was in bathing suits at the swimming pool and I seemed to be admiring my body all the time . . ." On he went, graphically capturing the immediacy of the dream, finally slowing down, stopping, falling asleep again.

[4] The drum turned, the pen traced a normal sleep pattern for another 85 minutes when the familiar signature appeared again. Soon another dream was trapped in the recording machine: "A and B [two Hollywood actresses] were with me in this room . . ." Then came another period of sleep and once again the EEG drum alerted the scouts, and the subject talked once more of his nocturnal fantasies.

[5] Two more times that night the scene was repeated and when morning came the dream hunters had five gleaming new trophies in their bag. As close as words—and science—could catch them, they were what the dreamer had dreamed, undistorted by the thousand and one gaps and disguises which usually mar the remembered visions of sleep. Running through them was a pattern which would be analyzed by those who use dreams as a clue to personality.

[6] If this kind of catch is the most exciting result of this new method of tracking dreams, there is another which is more fundamental and may well be more important. Prof. Nathaniel Kleitman of the University of Chicago's Sleep Laboratory reflecting on the technique his group developed, says: "Obviously

we haven't been able to monitor a night's sleep of each and every person in the United States. But when we find naturally recurrent dream patterns in every one of the subjects studied—even those who tell us they never dream—then we have a strong statistical case that everyone dreams every night."

[7] The fact that dreams are probably universal in their occurrence and happen as regularly as the motions of the planetary bodies has already been turned to practical use in psychiatry, medicine, and learning theory. A new "science of dreams" is emerging.

[8] Until Dr. Sigmund Freud applied his genius to the world of dreams some 60 years ago, little if any orderly scientific thought had been expended on the perplexing and fleeting nighttime phenomena; dreams were regarded as too trivial for study. Then, in the monumental works that were to change irrevocably man's way of looking at himself, the Viennese doctor threw a powerful searchlight into the dark recesses of the mind to illuminate its most mysterious product, the dream.

[9] For Freud the dream was a type of wish-fulfillment that took place in order to safeguard sleep. This theory, in part, can be verified easily enough with children who have simple, straightforward dream lives.

[10] Adult dreams are another matter. By morning, Freud explained, the usually painful memory of the unruly wishes paraded during the night may be suppressed. And while it is the psychoanalyst's job to draw from the patient the details of the wish-fulfilling dream, even doctrinaire followers of Freud wryly acknowledge the drawbacks.

[11] For one, they realize they may be getting an edited version, perhaps a completely rewritten script, as the patient protectively reweaves the story. Of course, the analyst, by establishing himself as a sympathetic listener rather than as a judge holding court, may overcome this obstacle. But there are dangers here, too, as the patient may go out of his way to please the doctor and make a "sensible, logical" story. "Just let them know what you want to hear about their dreams," an analyst reported last week with a tolerant smile, "and they'll go out and dream up a textbook full."

[12] Though it is a costly, time-consuming, laborious process, it would obviously be useful for the analyst to have some unedited dreams before him. They can be used for comparison with the patient's tailored versions, the relations between them could be studied, and a clue might be found as to exactly what processes a patient uses to censor his dreams. At the University of Chicago just such a study is now going on. A patient under psychotherapy spends an occasional all-night session in the sleep room where his dreams are recorded and sent to his doctor for analysis.

[13] Some medical doctors also have been quick to see the value of the new dream science. Certain illnesses such as bronchial asthma, cardiac failure, and crises in ulcers tend to strike in the middle of the night. In fact, there is one form of coronary trouble which hits so frequently at night (and rarely during the day) that it is known as nocturnal angina.

[14] "Can it be," asks Dr. Arthur Shapiro, an internist at the State University of New York's Downstate Medical Center in Brooklyn, "that the occurrence of dreams or their content may be responsible for these night ills?" With the new knowledge of the natural dream cycle, Shapiro expects to match up the onset of dreams with possible changes, for example, in muscle spasms or in acid secretion. "It's just a matter of adding some more electrodes," he points out. "If we find any correlations we plan

to wake the subject and find out if he is having an emotionally charged dream.

[15] "It may turn out that we have to treat some asthma, coronary, and ulcer patients as psychological cases even when their trouble seems almost entirely organic. And alternatively or additionally, we might use sedatives or drugs to keep the patient from reaching that distinctive stage in the sleep cycle which Kleitman found is essential to dreaming."

[16] Sustained interference with the dream cycle through the use of "no-dream drugs" may prove to be a remedy worse than the illness, Shapiro cautions. It may well be that dreams act as a necessary safety valve whereby civilized man gets rid of his destructive—though not strictly Freudian—impulses, harmlessly. "Maybe we would all flip our lids," one investigator said in all seriousness, "if we were deprived of our dreams over a period of time."

[17] Already there is some evidence that this is so. Soldier volunteers deprived of sleep for as long as four to eight days in Army experiments seemed to compensate for their loss of sleep time (and dream time) by developing dreamlike hallucinations during the experiment. Still others developed psychotic symptoms persisting long after the tests were over—in two cases as long as two years.

[18] The recent wake-athon of New York disk jockey Peter Tripp, for all its carnival atmosphere, yielded important information on the safety-valve theory. Tripp also experienced hallucinations during the last few hours of his 200-hour-long exploit. And when he finally went to bed, it was expected that he would descend into a sleep trough so deep there would be little, if any, dreaming. But first indications are that Tripp apparently had at least the normal night's quota of dreams—perhaps even

more than usual for the time he slept. It was as if he was trying to make up for the lost dreams by crowding in some extra episodes when sleep finally came.

[19] A somewhat harrowing experiment could check this idea. Volunteer subjects (kept unaware of the true purpose of the experiment) would be put to sleep with attached electrodes in the approved fashion. When the EEG pens signaled the emergence of dream thought, the buzzer would rouse the subject before the dream could begin to unfold. The subject would be given some plausible instructions and then allowed to go back to sleep. All through the night, whenever the curtain of the dream act was ready to rise, the buzzer would spoil the show. How much of this treatment the average normal man could take, and for how long, is anybody's guess at the moment.

[20] The convincing demonstration that mental activity goes on during sleep has given new hope to those who think that those hours of slumber can be used for some form of productive intellectual work despite Professor Kleitman's contention that dream cortical activity is of a low level. There has always been a lore which suggested that some of the most brilliant discoveries and solutions come during sleep, when insight, prepared by hard work, can pierce to the heart of a problem. Robert Louis Stevenson, for example, claimed that all his plots came to him in his dreams, including the celebrated tale of Dr. Jekyll and Mr. Hyde. Prof. Hermann Hilprecht, famous German Assyriologist, dreamed that a Babylonian priest gave him the key to two puzzling ancient inscriptions—and then woke up to decipher the text.

[21] In his work on sleep and dreams at Mount Sinai Hospital in New York, Dr. William Dement, one of the early collaborators of Kleitman, set out to

find if a solution to a complex problem in logic could be reached in a dream. Accompanying the problem were these instructions: Do not attempt to solve or even think about the problem until you are ready to go to bed. Then devote fifteen minutes, no more, to a vigorous attempt to solve it. If you have not solved it after fifteen minutes put it out of your mind and go to bed. Whether or not you reached a solution, if you have any dreams during the night try to remember them and jot them down, especially if they have anything to do with the problem. He found that about 80 per cent of subjects who reported dreaming at all, dreamed about the problem, some stumbling across the answer, but not recognizing it. One subject came up with the solution. "That's all we need to make the point," said Dement.

[22] The inadvertent hero of the dream science story happens to have been a nameless Chicago infant. In 1952, Kleitman and a young postgraduate Ph.D. named Eugene Aserinsky were making the rounds of Chicago homes observing the sleep cycles of newborn babies. They noticed that the eyes of the tots continued to move slowly under the lids after all other body movements had stopped. To find out why, the two sleep scientists decided to explore the entire phenomena of eye movements. Their original method, still the basis of most scientific dream research, was deceptively simple: Subjects went to sleep on austere, military-like cots. Attached to the sleeper's temples, either with adhesive tape or the collodion glue used to patch up bleeding prizefighters, were tiny electrodes. These gauged changes in the eye muscles' electric potential as they go from the resting to the moving state. Thin wires led out from the electrodes to a switch box over the cot,

and then into an electroencephalograph (EEG) machine.

[23] Night after night, Aserinsky monitored the EEG report. To his surprise he detected split-second, jerky bursts of eye activity in clusters averaging twenty minutes and occurring several times each night. Kleitman had the hunch ("just call it a hypothesis") that the rapid eye movements or REM's had something to do with dreaming.

[24] New EEG electrodes were hooked up to the scalps of the sleeping subjects to pick up and amplify almost a million-fold the tiny changes in brain electrical activity—or brain waves. Other electrodes recorded heart and respiratory rates. The subjects, mainly students or people from the neighborhood, slept peacefully despite the Medusa-like outcroppings leading from their heads. Distinct REM, breathing, heartbeat, and brain-wave patterns showed up in these EEG tracings—all at the same time during sleep.

[25] Let's wake them up and see if they're dreaming, Kleitman suggested. Out of 191 arousals during REM's, 152 dreams were reported—a batting average of .800. As a cross-check, wakenings in the absence of eye movements were made 160 times with dream recall taking place only eleven times. Left sleeping undisturbed during a night of routine and unmistakable REM bursts, most subject's were able to recall only a few dreams.

[26] Clearly REM's were a clue to dreaming.

[27] Gathering around him a group of young scientists—physiologists and psychologists from the university—Kleitman undertook to refine his techniques. A buzzer and tape recorder were added to the dream-room's paraphernalia. When REM's appeared on the graph, the buzzer was sounded, and the sleeper was asked to dictate his dream, if any,

into the recorder. But when to sound the buzzer? The REM bursts appeared to last anywhere from 5 to 65 minutes and it was impossible to tell when to interrupt without spoiling the dream. Awakened subjects were sometimes loquacious, sometimes terse. Were they anxious to get back and finish the dream they had started?

[28] Then Kleitman and Dement, in a key finding, discovered that all REM's were accompanied by a distinctly flattened brain-wave signature on the EEG graph. They found that dream recall, in the presence of the flat brain-wave pattern, was close to 100 per cent, *whether or not any REM's were apparent.*

[29] But if the flat EEG pattern was the true signal that dreaming was taking place, what part did the REM's play? Dement and graduate student Edward Wolpert went back over transcripts and graphs and noted that the end of eye movements were frequently accompanied by gross body movements, a shift in bed that sent the EEG pens racing wildly. Then eye movements would begin again. Could it be that the body movements represented the end of one scene and the beginning of another?

[30] To find out, Dement and Wolpert sounded the wake-up-and-tell-us-if-you're-dreaming buzzer the moment the body shift lines were spotted. One subject recalled: "I had the impression that the dream had reached its natural end, that the TV program I was watching had reached its fade-out point . . ." From such evidence, Dement and Wolpert tentatively concluded that body movements during dreams signal a shift in the dream activity.

[31] Then the final refinements were made. Again Dement and Wolpert retraced the records of graphs and tapes and found that eye movement related to active dream movement. In one case,

the last eye movement recorded on the graph was downward, and the last reported dream activity on the transcript was picking an object up off the floor. They were able to distinguish two categories of dreams—active dreams that are "watched" by the sleeper's eyes, and thought dreams with little or no eye movement taking place. Wolpert, working now with Dr. Harry Trosman, pinpointed how dreams swirl away from memory, first fragmenting (within five minutes after eye movements stop) and then evaporating almost completely in another five to ten minutes. At New York's Downstate Medical Center, psychologist Donald Goodenough found a paradoxical reason why at least some people say they never dream: Apparently they dream so close to the waking stage (as determined on the EEG machine) that they mistake their dreams for wakeful night reveries. Chicago's Dr. William Offenkrantz was able to record the dreams of a congenitally blind man (who dreamed of sound, touch, and ideas rather than things) by waking him during the flat EEG patterns.

[32] Thanks to these findings, sleep scientists can now bag a night of dreams with ease simply by checking the unrolling drum.

[33] First comes deep, probably dreamless sleep. The EEG traces the little-understood but characteristic hill-and-valley—a high-voltage pattern—perhaps caused by the intrinsic, rhythmic ebb and flow of nerve activity. After about 90 minutes, "sleep spindles" (so named because the patterns look like the wire unwound from a spindle) indicate dreaming is about to begin. Then the first act of the dream unfolds when the EEG lines trace the low-voltage pattern indicating the self-canceling chaos probably marking mental activity.

[34] The first dream act is short, averaging about eight minutes in length.

The night-long cycle averages four dream acts of gradually increasing length—19 minutes, 24 minutes, 28 minutes.

[35] All these historic findings go beyond the problems of treating illness. Now science can summon the evanescent shapes behind the logical mind.

For those who believe, in Freudian-disciple Ernest Jones' words, that "man's chief enemy is his own unruly nature and the dark forces pent up within him," there is hope, at last, of pinpointing the origin of these forces and achieving some measure of control over them.

WRITING ASSIGNMENTS

1. Summarize briefly but completely the events of a typical night's experiment on the dreams of a single sleeper. As specifically as possible, and using Mr. Diamond's article as a source of information, describe step by step what you think would take place.

2. Explain as completely as possible a dream, either pleasant or unpleasant, that you have had. In addition to narrating the story or plot of the dream, try to also explain why you think you dreamt it, and to what real events of your life it seems to be related.

3. This article briefly mentions the dream theories of Sigmund Freud, whom many people identify as the father of modern psychology. As a brief exercise in using materials of a library, find five books that discuss Freud's dream theories. List the titles and publishing information and then, using information from one or more of these books, write a brief explanation of how "repression" or "free association" (choose only one word to write about) is connected to the process of dreaming.

The Push into Space

[1] When the Soviet Lunik raced past the moon and free of the earth, it did more than win a triumph for its designers. It also marked a turning point in the multibillion-year history of the solar system. One of the sun's planets had at last evolved a living creature that could break the chains of its home gravitational field. After a few more moments on the evolutionary time scale, earth's restless social primate, man, can almost surely make himself felt throughout the system. Earth's life will no longer be confined to the earth.

[2] This startling development took place with explosive suddenness. Boys still in high school remember a time when sensible citizens considered space flight as impractical as hunting leprechauns. Ten years ago the altitude rec-

ord for rockets, 250 miles, was held a brilliant achievement. Several years ago, the earth satellite, that humblest of space vehicles, seemed an almost impossible project.

[3] But the basic rules of space flight have been known for centuries. The Chinese, who invented rockets about 1200, did not theorize about them, but Sir Isaac Newton's laws of motion, published in 1687, not only explained the principle that makes rockets fly but gave the essential sailing directions for spaceships of the future. When a U.S. Atlas or an even bigger (for the present) Soviet space rocket roars into the sky, it runs on rails devised by the ill-tempered Sir Isaac, who sat in his English garden nearly 300 years ago and wondered why things move as they do, and why things fall.

[4] When a rocket engine shoots a jet of gas out of its tail cone, Newton's third law takes over: *For every action there is an equal and opposite reaction.* Acting in the opposite direction to that of the racing gases, a mighty force lifts the rocket off its launching pad. As long as the engine fires, the rocket climbs faster and faster, obeying Newton's second law: *An unbalanced force acting on a body makes it accelerate in the direction of the force* . . . When the engine burns out, the rocket continues upward under the control of Newton's first law: *. . . A body in motion continues to move at constant speed in a straight line unless acted upon by an unbalanced force.* As it rises, it slows and curves because an unbalanced force, the earth's gravitation, keeps pulling at it in obedience to Newton's law of gravity: *Each particle of matter attracts every other particle with a force that is directly proportional to the product of their masses and inversely proportional to the square of the distance between them.*

. . .

[5] The best way to think of space as a navigable medium is to imagine the frictionless surface of a calm, glassy pond. Small objects drift across it easily, propelled by feeble forces. Scattered at wide intervals over the mirror surfaces are deep, sucking whirlpools. If a floating leaf drifts close to one of them, it plunges down to the bottom. A self-powered object, say a water insect, that gets sucked into a whirlpool has a terrible time battling back to the surface.

[6] Deep space, far from stars or planets, is like the pond's smooth surface. An object becalmed in its emptiness floats like a galleon in the doldrums. If the object is a spaceship with propulsive power, it can cruise in any direction, meeting practically no resistance. But it must keep away from the whirlpools: the gravitational fields that surround stars and planets. If it plunges into one of them, it may end as a puff of gas in a star or a brief streak of fire in a planet's atmosphere.

[7] Looking at it from the other end, a spaceship that starts its voyage on the surface of a planet has a hard time climbing out of its gravitational pit. Once it has reached untroubled space, it can coast for millions of miles on its unopposed momentum.

[8] To fight free of the earth, the space navigator must reach a speed called escape velocity. Figured at the surface of the earth, this is 25,000 m.p.h. But rockets do not start suddenly. They accelerate gradually, keeping their speed fairly low while still in the atmosphere, then spurting quickly. If a rocket is moving 24,000 m.p.h. when it is 300 miles above the surface, it will escape from the earth's gravitation. When the Russian Lunik launchers, watching their bird with Doppler (speed-measuring) radios, saw it pass the critical speed,

they knew it would never return to earth. A lesser speed than escape velocity sets a satellite revolving around the earth just free of the atmosphere. A satellite can be compared to a chip or leaf circling around the sides of a whirlpool without escaping from it or immediately being swallowed.

[9]   Near the rim of the earth's gravitational pit is a much smaller pit belonging to the moon. An object shot away from the earth at 24,800 m.p.h. will reach the boundary, about 34,000 miles short of the moon, where the moon's pull is as strong as the earth's. If it reaches this point with a small velocity, it will fall on the moon. If it crosses the line at good speed, it will shoot past the moon, its course merely deflected. This is what happened to the Lunik.

· · ·

[10]   Perhaps the most striking thing about space navigation is the ease of long-distance travel after successful launching. Mars never comes closer to the earth than 34.5 million miles, Venus never closer than 25 million miles. To cover these great distances, it takes more time (146 days to Venus, 260 days to Mars), but only slightly more speed than is needed to go to the moon, which is only 230,000 miles away. This is because space between the planets is comparatively smooth. It is only slightly affected by planetary gravitation, and the great pull of the sun is countered by the orbital speed that a spaceship inherits from its home planet.

[11]   Full escape from the gravitational pull of the sun would be tougher. Starting from the earth's surface, a ship would need 36,800 m.p.h. Soaring past Mars, Jupiter, Saturn, Uranus, Neptune and Pluto, it would reach the outer limits of the solar system with almost no speed left. Then, like a chip on a glassy lake, it could drift for millions of years before it approached the nearest star,

Proxima Centauri, which is 25 trillion miles away from the sun. Man's spaceships can probably reach interstellar escape velocity in a generation, but there will be little profit in interstellar voyages. They will take too long. The barrier that protects the stars and their planetary systems from human invasion is not space but time, and the shortness of man's life.

[12]   How close is interplanetary voyaging? The great weight (2,925 lbs. of instrumented payload) of Sputnik III proved to the space-wise that the Russians had practically licked the initial problems of interplanetary flight. U.S. scientists reckon that the Soviets' Lunik, with only a little more speed, would have swooped past Mars and soared out toward the asteroids. George Paul Sutton, professor of aeronautical engineering at M.I.T., believes that present propulsion systems with a little refinement can send a space vehicle as far as Jupiter or even to Saturn, 750 million miles from the earth.

[13]   Astronomers can hardly wait for the day when these first space scouts are launched. For oddly enough, they know less in many ways about the planets, the earth's neighbors, than they do about far-distant stars. The reason is that stars shine in their own light, revealing much about themselves to astronomers' spectroscopes. The solar system's planets are visible only in the reflected light of the sun. Their spectra carry little firm information, and the details that can be seen on their surfaces are clear enough to excite but too vague to satisfy human curiosity.

[14]   The moon is an exception. It is so close that it shows a wealth of detail that astronomers have studied for centuries. They have also argued bitterly over many questions presented by its serene face, e.g.: Are the ring-shaped

craters the result of volcanic activity or meteor impacts?

[15] Dutch-born Astronomer Gerard Kuiper (rhymes with hyper), head of the University of Chicago's Yerkes and McDonald observatories, thinks the moon was formed at the same time as the earth (5½ billion years ago), but at first it revolved only about 20,000 miles from the earth's surface. Beyond it were a lot of smaller satellites arranged in a disk somewhat like the rings of modern Saturn.

[16] This situation did not last. When the earth acquired oceans, the great tides aroused in them by the nearby moon made the earth rotate more slowly. This made the moon spiral outward. As it moved, it crashed into the lesser satellites, each of them blasting an impact pit in its surface. The bigger pits punched through the moon's crust and were filled with lava from the molten interior. The biggest satellite of all, about 100 miles in diameter, hit the present site of the lunar plain called Mare Imbrium—the right eye of the "man in the moon."

[17] After this climactic event Astronomer Kuiper thinks the moon led an increasingly peaceful life. It picked up the rest of the small satellites, which made the fresh-looking pits on its surface. Cosmic rays and other high-speed particles bombarded its surface, riddling the material with microscopic holes. This beaten-up stuff is only an inch or so thick, says Kuiper, and it is not dust. He thinks it would feel underfoot "like crunchy snow."

[18] Nobel Prizewinner Harold Urey of the University of California at La Jolla, another leading moon authority, agrees with Kuiper about there being lava on much of the moon's surface, but he does not think that it welled out of a molten interior. Instead, he contends, it was formed on the spot by the energy

of great meteors that hit the moon and melted both themselves and the local lunar rock. He thinks that the present surface material may be something like sand or gravel.

[19] The newest and most radical moon theory was developed by British Cosmologist Thomas Gold, now at Harvard. Professor Gold agrees that the moon was pockmarked long ago by large meteors, and it may have been built up entirely by such accretion. But he does not think that the smooth, dark areas that are called *maria* (seas), because early astronomers thought they were exactly that, are filled with lava. He thinks that they are low places full of fine dust that was removed by a kind of erosion from the moon's highlands. In some places it may be more than a mile deep.

[20] There is no water on the moon, so Gold's erosion cannot be like the kind that wears down earth's mountains. He thinks that the chief eroding agent is high-energy radiation from the sun helped by cosmic rays and meteorites. They slowly chewed a flour-fine dust from the moon's exposed rocks and kept it stirred up so that it gradually flowed into low places like the interiors of old craters and the *maria*.

[21] Whether Gold's theory is correct or not, it threw something of a scare into space-minded military men who hope some day to land on the moon and do not like the idea of sinking into a mile of loose dust. Their fears were calmed by simple tests made in the laboratories of their contractors. North American Aviation, Inc., for instance, shows two sealed glass tubes. One of them contains air as well as fine dust, and a small steel ball sinks deeply below the surface. The other has a vacuum. The dust particles, no longer lubricated by air between them, pack tightly and prevent the ball from sinking. On the airless moon, it is

likely that dust has compacted in the same way.

[22] Russia's Lunik carried an instrument to measure the radioactivity of the moon's surface. Neither Kuiper nor Gold believes that it could have worked at the distance (4,660 miles) at which the Lunik swept past the moon, but they would be grateful for any information that the Russians choose to release. Dr. Kuiper believes that the moon's surface is blazing with radioactivity. On the earth, he says, the thick layer of air is the shielding equivalent of 3 ft. of lead or 33 ft. of water, protects the surface from many kinds of tough radiation beating down from space. Kuiper believes that the moon is radioactively contaminated to a depth of 30 ft. below the surface.

[23] Nearest planet to the earth is Venus. It is about as big as the earth and has an atmosphere, but it seems even less attractive as real estate than the airless, sun-seared moon. Its atmosphere is so cloudy that outsiders, peering from the earth, can see only its slightly yellowish cloud deck, which sometimes shows faint, impermanent markings.

[24] The Venusian atmosphere contains carbon dioxide. This information does not mean (as many science-fiction writers seem to think) that Venus under its clouds is covered with lush jungles. Earthside plants need carbon dioxide, but their flourishing presence on earth is the reason why the earth's modern atmosphere contains only a trace of CO_2. This abundance of carbon dioxide in the Venusian atmosphere is excellent proof that the planet has no earthlike plants on it.

[25] Probably it has no life at all. Dr. Kuiper thinks that it has no water or free oxygen. Radio waves, which penetrate the murky atmosphere, hint that the temperature of the invisible surface is something like 500° F., which is much too high for the earth's kinds of life. Venus rotates only once in several weeks, making the sunlit side much hotter than the dark side, and causing violent storms that sweep perpetually over its hot, dry deserts.

[26] Dr. Urey still thinks that the clouds in the Venusian atmosphere may be made of water droplets like clouds on earth, but few astronomers agree with him. Dr. Kuiper thinks they are made of fine dust particles of carbon suboxide (C_3O_2). In an attempt to prove this theory, he made a mixture of carbon dioxide and carbon monoxide and exposed it to assorted radiation at the Argonne National Laboratory. Sure enough, carbon suboxide formed, and its molecules stuck together to make particles of yellowish polymer.

[27] Mars is more interesting than Venus because its atmosphere is transparent enough to permit its surface to be seen. But astronomers do not agree about what they see on it. All of them see white patches at the planet's poles, which they accept as thin layers of ice or hoarfrost. All of them see irregular light and dark markings that change with the Martian seasons. Only a few of them still see the network of straight, artificial-looking lines that was widely believed a generation ago to be a system of irrigation canals built by highly civilized beings to distribute the failing water supply of their aging planet.

[28] Even stern astronomers regret to see the Martians abolished, but they can do nothing to save them. They have to insist that even if Mars is really covered with fine lines at the limit of vision, they cannot be irrigation canals, since they are not arranged in a way that would distribute water from the icecap, and they follow no logical contour lines. With this notion lost, there is no further support for the civilized Mars theory.

[29] The Martian atmosphere is thin (8% of the pressure on earth) and may have no oxygen. It contains a little carbon dioxide and probably nitrogen and argon. The daytime temperature may occasionally rise above 86° F., and at night it may fall to minus 150° F.

[30] These are tough conditions for life, but life is tough. Mars's seasonal changes of color suggest strongly the growth of something like vegetation in the Martian spring when the polar ice-cap melts or evaporates and spreads its scanty moisture over the nearby surface. And only this year new evidence was found that some kind of life exists on Mars—perhaps at the level of lichens. Dr. William M. Sinton of Lowell Observatory took spectrograms of Mars in infra-red light, found dips in three places where infra-red waves are absorbed by chemical compounds containing hydrogen atoms bonded to carbon. Earth's living plants and animals are made almost entirely of such compounds.

. . .

WRITING ASSIGNMENTS

1. Why would you or would you not like to take part in the exploration of outer space? Do you think it is a valuable program? Why?

2. By doing some research in magazines at the library, write a report on the latest rockets of the United States and Russia.

3. Space travel has been a lure for writers for many years; you might as well try your hand at it. Using the information in this article and a good dose of imagination, describe the events of an imaginary flight to and landing on a distant heavenly body.

PART 4

Reading the

OPINION

INTRODUCTION

Many (in fact, probably most) of your opinions are not your own. Very few of us have the time or ability to think through every question that confronts us and arrive at a personal solution or opinion. Instead, we usually take over opinions from someone else—parents, teachers, government leaders, writers, celebrities. These opinions then seem to become our own, and, in fact, guide and control our lives.

It is important, then, for you to recognize the opinions in material that you read. You need to recognize, for one thing, that they are there. You need to recognize exactly what they are, and to recognize how well they are defended or proved. Only in this way will you even be aware of where your opinions come from and, more importantly, of what arguments they are based on. For not every opinion that gets printed is a right one or even a sensible wrong one. You have to learn to judge arguments that you read, but before you can judge, you have to learn to understand them.

Asking Why

Opinions can come to you in many disguises. Sometimes they are openly revealed, sometimes they are hidden. You have already seen how many of the stories, descriptions and explanations in this book have contained implied opinions. Sometimes these opinions are intentionally hidden, so that the reader will think he is reading facts only, but is nonetheless being persuaded to think about the facts in a certain way. Here we will be concerned only with those opinions which are openly revealed, with writing that clearly and intentionally is meant to persuade you to agree with the opinion of the author. For you the reader there is a choice involved; there are two or more opposed beliefs which you may hold. The writer's job is both to support his position and attack the other, though he will not usually do both in equal amounts.

Asking What

In determining *what* the opinion is, you have to be able to recognize exactly what specific position the writer is taking within the broader scope of the conflict. What specifically is he for or against? Despite the familiar saying, there are usually *more* than two sides to any argument. The writer may be taking an extreme position or he may be taking a more moderate, compromising one. He may be defending only certain parts of a more general position; he may even be accepting certain parts of the opposing position. What, specifically, is he trying to prove?

Asking How

Even when the attempt to persuade you is apparent, and the exact opinion clear, the method of argument employed may not be so apparent. I will describe the four most common *methods of argument:* logical, emotional, satirical, and critical.

The *logical argument* clearly defines the issues involved and makes clear the meaning of certain key words. It both presents its side of things and criticizes the opposing arguments. In so doing, it stresses the evidence that supports its contentions and attempts to interpret the evidence in an intelligent, reasonable manner. It is aimed at the reader's intelligence.

The *emotional argument,* on the other hand, is aimed at the reader's feelings. It plays on such basic emotions as hatred, love, fear, greed, selfishness, happiness, sadness. The reader is not asked to think; in fact, great care is often taken to keep him from thinking. Words and issues are not clearly defined. Emotional words or slogans are constantly used. Those with positive values (popular, patriotic, progress, justice, truth) are applied to "our" side; those with negative values (dangerous, un-American, reactionary, socialistic, dishonest) are applied to the other side. Often more of the argument is devoted to an exaggerated attack on the opposing viewpoint and the opposing people than to a defense of the author's own position. Evidence, if used at all, is often not very convincing once you separate it from the catchy slogans and emotional words.

The *satirical argument* is actually a special kind of emotional approach. It attempts to persuade you by ridiculing, by kidding those ideas, attitudes or people it opposes. It intentionally exaggerates errors and faults, hoping to make you laugh at them and thus see the "Truth." In fact, the most apparent trait of this kind of argument is that it is supposed to be funny as well as persuasive. The writer knows he is exaggerating. He knows you know it. And hopes you will laugh at it. Much of our best comedy is satirical to some degree. Sometimes the main purpose of this comedy is the humor itself, but sometimes the real purpose is an argument, with the humor used as a device to get the opinions across to you.

The *critical argument* is an attempt to evaluate and interpret a work of art—popular or serious. At its simplest judging level it merely says a work is good or bad, worth seeing or not seeing, worth reading or not reading. It cites evidence from the material itself or the performance of the material to back up its contention. It may also support its contention by reference to other works of the same type or to certain standards for works of the same type. But often the judgment is mixed with an interpretation. The interpretation may explain the possible meanings—or comments on life and people—suggested by the work itself, or it may explain the significance of the work (and others like it) in its society—that is, what it represents in the life of a people and time. Finally, in the case of works whose value is generally assumed, only the interpretation is made.

Of course, you will not always find arguments neatly fitting into one of these types. Many arguments will mix, to one degree or another, two or even more of these approaches, and you, therefore, have to notice when this occurs.

Finally, you need to determine and judge how the writer supports or proves his general contention. What *sub-arguments* or reasons does he mention? Does he provide *evidence* for each of these sub-points? What kind of evidence is it? Does he use facts which we would have to admit are true (even if we didn't want to); does he refer to authorities, that is, prominent people and experts, who agree with him; does he merely use more opinions to support his original opinions? When you are not an expert yourself, it is difficult to judge evidence in this critical manner, to determine if it is accurate, relevant and complete. But you can at least make a beginning by learning to tell the difference between the evidence and the argument it is supposed to support, by learning to tell a fact from an opinion.

IN READING THIS SECTION—

1. Be sure to determine just *what* the author is trying to prove.

2. Notice *how* he is going about it: the method, or methods, of argument and the organization of the sub-arguments.

3. Notice and try to evaluate the kind of supporting evidence used.

Civil Defense Is a Farce

INEZ ROBB

[1]   Sure, I like to play games: Spin-the-Pan, Croquet, Post Office, Hearts, Footsie—you name it.

[2]   But Russian Roulette is not my dish. Nor am I in any mood to play games, no matter how elaborate, with Civil Defense in which the stakes are life and death for millions of Americans.

[3]   I don't know how Civil Defense operated in your home town last week when the Federal Civil Defense Administration decreed a mock hydrogen bomb attack across the nation. But in my home town, which is New York, it was a farce.

[4]   Oh, yes, it was pronounced a great success by the authorities because eight million New Yorkers disappeared from the sidewalks for from eight to ten minutes, the length of this "serious" test. In that interim, you could have shot a cannon (how quaint in this atom age!) up or down Broadway or Fifth Avenue or Riverside Drive and never plugged a soul except police and Civil Defense wardens.

[5]   And where were all the obedient millions who so promptly "took cover" once the warning sirens blew? Well, an appalling percentage of them were standing placidly behind plate-glass windows in the store fronts of Fifth, Park, and Madison Avenues and Broadway, Maiden Lane, Lexington Avenue, Forty-second Street and the Bowery. Or in

equally flimsy "cover" all over the city.

[6]   What this "mock" drill—and what an apt word!—proved is that the sidewalks of New York can be cleared in nothing flat. What that fact itself proves is beyond my grasp.

[7]   Why Civil Defense authorities had to prove once more that New Yorkers—and, presumably, all town dwellers—will quickly clear their streets by stepping through the nearest door, as ordered, is also beyond me. They proved this fact conclusively on November 28, 1951, when the first city-wide atom air raid test emptied the streets in two or three minutes.

[8]   As a survivor of a little wartime bombing, I thought the 1951 drill a fiasco completely divorced from reality. It was obvious that time that somehow the safety of the individual had been confused with cleared streets and empty sidewalks!

[9]   In the intervening three and one-half years, I had every confidence that Civil Defense had devised some really adequate, horse-sense safety measures.

[10]   But the most recent drill was a dreary and frightening repetition of the initial drill of 1951. As far as this participant in both drills could see, nothing new had been added.

[11]   Why, ten years after the explosion of the first atom bomb, are there

no adequate, intelligent drills or plans to protect as many persons as possible? Why, after a decade, is Civil Defense still Playing Games?

[12] It is ridiculous for Civil Defense to pat itself on the back because it can clear streets. A hydrogen bomb is not needed for that. Anyone can do the same thing, given enough stench bombs.

WRITING ASSIGNMENTS

1. What is a good procedure for Civil Defense preparation against atomic attack? Or, if you like, why is no procedure a good one? In explaining what a good pro- cedures is, discuss what the individual should do both during a test and at other times; what the authorities should do and what their aims should be? Agree or disagree with Miss Robb.

2. Direct an attack against the procedure of some branch or department of the government. This might be some specific action taken or some general, standing sys- tem or process. Explain the procedure fully and then point out why it is foolish, un- just, dangerous, etc.

3. What kind of drills have you participated in? Select one or several and describe what went on during the drill (or drills) and judge whether or not anything was achieved.

Go Western, Young Writer

FRANK R. PIERSON

[1] A little more than 25 percent of all the movies ever made have been Westerns, and television is approaching the same proportion. It is all mystifying to the producers. No one understands why Westerns are so popular, and when men are investing millions in making a product it unnerves them not to know why people want it and what they use it for. Every *Variety* announces some- one's new theory: people like the vio- lence, they like the simplicity, the maleness of the symbolism of gunfights, the release of tension. The consensus at the moment seems to be that audiences like escape into what Stanley Kauffmann referred in these pages as "that lovely uncivilized feeling." James Garner, who plays the lead of *Maverick*, an hour Western, once explained it thus: "The heroes have perfect socio-economic mobility."

[2] The adult television Western rep- resents a flight from reality all right, but

I suspect it is not the public fleeing so much as it is the creators. Television is fenced in by so many vexations in handling honest drama that its only solution is to make Westerns.

[3] Consider the conditions under which television drama is made. The first rule in testing an idea for a story or a series is to think of who might object to it. If it could offend a government bureau or lobby, no sponsor with government contracts will want it. Thus stories about farmers, generals, Indians and lobbyists are difficult to sell. Most stories that touch however remotely on government matters are cleared with the government as a matter of routine. Nothing critical of generals is going to get on the air.

[4] Try a story about a lynch mob. It might offend members of lynch mobs, who also smoke, wash and support the economy by taking pills for their headaches. A producer approaches such a story in the spirit of a veterinarian debarking a dangerous dog. He decides it's all a misunderstanding; the mob repents; instead of lynching the man they elect him to high public office. This is not as silly as it sounds. *Noon on Doomsday*, an undistinguished but good hearted drama that suggested the Emmett Till case was relocated in New England and the victim rewritten into an unidentifiable vagueness. During production a Coca Cola bottle was removed from the set, because Coca Cola, as everybody knows, was invented in the South. Reginald Rose's *Thunder on Sycamore Street* was fixed up by changing the key figures from a Negro to an ex-convict, and an unjustly convicted convict at that.

[5] Or the producer can take the story back to the frontier, where flotsam of the "Civil War, renegades, ranchers and sodbusters forge the history of a nation against the beauty of the savage

Tetons. Back there it no longer appears to relate to reality. The writer can say almost anything about Cavalry generals without consulting with the Pentagon. It is the writers who flee the present, taking with them most of the real moral conflicts television cares to confront.

[6] This has nothing to do with the sort of Westerns whose heroes are characterized solely by whether they pick off their enemies with a rifle or club them to death with canes. It has everything to do with the superiority of *Gunsmoke* over the fatuity of the *Loretta Young Show* or the flaccid nonsense of *GE Theater* and the rest. *Gunsmoke* is the most popular show on the air, and it is one of the best by any standards. Its characters have a sense of humor about themselves. They convey a rudimentary idea of place, of people sorely tried, who sweat and suffer. *Gunsmoke*, *Maverick*, and occasionally *Have Gun, Will Travel*, are apt to give wry and revealing twists of character to standard plots. Their sodbusters are vicious because they're hungry, their villains dangerous because they're scared. Their dancehall girls are unmistakably businesswomen. Perhaps the reason they are so popular is that they are more honest, varied and interesting than anything else on the air.

[7] This is heresy. For despite *Gunsmoke*'s dazzling financial success, the industry is oddly resistant to its lesson. Even the first producer of *Gunsmoke*, Charles Marquis Warren, is baffled by it. "It just shows people will go for that go-nowhere dialogue," he has said. Professional Western writers are worrying about psychology and modern overtones slowing down the action. They seem to believe Westerns' appeal lies exactly in their unreality, which is the same reason their strongest critics attack them. The producers stick rigidly to form, as though Westerns had to be the same

story over and over again. They all miss the point: Westerns are only a highly stylized set of theatrical conventions, within which tales of vastly varying sophistication may be told. The really successful Westerns fictionalize reality, which is not at all the same thing as falsifying it.

[8] Both the hope and despair of Westerns is that audiences will accept any sort of story, so long as there is virtuosity in the performance. They know who is going to be shot from the moment he steps on camera, but they must be surprised when it happens. It is like a *pas de deux* [1] of classical ballet. And it is almost the only common theatrical event where audience and artist are meeting on common ground, where, once the conventions are satisfied, some semblance of human truth can be intimated. If someone is going to write a true tragedy [2] for the popular theatre it is almost certainly going to be a Western. On television it is the only way it could be tried.

[1] A duet that has set routines but many variations.
[2] Generally considered the highest form of dramatic art.

WRITING ASSIGNMENTS

1. Explain the reasons for the popularity of a type of television program. Like Pierson, discuss what type of audience it appeals to and why it appeals to that audience; compare it to other types of programs; try to guess the producers' motives; judge its value. You might deal with some other type of program than the Western, or you might try the Western, giving your version of its value and popularity.

2. Defend a form of public entertainment that is often looked down upon by many people (including teachers). Try to show what its appeal is, what its worth is; and try, too, to mention and attack some of the usual criticisms made of it.

3. Television reaches an enormous audience, which is growing yearly. Argue that this great force is a powerful influence for good in our society or that it may not be now but can be. Refer to specific programs and types of programs that help to make it so or are needed to make it so.

Good Grief, More Peanuts!

GERALD WEALES

[1] The debut of *Peanuts*, Charles M. Schulz's comic strip about the adventures of Charlie Brown and his friends, occurred modestly in October, 1950, in eight newspapers. Since then, as an examination of the six published

Peanuts books shows, the characters have become clearly defined and differentiated, the drawing sharper and more detailed, the wit more personal. The standard comic strip gags—cute-child variety—that shared space with originality in the first of the collections, *Peanuts* (1952), have given way to fantasy and a slightly satiric, slightly satanic logic.

[2] As the strip has developed, its popularity has grown. The six paperbacks have, in the good round figures of the publisher, sold over a million copies, and the strip is carried—daily or Sunday —by more than 450 papers. Vinyl figures of Charlie Brown and the dog Snoopy —which without seeing I know I do not want on my desk—are about to flood the drugstores of America. A popular song about a Charlie Brown, which has no connection with the cartoonist, his publisher, or United Features, which handles the strip, is cashing in on the *Peanuts* excitement and at the same time helping to feed it. Schulz has stirred up more adherents among intellectual comic-strip readers than any of the younger cartoonists except probably Walt Kelly; and *Peanuts*, like *Pogo*, commands intense loyalty. The staunchest followers, on and off college campuses, have even substituted Charlie Brown's exclamation of exasperation, "Oh, good grief," for meatier curses.

[3] When the first of the *Peanuts* books appeared, a note at the front, an interior blurb, declared that "*Peanuts* is just about the most original strip to appear since George Herriman's *Krazy Kat* in its prime." The claim is a little misleading. It is Walt Kelly and not Schulz whose work bears comparison with Herriman's, but perhaps that is what the blurbist meant by "just about." *Pogo*, like *Krazy Kat*, is a complicated creation that develops situations over a period of time; *Peanuts*, although there are occasional variations on a theme, is a one-

strip-one-joke affair. Kelly, like Herriman, has a remarkable sense of verbal play; Schulz, when the language is at all unusual, depends for his humor on the incongruity of adult jargon in the mouths of children. The antecedents of *Peanuts* are not in Herriman. Schulz's distinction is that he has taken over the familiar comic strip about children and turned it into something peculiarly his own.

[4] Ordinarily, the child strip has taken one of two forms. Either the child, as in the classic *The Katzenjammer Kids*, is pitted against the adult world in a violent antagonism, or else his mishaps and pranks are indulgently considered. Hank Ketcham's popular *Dennis the Menace* manages to combine both, having softened the Katzenjammer monster into a recognizable brat and having laced the whole concoction with a sentiment that is only occasionally cloying. In either case the child is seen only in relation to the adult. Schulz's originality lies in his having banished adults from his strip. Parents have dwindled to offstage voices, like distant gods, as impersonal as the weather and demanding the same kind of adjustment from the characters.

[5] Charlie Brown and his neighbors are interested in the things that preoccupy all children—sports and games, rain and snow, candy and ice cream— but the realistic concern is only a point of departure. The world is a fantasy one. The wonderfully efficient Linus can stand in the outfield, catch sight of a high fly ball, calmly fold and put down the blanket that he carries for comfort, and still make his catch. The variations that Schulz has played on this one gag indicate the increasing whimsicality of his work. Linus has stopped to remove his shoes and climb into the wading pool, or to build a high and improbable sand castle, before catching the always on-

coming ball. In the same way Charlie Brown's insistence on playing baseball even in the rain has become more frenetic over the years. In the early, almost realistic, strips he stayed on the field, though the rain was so thick that he could not have seen his opponents had they still been there; now he stands on his pitcher's mound, calling for the cowards to come back, while Snoopy swims by or Linus poles in on a raft from the outfield.

[6] If the strip were simply concerned with this kind of comic overstatement, it would be amusing and no more. Often, however, the extravagance hinges on some immediately perceptible personality quirk. The jealousies, the triumphs, the defeats, the ambitions of the characters in *Peanuts* are all those of real children (and, more important, of real adults); and if they are displayed obliquely, seen in unlikely contexts, voiced in improbable words, that in no way lessens the force with which they strike the reader. This can be seen most clearly in Charlie Brown, the strip's hero (or anti-hero, to use a currently fashionable critical term). Although the things that happen to Charlie Brown's kite—down a sewer, for instance—are unlikely, his failure at checkers, at football, at almost everything, defines him quickly and easily as the perennial patsy. It takes more self-assurance than most men have to keep from suffering the shock of recognition when, once again, Charlie Brown runs trustingly toward the football that Lucy holds, knowing and not knowing that she will pull it away and that he will fall once again full length and defeated. Schulz wisely makes his comments indirectly, in terms of the action of the strip, but once in a while he speaks directly. One of the most impressive of the strips, which unfortunately has not been included in any of the books, finds the children discussing their plans for the distant future of adulthood; asked what he is going to be when he grows up Charlie Brown answers, "Lonely."

[7] The figures are all reminiscent of the stock comic types of old farce. Charlie Brown, as I have indicated above, is the fall guy, the butt of everybody's jokes. The girls plan parties so that they can fail to invite him, or, if they do ask him, as Patty did in one of the strips, and he calls to say that he will be late, the hostess has to admit that she did not notice that he had not yet arrived. He is regularly in search of signs of affection and just as regularly he is deserted (even by the dog) or chosen last or accepted reluctantly. The title of two of the books, *Good Ol' Charlie Brown* (1957) and *You're Out of Your Mind, Charlie Brown* (1959), indicate the condescension or the belligerency with which he is received. Since it is ordinarily the girls, particularly Lucy, who make Charlie Brown's life miserable, it has been suggested that the strip is a microcosm of America's female-dominated society, a possibility which has to face the problem of Schroeder's systematic rejection of Lucy and Linus's occasional rebellion.

[8] Lucy, the second most important figure in the strip, is a mixture of stock types. She is the fuss-budget, the business minder, the henpecking woman; she is the perfect top sergeant; she is also the comic pedant. In her early appearances (she does not turn up until the second book, *More Peanuts*-1954), she is busy counting the stars and the raindrops, later in misexplaining natural phenomena to her brother, finally in offering, as the back of the new book shows, "Psychiatric Care, 5¢." Since the comedy stems from the simplicity of the characters, a relatively small number of situations are used and reused. Schroeder, who plays Beethoven on a toy piano,

can be depended on for some jokes in which his artistic soul is tried by his Philistine friends. Linus, who cannot kick the blanket habit, is regularly seen defending his security fetish and describing it in psychological terms that he probably picked up from Lucy. Snoopy, who dreams of being more than a dog, has finally claimed a whole book to himself—*Snoopy* (1958)—in which some of the Snoopy cartoons from earlier books have been reprinted along with a host of new ones illustrating Charlie Brown's complaint that he cannot draw a picture from a real dog model because he does not know any real dogs.

[9] *Peanuts* is constructed within a narrow formula. If one sits down in cold blood—as I have just done—and reads through all six books, one after another, the repetitiveness becomes apparent. In a sense, the test is unfair, since the books are designed to be opened at random, poked at casually, built as they are of strips that appeared with at least a day between them. The amazing thing is that, despite the repetition, the work as a whole gives off a sense of invention and imagination which is perhaps heightened because the individual characters set up an expectation that has to be both met and avoided. Charlie Brown has to act like Charlie Brown and still, somehow, surprise.

[10] So far Schulz has managed to produce the surprises. The latest book, *You're Out of Your Mind, Charlie Brown,* is funnier, richer, in some ways sadder than the earlier books. Perhaps, one day, invention will flag, mechanical effects will begin to take over, *Peanuts* will become simply a comic strip and not a work of imagination. So far that has not happened.

WRITING ASSIGNMENTS

1. Explain how some other comic strip besides *Peanuts* makes some comment about people and society. Following Mr. Weales pattern, you might discuss what the humor is based on, what subjects it is concerned with, what kind of personalities the characters have, what makes it different from other comic strips.

2. Comic strips are probably read by more people than are any other kind of writing. Do you think comic strip writers in general are living up to the responsibilities the vast readership places on them? Use examples of specific comic strips.

3. What is your favorite form of humor (books, television, radio, comic strips, cartoons)? Or, who is your favorite humorist? Why? What is unique? What is more effective? Is there more than mere amusement present in the humor?

The Egghead Vs. the Muttonhead

J. DONALD ADAMS

[1]   About fifty years ago, Americans began to use a new word: people would say that so-and-so was a "highbrow." The term carried with it a tinge of contempt. The highbrow, it was suggested, set himself apart from other men. His sincerity was suspect; he was "putting on airs."

[2]   We still talk about highbrows, but a few years ago we began to give them another name. The word "egghead" came into play, and it, too, had a note of derision.

[3]   We are, so far as I know, the only people who have gone to such extremes in inventing words to suggest that to be interested in the things of the mind is somehow reprehensible. No European or Asiatic people, including the Russians, has ever made fun of its college professors to the extent that we have.

[4]   On the other hand, I doubt whether any other nation has concocted as many words to characterize ignorance and stupidity: "dope," "boob," "nitwit," "saphead" are only a few. There's an old word I'd like to see revived and placed in opposition to "egghead." The word is "muttonhead." "Egghead" seems here to stay and we need a term to balance it, because there is a war on between the eggheads and the muttonheads.

[5]   The war has its roots and antecedents in certain American attitudes which have been with us ever since we became a nation. But it was once confined to the frontier—something we no longer have, except for outer space. Now it raises its ugly head everywhere—in our speech, in advertising, newspapers, magazines and books, on the radio and TV. The muttonhead would like to drag everyone down to his own level and he doesn't seem to want to raise his own. He resents superiority, mental superiority especially, and that old American curse —the fear of what the other fellow will think of us—causes too many people to adjust their standards to his.

[6]   Let's go back, for a moment, to the beginnings of the muttonhead attitude. It developed out of the "I'm as good as you are" feeling which came naturally to a people who had turned their backs on kings and nobility. It flourished on the frontier, where the door was wide open to self-reliance and strength. Where you came from and who your father was didn't matter. What mattered was what you could do.

[7]   Now, that in itself was a healthy attitude, but along with it came an intolerance for those who felt there were things as important as material progress. Of course, the practical skills were those most needed in the work of opening up a continent. But the feeling of distrust which the frontiersman had for "book-

119

larnin'" has lingered on long after there was need for it.

[8] In this, our history has been different from that of other people who have moved into and occupied great spaces of the earth. I am thinking, naturally, of the Russians, who in some ways are so like us and, in others, worlds apart. The Soviet citizen, slave of the state though he is, would be puzzled by and incredulous of such terms as "highbrow" and "egghead." One of the most frequent terms of disapproval of a person or an act in Russia is *ne kulturni*—not cultured.

[9] Perhaps the greatest threat which Russia has delivered against us is the recognition and rewards she gives to her intellectual workers. Her élite, outside the Government, are not movie and television stars, but teachers, scientists, artists and intellectuals. American families often make severe sacrifices to send their children to college; the Russian state underwrites the needs of its gifted children.

[10] Rightly, we deplore the restrictions under which the Russian writer or artist must work. His book, his painting, his symphony, must tend to glorify and uphold the Socialist state. But in our war between the eggheads and the muttonheads, we are developing our own kind of intolerance. We are producing a kind of writer who, though he is indeed free to criticize the Government in any way he wishes, does glorify the muttonhead and hold him up for our admiration.

[11] There is a recent novel by James Jones in which the central character is a writer. We are told he is a good writer, so good that a story of his is one of the best things written in his generation. And how does this young genius express himself? "I ain't written nothin' since I left here," he remarks at one point, and at another: "I ain't lookin' no gift horses in the mouth." These are representative

samples of his conversation. He takes pride in being semi-literate.

[12] Similar attitudes are shared by many Americans. A lot of the carelessness in our speech is deliberate. We know better, but we don't want to be thought of as putting on the dog.

[13] The curious thing is that often these self-conscious efforts at being considered "a regular guy" are resented by those to whom they are addressed. The truth is, nobody likes being talked down to. It was one of the measures of Franklin Roosevelt's shrewdness that in his fireside chats he never tried to abandon the manner of speech to which his environment and education had conditioned him.

[14] At this point you may say: "How do you account, then, for the fact that colleges are overcrowded, that more and more boys and girls have their sights set on higher education? How does that fit in with your idea of a war between the eggheads and the muttonheads?"

[15] I don't think the answer is too difficult. I don't believe that the love of learning, or respect for it, has increased. I would guess that more than half the students in our colleges are there because they or their parents know that by going to college they can better their financial and social prospects.

[16] The muttonhead attitude is being encouraged in our society because of the constant search for the lowest common denominator—for what will sell to the largest possible number of people. Now there is nothing wrong with the profit motive in a society based on free enterprise. But there is something wrong when the purveyors of entertainment, for example—whether in the form of TV, radio, the movies, newspapers, magazines or books—put too low an estimate on the level of quality to which people will respond. By so doing, they foster

the muttonhead attitude. And, frequently, they fool themselves.

[17] Why do you think the Hollywood moguls discovered that their dwindling audiences are composed more and more of teen-agers? Why are increasing thousands turning away from their TV sets in boredom or disgust? Isn't it because the producers put too low a rating on the intelligence of the people to whom they are appealing?

[18] Actually, nobody wants to be a muttonhead. What the whole matter boils down to is the old fear of having others think that you are setting yourself up as superior. All of us resent condescension, but everybody respects those who know what they want and prefer. And that can be shown without looking down your nose at the other fellow. If we could all be ourselves, with understanding of one another's limitations and of one another's potentialities, there would be no war between the eggheads and the muttonheads.

WRITING ASSIGNMENTS

1. Which do you believe are the most important benefits of a college education—practical skills or intellectual and cultural gains? Apply your answer to your own personal situation.

2. Which do you believe the American people admire and respect most—financial success or intellectual and cultural growth? Do you find this a satisfactory state of affairs?

3. Using typical programs and films as examples, sketch in what the producers of television and motion pictures seem to think the taste and intelligence of the public are. Do you believe they are correct?

Why Not Let Pay TV Have a Trial Run?

[1] Commercial television has been running into heavy weather of late. Nobody seems completely satisfied with it. The sponsor, who is paying important money to sell his cigarettes or motorcars, wants to be sure that the program he is paying for not only reaches people who are interested in cigarettes or motorcars but gives a helping hand to the salesmen. The public, or at any rate the part of the public that worries about such matters, wonders whether television programs wouldn't be better if there weren't any commercials.

Background problem in TV

[2] This sounds as if commercial television had never given its audience a good play, a first-class fight or a World Series ball game. Of

course, this is not true (cf. *Wonderful Town,* the Army-Navy football game, the McCarthy hearings, Leonard Bernstein's expositions of symphonic music, the Kentucky Derby, A Night to Remember, and so on). But television's critics declare that the more esoteric programs, like Bernstein and What in the World?, are becoming infrequent for the simple reason that people with something to sell have to go for the mass-audience attractions.

[3]   The answer of those who want to do something about all this is, "Give us pay TV!" These reformers, of course, include manufacturers of devices to make pay TV a practical possibility. They include, also, some Hollywood producers, who see a way out for their business if first-run movies can be seen by a vast television audience which has paid to look; not to mention Broadway and "off-Broadway" theatrical producers, and an impressive section of our dramatic and musical "talent."

[4]   Opposed to pay TV are, of course, the broadcasting networks, most of whose income is from the sponsors of the network shows now produced, an influential group of advertising agents whose interests are similar, and the owners of motion-picture theaters who fear, with some justification, that pay-TV entertainment, including the promised first-run films, would darken their houses darker than they are now.

[5]   The argument has produced varied and contradictory opinions. John Crosby, the TV columnist, declares that TV is "being run by business and ad-agency men who are afraid of excitement and risk. The creative people who thrive on danger simply aren't around any more." The claim of pay-TV advocates is that if producers were permitted to sell their entertainment directly to the public, instead of to advertisers, things would be greatly improved. They promise Broadway shows, first-run Hollywood or foreign movies, symphony concerts, top sports events—all for a fraction of the cost of enjoying these treats in a theater, a stadium or a concert hall. It is argued that, in the absence of an advertiser, whose interests come first, entertainment or instruction via TV could be something completely new to the American public. Proponents of pay TV insist that the idea ought to be tried.

[6]   The Broadcasting networks and their supporters argue that pay TV not only would injure their business but that it would not produce the video millennium promised by those who are promoting it. They agree that sponsors with soap to sell seek to attract a mass audience rather than one which goes in for abstractionist drama or ballet. However, as Robert Sarnoff, president of the National Broadcasting Company, has sagely pointed out, "the economics of pay TV—like those of free television—compel it to seek the largest possible subscription audiences."

[7]   Even if Mr. Crosby's "creative people who thrive on danger" might do better under pay TV than they do at present, the more serious objection raised by Mr. Sarnoff is that pay TV, by shutting off the income of the networks from advertising, will make it impossible for them to put on what Mr. Sarnoff describes as "service" programs, that have become so important a feature of radio and television presentation: world-wide news coverage, play-by-play reporting of national political conventions,

Marginalia (left column):

Specific topic to be argued

Some pro-TV people

Some who oppose Pay-TV

Pro-Pay-TV arguments

An argument against

A second argument against

sports events and interviews with important political figures. This type of program is often sponsored, but by and large is operated at a loss, which the nationwide entertainment programs are relied on to overcome.

[8]   It is obvious that if *My Fair Lady* or *The Music Man* could be presented in full over pay TV from eight to eleven p.m., the networks would have a hard time selling those evening hours to any advertiser who wanted an audience. Thus, with their best performers working on pay-TV programs and the best night hours taken over by some popular Broadway play or Hollywood movie, the networks would have far less to sell than they now have and, in consequence, far less income to spend on unprofitable service programs which the public has come to expect.

Illustration of argument in previous paragraph

[9]   Should pay TV produce the income which Mr. Sarnoff thinks it may, there ought to be money enough to support public-service presentations. Indeed, the FCC might well insist, if it has the authority, that producers of pay-TV programs should devote some of their time to news, addresses by the President and other officials, charity appeals, and so on. After all, somebody has to provide these services and, if the present means of doing so becomes impossible, we should have gone a long way toward Government radio and TV. That would be a high price to pay for the benefits that pay TV promises.

[10]   The most effective opposition to pay TV just now comes from the House Committee on Interstate and Foreign Commerce or, more specifically, its chairman, Democratic Rep. Oren Harris, of Arkansas. Chairman Harris' dim view of pay TV springs from his belief that it would kill "free," or commercially sponsored, TV. For this reason, nine bills were introduced in the last Congress forbidding the FCC to authorize pay TV. In May of 1957 the Federal Communications Commission, which had been making a prolonged study of the situation, expressed the opinion that "it is now timely and desirable to determine the conditions under which trial demonstrations of subscription television could properly be authorized."

Fear of Rep. Harris

FCC proposal for Pay TV

[11]   Chairman Harris promptly threw a block into this proposal in a series of letters to the commission in which he clearly indicated skepticism, to put it mildly, as to the practicality of pay TV. He also appeared to believe that pay TV would end free TV for good and all. In a letter to the then FCC chairman, George C. McConnaughey, Mr. Harris asked rhetorically what he should tell his constituents "when they come home in the evening and find a channel upon which they once viewed a free program and find it blurred until they purchase a gadget of some sort and pay to see the program."

Harris' protest

Illustration of Harris' argument

[12]   Mr. Harris insisted that the whole thing should be postponed until Congress could explore the situation further and, if necessary, amend the Communications Act to straighten out any legal difficulties in the way. The Federal Communications Commission therefore decided in February of 1958 that "authorizations for subscription television" would not be issued until congressional opposition was ended. That is where pay TV—or any adequate experiments with it—stands or, rather, sits, today: firmly in the lap of Chairman Harris and Congress.

FCC changes its mind

The Post's
opinion

[13]   It isn't necessary to accept all the roseate predictions for pay TV as a means of leading America up to a new cultural plateau in order to believe that this new idea should have a chance to prove itself. If there is an audience which is willing to pay for full-length Broadway plays, Wagnerian operas, first-released Hollywood or imported moving pictures, or boxing matches—all without an interpolated order to dash out NOW to the drugstore for a six-way cold cure—should these innocent desires be denied? If there are not enough such people to make pay TV a success, then it will be a flop. If pay TV proves to have the predicted audience, we shall see a "new dimension" in communication, to which the existing system will have to accommodate itself.

The Case Against Pay TV

JACK GOULD

Background
to the
debate

[1]   The Federal Communications Commission recently issued its latest pronouncement on the liveliest controversy in television: pay-as-you-see TV. With its accustomed grace in using the English language so that the words will have no meaning, the commission declared that it was getting ready to accept applications for a test of toll television but warned that this step did not mean any applications would be granted.

[2]   Such firm indecision has been characteristic of the years of debate over the idea that the viewer at home should pay the cost of the programs that he watches. Few schemes in the realm of electronics and show business have occasioned such a deluge of excited double-talk and such a paucity of tangible fact.

[3]   But the mere thought of making every home a box office is either so tempting or so frightening to assorted industries that no lull in the war of the mimeograph machines is to be expected. The repercussions from the latest F. C. C. announcement suggest the magnitude of what is at stake.

Some brief
arguments—
pro and con

[4]   The Hollywood motion-picture industry has said it believes that toll TV will be the solution to its economic ills arising from free video, the mass movement of millions to the suburbs and the high cost of baby sitters. But exhibitors of films—the theatre owners—have said that toll TV threatens to leave them the destitute victims of an outmoded means of distributing Marilyn Monroe.

[5]   The Giants and the Dodgers, in their interminable comparisons of the relative economic attractions of New York and the West Coast, have expressed hope that toll TV ultimately will make baseball fans pay much more for their loyalty to the national pastime. A covey of intellectuals has insisted that a TV box office is the divine key to a cultural renaissance that will make mediocrity obsolete.

[6]   The existing broadcasting industry, sidling up more cozily to sponsors, has insisted, ever more loudly, that if toll TV comes their only course will be to audition pallbearers. Some elements of the advertising industry, with their keen appreciation of television's present role in coaxing the consumer to invest in a whiter white, are weighing a survey in depth. In Washington, a scattering of Congressmen have promised resolutions, investigations or laws to set matters aright in conformance with their independent partialities. In the background quietly sits the American Telephone and Telegraph Company, wondering whether someone will ask it to rewire the United States.

[7]   The case against toll television is rooted in the belief that a box office will mean that the public will be asked to finance what it now gets without charge and that the structure of today's public medium will be destroyed.

The case against begins

[8]   If pay-as-you-see TV can overnight mean huge grosses at a box office, today's top TV talent will move en masse to the new form, it is held. The enlightened performer, normally a canny business man, will not give away his wares for the greater good of Procter & Gamble if he can declare himself in for a percentage of millions of dollars.

[9]   The entertainment programs that carry the freight for todays' advertising-sponsored TV, in short, will be siphoned off. Accordingly, the broadcasters will be unable to afford to present those events—news, documentaries, a Khrushchev interview, religious programs and the like— which the Government decrees is part of a balanced station schedule.

Loss of revenue for regular TV

[10]   Qualitatively, the broadcasters ask what is to be provided by the toll supporters that doesn't currently exist. Movies are offered in abundance; sports are well represented. Drama may be uneven, but is it not also uneven on Broadway and in films? The proponents of subscription television have not come up with any answer to TV's basic problem. The need for so much material inevitably leads to creative difficulties. So, they say, the promoters of subscription TV are only out to fool the public with their persuasive claims for superior quality; they are going to be subjected to precisely the same pressures and will still be relentlessly pursuing a mass audience.

Will offer nothing new

[11]   Television's basic limitation is a shortage of facilities, born of both technical and economic considerations. The introduction of a box office will not change the way of life inherent in a mass medium. If there is a pay-as-you-see TV channel, will its operator be content with the limited income from an esoteric ballet or will he go after the maximum dollar in association with Jayne Mansfield? Hucksterism is not peculiar to Madison Avenue; it has existed at the corner of Hollywood and Vine and also at Ebbets Field and the Polo Grounds.

Will seek mass audience

No service programs

[12]   The toll TV faction has spoken glowingly of the opportunities for more grandiose productions, which advertisers cannot afford. But they have been strangely mum on what proportion of their proceeds will be allotted to carry addresses from President Eisenhower, to cover political affairs and give Senators a forum, or to report events such as the tour of Queen Elizabeth. The toll operators, it is held, subscribe to an odd concept of public responsibility: they'll be delighted to absorb the medium's assets and give away its losses.

Commercials

[13]   One selling point for toll TV has been the implied suggestion that there will be no commercials. The record hardly warrants such optimism. Commercials have been commonplace in motion-picture houses where the public pays. One toll operator has reported that a box of soap flakes might contain a slug. The slug would then operate a coin box which would make available, free of charge, a so-called toll attraction.

[14]   If several sponsors should step forward with a tempting kitty of $1,000,000, such as they spend in a single evening on TV today, will the toll operator shyly turn his head in the other direction and exclaim, "Why the very idea!"? The broadcasters cordially invite the toll idealists to read up on the twentieth century.

Some problems ahead

Legal maneuvers

[15]   The future of toll television is wrapped up in many uncertainties and problems. First, if the commission does authorize a three-year test of on-the-air toll television, it is widely believed that this will mean an opportunity to see if the new medium can get off the ground. If it flops— the F. C. C. can relax. If it succeeds the F. C. C. would hardly be able to stop it. It is for this reason that some Congressmen and broadcasters would like to drag the issue away from the F. C. C. and take it up to Capitol Hill, where toll TV would probably perish in delay.

An experiment

[16]   As for closed-circuit television, attention is now focused on a test in Bartlesville, Okla., where a film exhibitor is wiring up the town to show first-run motion pictures. The outcome of this experiment may not be known for some time, until families react to the idea of a monthly bill of $9.50. In Bartlesville the toll operator also controls all the film houses, so that in this instance there is no conflict of interest between media.

[17]   But toll TV more basically faces the medium's familiar dilemma of trying to decide whether the chicken or the egg comes first. All systems for scrambling and unscrambling toll images involve an initial installation cost; so, too, do closed-circuit methods. With millions of potential viewers involved, the charge will be passed on to the public in one form or another.

Money problems

[18]   Meanwhile, even if toll TV enjoys nothing but green lights, it will take time to get the operation going on a substantial scale.

[19]   This, then, is the rub: Will the public invest in toll TV until, as and if it knows precisely what its attractions are going to be? And will film producers or sports promoters invest in toll TV until they are sure there is a paying audience in existence? Toll TV's troubles really begin when somebody says go ahead and start.

WRITING ASSIGNMENTS

1. After reading the two articles in this book on the subject of Pay TV, you should now be able to form an opinion of your own. Write an essay in which you defend or attack Pay TV, using whatever arguments you have found most convincing in the two articles and whatever arguments you yourself might be able to add. Remember that one sentence or statement does not usually serve as a good argument. You have to explain it further with details and examples.

2. Another argument is also suggested by this article: What is right or what is wrong with commercial TV today? Take a stand on either side and first be sure you define clearly exactly what it is you are praising or criticising about TV. Then support this over-all statement with examples from TV. Do not merely mention names or titles, but try to describe and interpret what they mean to you.

3. Have you seen one television program, or possibly one motion picture, that stands out above the usual program or picture? Write a review of it in which you explain just what was unique and impressive about it. Do not merely tell the plot. Instead, interpret what that plot showed, analyze the characters, discuss the action, etc.

The Real Delinquent—The Parent?

JACOB PANKEN

[1] We have always had some delinquency on the part of children, we probably always shall have some until we root out the basic cause of this social disease. The best we have done so far is to attack the problem obliquely, seeking to cure and rehabilitate children who are already delinquent. Judges, social workers, psychiatrists and psychologists have developed techniques for their treatment, and these children should be treated by all techniques available.

[2] But all delinquents cannot be cured by the methods at hand, nor do these methods eradicate the original cause and thus prevent development of new delinquencies. In the last five years juvenile delinquency has increased alarmingly, rising in some urban centers by more than 100 per cent. In New York City the number of court cases involving delinquent children jumped from 4,379 in 1940 to 6,975 in 1945, a rise of more than 50 per cent.

[3] Obviously we have not been very successful in preventing juvenile delinquency. I think we can succeed in solving this community and nationwide problem with a long-range, permanent program of prevention. But, first, we must accept this fundamental premise: No child is born into the world to be bad or to be

good. He is as bad or as good as we make it possible for him to be.

[4] Under this premise the question, "What causes juvenile delinquency?" instead becomes, "Who, in the first instance, makes it possible for a child to be bad or good?" And there is only one answer—the parent.

[5] It may appear to be oversimplification to recommend improving the parent in order to bring up a younger generation that will not, except perhaps for a normal allowance for exceptions to the rule, become delinquent children. Yet a brief examination of the influences that shape the development of each of us, through childhood to responsible—or irresponsible—citizenship, supports this contention.

[6] Most delinquent conduct and crime stem from neglect of children. Neglect is not merely failure to provide the physical needs, the clothing, shelter and medical care needed. Failure to provide proper supervision, leadership and guidance within the home is a more serious form of neglect; its consequences are often the most telling factor in the development of delinquency patterns in the child. The community may step in to cure sickness and supply physical needs; that is fairly easy. But anti-social characteristics learned in early childhood in the home are not easy to eliminate or even to modify. They are too deeply rooted.

[7] For it is in his very early years that the child acquires the characteristics which fashion his personality and pattern his life. It might be said that he begins to learn how to live and how to act and react, and his personality begins to form at his mother's breast. The child's earliest teachers are his parents and his siblings.

[8] His gods are his mother and father. If his gods are bad, he is going to be bad. If parents are inadequate to their responsibilities, their children will

be the victims. If, therefore, parents are unfit because they were never taught how to guide their children, or if by their acts they inspire anti-social attitudes, prevention of juvenile delinquency by the community becomes—as it is now—merely an unrealized bit of wishful thinking.

[9] Often delinquent conduct is a form of exhibitionism to compensate the child for a lack in his daily life—a feeling of rejection and insecurity. The human being is gregarious and the child wants to belong. We must bear in mind that children, no less than adults, are subject to conflicting emotions. There is always a conflict between the good that is awakened and the bad that beckons, the bad that gives a sense of belonging, of being sought after, or a sense of loyalty to the gang that provides interesting activity.

[10] The resolution of this conflict decides where the child is to belong—with the good or the bad—and the direction, whichever path he takes, he learns from his home environment and the example and influence of his elders. He can be taught, and with not insurmountable difficulties, to respond to the finer things rather than to the evil in life.

[11] Most delinquent children are asocial rather than anti-social; they have no moral sense because it was never taught them. They have no sense of responsibility, no consciousness of social cooperation, because these essentials were never taught them. But children can be taught not to become delinquents. There are exceptions, of course, where the individual is incapable of distinguishing right from wrong and is unable to appraise the quality of his acts because of mental defects or insanity.

[12] Since it is the parent who makes it possible for children to grow up good or bad, training for parenthood is the road to prevention of juvenile delin-

quency. Parents, being the first teachers of children, must themselves be trained in their duties. We who work with children realize that anew as each delinquent child and his parents appear before us. Daily we see proof that the mere fact of parenthood does not automatically endow men and women with the knowledge and understanding mothers and fathers need.

[13]   I recall a boy who came before me charged with delinquency for having at the point of a knife robbed another child of his pennies and then beaten him. The relationship between his mother and father was revealed as contributing materially to the child's misconduct. The husband beat her repeatedly, the mother told the court. The husband denied this, explaining, "I only slap her."

[14]   "Do you think it proper for you to slap your wife?" he was asked. "You know that has a bad effect upon your children." His reply was shocking: "I think a woman should be slapped once in a while any time."

[15]   He had learned this precept, he said, as a child, from watching his father slap his mother "once in a while." And now his son is learning the "facts" of human relationship from his father, who learned them so badly from his father. A vicious circle!

[16]   So, too, is the case of a juvenile delinquent in which I punished the father —actually sent him to jail. I do not like to send anybody to jail, but this father had purchased from his son's friends the goods that they and his son had stolen. Children cannot be helped by punishment, nor can adults, but when an adult contributes to a child's delinquency it is a good thing to take him out of circulation for a while.

[17]   And yet I do not know that it was right. Can it be said that these untrained parents who contribute to the delinquency of their children by neglect or example are at fault? Were they not also neglected by their parents and by society so that they grew up to be maladjusted and in turn exposed their children to maladjustment?

[18]   Some think that the answer is schools for parents. San Francisco has established such a school. But in many cases it is too late to teach parental responsibility to those who are already parents. Many have first to unlearn bad techniques, others refuse to learn and many more cannot or will not attend such schools.

[19]   As I see it, the solution is to teach men and women how to be good parents before they become parents. The place to begin is with our children, teaching them now how to teach the children they will some day have. And the place to do that is in the schools.

[20]   Our high school pupils take courses in botany, science and higher mathematics. That is good. But only a small percentage of high school pupils carry on their studies in college, and a smaller number make use in later life of the knowledge they acquire in these subjects. I do not propose the elimination of these subjects from the curriculum. They are part of the process of education.

[21]   It is even more important, however, that our children receive training in the marriage relationship and parenthood, since nearly all of them will marry and have children. Yet nowhere in the high schools or junior high schools throughout the country are courses given to fit our young for the responsibilities of marriage and parenthood.

[22]   We train men and women to improve agricultural products, to become expert in animal husbandry and the care of trees. But we do nothing about preparing prospective fathers and mothers for the most important of all life's functions: the bringing-up of the next gen-

eration. If we would end juvenile delinquency, we must train parents-to-be in the art of helping their children grow up into good boys and girls rather than bad ones. To that end we should require all high school pupils to take courses in parent responsibility and child guidance. They should be taught child psychology, hygiene, the care of the physical needs of the child; the effect upon children of the relationship of parents to each other; the ability to discover and encourage the child's talents and special interests; the child's proper place in the home as a personality and as a member of the social unit. It is in the latter field especially that the child develops a sense of security and respect for himself and for those around him.

[23]   What this amounts to is that, while teaching our children how to be good citizens, we teach them also how to be good parents. A comprehensive course covering the subjects mentioned above would awaken interest in the high school student body. The course should be required, and graduation from high school should depend upon its satisfactory completion.

[24]   This may not be a cure-all, but it is certainly a long step in the right direction. In one generation we should be able to eliminate a high percentage of the original cause of juvenile delinquency—the delinquent parent—and thus solve the problem, in time, at its source.

[25]   While following such a program we must continue to work toward the cure and rehabilitation of the present generation's delinquent children. Elimination of poverty would help. Clearance of slum areas would contribute to rehabilitation and to permanent prevention. The use of public schools as cultural centers for parents and children, and as play, dance and sports centers under proper supervision would help to keep children off the streets. Another technique I have found to be valuable is suggested reading. This serves to improve the mind and to inspire the child with ambition by leading him to identify himself with the fine characters of history and literature.

[26]   But these, at best, are halfway measures. The heart of the problem of juvenile delinquency is delinquent parents. Left to chance and to themselves, good parents are more apt to have good children than bad; bad parents are more likely to have bad children than good. We can no longer leave it to chance. We must make it our business to see that all our children have good parents.

Parents and Juvenile Delinquency

BERGEN EVANS

[1]   In spite of the popular faith in our new Age of Religion, juvenile delinquency is often attributed to the decline of religion, and judges frequently make the headlines by requiring some young hoodlum to memorize the Ten Commandments or to attend Sunday school. More often, however, it is insisted that delinquent juveniles are the product of delinquent parents. This is a smug generalization that serves to relieve the utterer of any responsibility and, by implication, casts a warming halo around his parents' and his own head. It is rarely uttered by the parents of convicted delinquents.

[2]   Actually, there is even great uncertainty as to what constitutes juvenile delinquency. Much of what is now called that used to be called "boys will be boys". Half the youthful male heroes of fiction would certainly be classed as delinquents today if they stepped out of the pages of the classics and the police could lay hands on them. In the older world of fewer people and more space they—and their counterparts among the actual living—didn't come as inevitably into collision with the law or their own kind as they would today. Some went to jail to be turned into hardened rogues; but most, after sowing a few wild oats (a jocular euphemism for being delin-

quent), settled down and often made good citizens.

[3]   The commonly received "causes" of youthful criminality today were investigated by a subcommittee of the United States Senate, which issued a special report in 1957 summarizing all previous studies—and rejecting almost every conventional explanation of juvenile delinquency.

[4]   It found invalid such widely assumed causes as poverty, poor housing and lack of sports and other recreational facilities.

[5]   If poverty were the cause of juvenile delinquency, the committee pointed out, we, the richest nation in the world, should have comparatively little. But we seem to have, if anything, more than many poorer nations.

[6]   If slum housing were the cause, there ought to be a marked absence of juvenile delinquency in the housing projects. But there is a great deal of it in the housing projects, where a new boy will often find a ready-made gang waiting to receive or harass him.

[7]   Devout believers in the moral and "character building" power of sports (one of the most vociferous and absurd delusions of our day) never cease to urge organized and supervised recreation as the sure cure for juvenile delinquency. But muscles can be used for ill as well as

good, and the fatuous moral talk of the ordinary supervisor is hardly likely to increase a suspicious, sneering adolescent's respect for authority. Studies have shown that delinquents are *more* interested in and more successful at sports and games than nondelinquents. They *love* clubs and recreational groups. In fact, says the subcommittee's report, it is partly through his group interests and activities that the juvenile delinquent gets into trouble in the first place. Nothing has closer teamwork and higher *esprit de corps* than a gang.

[8]   That would seem to leave only the parents. It is easy to blame everything on them.

[9]   When the experts—the psychologists and the psychiatrists—study a young criminal they are almost certain to find something wrong with his parents. The child, being a child of today, usually describes his problem to them in terms of conflict with his parents (just as the young wretch at Tyburn two centuries ago, under prodding by the clergy, ascribed *his* crimes to the Devil). And the psychologists and the psychiatrists—like the clergy and the commissars—run the risk of accepting the echoes of their own prompting as an unbiased confession.

[10]   Of course, the setting of the delinquent's problem in terms of conflict with his parents has some truth in it. Almost all of the pressures and restrictions of the world the child must live in come to it, at first, through the parents. It is the parents who must tell the restless growing boy that he is not to play with matches, not to break the neighbors' windows, not to take too great liberties with the neighbors' daughters.

[11]   The parents, however, did not create the rules, and to blame them for the conflicts that enforcement of the rules engenders is stupid. One has to ask whether the parents of our juvenile delin-

quents were negligent beyond the norm in training them. Are more parents today than formerly neglecting their children or abusing them?

[12]   The answer to these questions is No. Never in history have parents so devoted themselves to their children. Hundreds of millions of copies of books on how to bring up children have been bought by the parents of this delinquent generation.

[13]   The typical modern parent, far from being negligent, is anxious about his children to an extent that would have amazed his grandfather. The thought, for instance, of ordering a delinquent from the house—in the *Way Down East*[1] manner—as being unworthy to associate with his parents would never enter a modern parent's mind. More likely he would feel that the fault was in some way *his*, not the child's.

[14]   Now *this* attitude is very new. Formerly the responsibility was all the other way; children owed everything to their parents—honor, love, obedience and support in their old age, whether merited or not. "Training," as it was called, was often brutal. Sons were regularly thrashed and daughters were locked up in dark closets or turned out of the house. Children were frequently denied food (unthinkable in a modern middle-class home) and sent to bed without supper because they had been disrespectful.

[15]   But the society of that day wasn't cursed with juvenile delinquents. Or at least it didn't view the problem in quite that way. It was well known that Satan was most active among the immature and a great many of his youthful followers were hanged, deported, killed in the wars or turned whores and pirates. Cities were so infested with murderous gangs and robbers—most of them young

---

[1] An old melodrama of stage and screen, silly and unreal by today's tastes.

men—that every man, of necessity, carried some instrument of defense. But no one thought that youth was any more delinquent than usual; the Devil simply had his normal complement of assistants.

[16] The parents of these earlier ruffians were by modern standards extraordinarily unconcerned about their young. The modern parent feels *much* more responsibility for his children. He is kinder than parents used to be. However ignorant, he is more anxious to learn than his forefathers were.

[17] If parents are not to blame for current juvenile delinquency, the cause must lie in the larger world that the parents must prepare the child for. One could suspect many things, from the public schools to the atom bomb. But the really significant thing is our present lack of standards, guide lines, norms. Morals, if you will. And that is why the claim of a great increase in religion accords so ill with a parallel claim of a great increase in juvenile delinquency.

[18] The parent of the old days had a clear notion of what constituted an upstanding citizen and what attitudes a child should learn to become one. It didn't matter that the parent was as grossly ignorant in this as in almost everything else he believed. His certainty —shared by everyone he respected in the community—served in itself to create the stability it postulated. The stern father could belt hell out of his sons in sadistic righteousness without doing them more than physical harm. For they believed as much as he did that in so doing he was upholding a clearly perceived moral order. By creating Jehovah in his own image and then acting like Jehovah, the

paterfamilias presented the child with a stable, organized, intelligible world with which he had to come to terms.

[19] No modern parent, in contrast, can have this certitude. And because he does not want to mislead his child or teach him inappropriate attitudes (and perhaps because the world has developed wholly new standards of honesty), he has constantly to say "I don't know." And he has to say this—often to his own anguish and dismay—about the most important things in life. He doesn't know, even, whether he should encourage the child to be self-seeking or self-effacing, to accept and obey authority or to reject and resist it. All the intelligent parent knows is that the world is changing so rapidly that his own experience is an uncertain guide for his children.

[20] Of course many parents are still convinced that they can get along by teaching their children what they themselves were taught. But they may be preparing their children for trouble and forfeiting their respect. For the problems of the modern world cannot be met by the old values. And the child of parents who have assumed that they can, begins to learn in the first grade that his parents are either ignorant or dishonest. At best, he reaches adolescence convinced that everything his parents taught him is inappropriate, with no idea of what life is like or what his part in it should be.

[21] The child of brighter, less certain parents is at least spared the shock of realizing he can't communicate with his parents; they may share only a common ignorance and helplessness, but it is at least something shared and there is comfort and strength in the sharing.

WRITING ASSIGNMENTS

1. What do you blame juvenile delinquency on? To simplify matters, do not try to be all-inclusive; limit yourself to three things—anything from comic books to disbelief in God; from parents to television—and show how they can produce delinquent behavior. Refer to specific cases if possible.

2. Rather than discuss solutions to the problem in general, set your mind to a solution of this specific case: A sixteen-year-old boy has robbed and beaten severely a liquor store owner. Provide him with an appropriate background and personal history, and then discuss what you believe should be done to him and for him.

3. Juvenile delinquency does not exist in a vacuum. Mr. Evans recognizes this when he refers to "our present lack of standards, guide lines, norms. Morals, if you will." What examples from American life today can you present that illustrate this lack of or confusion of moral standards? These might be examples of actual "adult delinquency" or they might be examples of the types of uncertainty that plague everyone today.

Why Are Americans Unhappy?

ALAN DUTSCHER

The basic
general
position

[1]   There is a minority report to be made of the American scene— a report which, despite the constant barrage of facts and figures "proving" the contrary, states candidly that our domestic scene is something less than an idyllic, paradisiacal "triumph in technicolor." There is a large fund of social unrest, of unhappiness in America, and if we are more or less blind to this situation that is only because the manifestations are

But why?

somewhat unfamiliar. The problems involved may be indicated very broadly as follows:

A brief
summary of
the problem

[2]   There is too much surface "happiness" in America today, too much real unhappiness; our standard of living is always rising, our leisure ever-increasing, we are forever "saving time"—still we never seem to have enough goods or time; we "save time" in order to "kill time" to use two expressions characteristic of our age, and since time is only a measure of life, the phrase "kill time" once again proves that language has a wisdom of its own, for time killed is man killed.

[3]   People are "able" to, and do, buy more commodities than ever before, yet the itch for possession only grows worse instead of being

134

sated. The rising standard of living, which we were brought up to regard as the touchstone of personal happiness and of the successful social system, often appears as a demonic force which will not let us rest, which forces us somehow to buy, buy, buy: After the car is bought, the house "must" be bought, after the house is bought, the giant refrigerator "must" be bought, then the combination washer-dryer, the "hi-fi" set, the backyard swim pool, and just about that time we are ready for a new car again, or a second car, and a new house for the new "additions."

[4]   The "welfare" state has given more "social security" than we ever had before, yet if there is one thing that haunts us in the midst of our plenty it is insecurity. And it is in fact statism which generates most of our fear, for it is the state which enforces conformity, wages, war, etc. We chafe at the bureaucratization of modern life, but more and more of us become bureaucrats; we mutter about high taxes and have little conviction that tax money is doing us or anyone else much good, but we either pay our taxes or find respectable ways to cheat. Rarely is taxation considered as a *social question*. And despite recurrent "economy drives" (always based on the most picayune considerations) taxes continue to grow; we would like the whole damn machine to stop for a while, so that we could look around, compare, consider, weigh, perhaps start on a different tack altogether. Yet despite "increased leisure time" individuals rarely have a chance to put on the brakes before it is too late.

[5]   To some, all of the aforementioned complaints will appear as simply another manifestation of the infinite human capacity for griping, for confusing individual shortcomings with real social problems. But there is too broad a consensus about these matters for them to be merely personal irritations.

[6]   This is the first illustration of what is meant by the previous statement that social unrest manifests itself in unfamiliar ways. Contemporary social grievances often appear less objective than they ever did before. In the '30's, for example, the grievances were "classical," tangible, somehow more "real" than they seem to-day. Hence the social and political demands of the sufferers were no less tangible: more jobs, better working conditions, higher pay, less working hours, more job security. Today the grievances frequently strike one as petty, intangible, remote, irremediable, a matter of *individual* aberration, and the general insecurity appears as mere *psychic* insecurity (the corresponding remedy being "positive thinking," tranquillizer drugs, etc.)

[7]   This is in part due to bureaucratization of modern life, which makes it unclear who or what is to blame for any given social irritation. On whom is one to blame higher taxes, for example?—there are so many social agencies and institutions involved. Ultimately, the official line is either to blame the Russians who "force" us to spend billions on defence (and how convenient this is, for one can "of course" do nothing about the Russians), or to conclude that all taxes are justified and there is something wrong with those who complain about them (probably, they should be psychoanalyzed).

The unrest is now different

Hard to pin down what is wrong

Part of the reason

We are
better off
and
should be
happier

[8]   After all, the question is sometimes asked, how can one complain about anything? Compare our lot, as individuals, with what it was in the '30's: automatic pay raises, diminished work week, "pleasant" working conditions ("soft" music piped in all day long, air conditioning, etc), increased job security—and all seemingly without our having to lift a finger to obtain them, for, compared to the '30's, we have no real labor-capital battles any longer.

. . .

New idea
for difference:
suffer because
of too much

[9]   It would appear therefore that we have social problems, though they are somewhat different from what they once were. One difference, already noted, consists in the difficulty of concretizing grievances and putting our finger on the cause of the trouble. Yet another difference is that instead of suffering from social deficiencies we seem to suffer from diseases of excess. The very apt title of Russell Lynes's provocative book, A Surfeit of Honey, already tells much. As odd as it may seem, we are less the beneficiaries of a rising standard of living than its victims. Stratified societies have social boundaries that are apparent. This means that people are kept in their places—a notion uncongenial to us. On the other hand, it also means that since beyond a certain point in the social system there is no place to go, people of all classes can "take it easy," or easier, can relax a bit. Sociologists like C. Wright Mills tell us that, in reality, our social order is far more stratified than appears on the surface. Nonetheless, because the stratification is not apparent, many of us draw the conclusion that "the sky is the limit." Thus, there is very little relaxing and very much pushing and climbing. This is no defence of social stratification; it is, however, a defence of rational limits on personal ambition.

Need for
balance

[10]   How does one determine rational limits? Which needs (for commodities, etc.) are genuine, which artificial? There is no pat answer, no magic formula. The secret is balance. But balance is a peculiar "secret"—one that must be learned again and again, for it is a very concrete thing. However, none of us are wholly independent of our environment, and that environment is hardly conducive to balance.

Advertising
keeps us
itching

[11]   An enormous part of commercial effort—advertising—is designed to inculcate an insatiable hunger for possession, useful or useless as the case may be, in the general population. The notion of unlimited need is insane and must lead, in practice, to collective and individual insanity. The insatiable itch for possession is as pathological as insatiable hunger or thirst. It results in a general psychic rootlessness, restlessness, and insecurity to which everyone is more or less subject.

[12]   Nor is such rootlessness the desideratum of progress, as some would have it. For progress presupposes a goal however relative toward which one is progressing. The "aim" of the whole economic apparatus today is—aimlessness; production and consumption not to satisfy human need, but for their own sake. There is no relaxing, no point to the story of modern life, and that is why the story often seems so senseless.

Transition

[13]   Then the question (and a very peculiar question it must appear to many) to which we must address ourselves is: Is an ever-rising stand-

ard of living a good thing, or is it perhaps symptomatic of social pathology? Has anyone ever proven that expansion *as such* is positive? There is another question that we will have to ask soon: Is eternal expansion *necessary* to keep our economy going? But for the moment let us consider the general and usually unquestioned assumption that necessary or not expansion is a good thing.

[14]   One result of the "surfeit of honey" is a terrible vulgarity. It is perhaps not generally realized that poor taste is a phenomenon *par excellence* of excess rather than of deficiency, of the haves rather than of the have-nots. The latter have very little choice in their possessions. The former, however, have the means to gratify almost any whim. Moreover, it is the haves who create the style that filters down to become the general pattern. The "style of life" of the haves of any period is a well-nigh infallible index to their reasonableness and thus to the reasonableness of the social order they head.

[15]   To be sure, "conspicuous consumption" has been with us a long time. What is new is that seemingly our whole middle-class society is consumed by the itch for possession—of the tasteless, the useless, the big, the shiny, the new, the loud, the exaggerated. Yesterday's newspaper carried an advertisement for "perfumed ink . . . that leaves an air of delicate fragrance on your correspondence." The day before an ad appeared reading (whether tongue-in-cheek or not is beside the point): "Buy a gold toothpick for the man who has everything."

[16]   The man who has everything! One can just imagine this man— surrounded by knicknacks—bored, restless, frightened. The urge to possess begins as vulgarity and ends as mania. It is the antithesis of the human point of view that it is not what a man has which is important but what he is.

[17]   The tastelessness extends beyond the realm of material possession to that of spiritual encumbrance. People now supposedly have the money to travel, and travel, one would imagine, is an educational, broadening experience. One would imagine . . . We do not say that scenic attraction described below is a typical vacation paradise of our nouveaux riches, nevertheless the mere fact that the staid *New York Times* devoted a long article to it is indicative of the kind of humorless, tasteless, fundamentally uncritical approach to things so current today. Moreover, it evinces a little of the spirtual counterpart of the urge for material accumulation—the drive to "see everything."

[18]   The article referred to appeared in the Travel Section of *The New York Times* of 6/9/57 and was written by reporter Galdwin Hill. The headline read: "Watching the bombs go off—Tourists can see blasts in Nevada test area this summer." The report read, in part, as follows:

. . . for the first time, the A.E.C. has released a partial schedule, so that tourists interested in seeing a nuclear explosion can adjust itineraries accordingly. . . . The best base for bomb-viewing expeditions is Las Vegas which has a couple of hundred motels and hotels of all types, with fairly standard rates.

Marginal notes:
- The specific form of his argument
- A second question
- First bad result of rising standard of living
- The new factor
- Examples
- Applies to spirit too
- Example

A perennial question from people who do not like pre-dawn expeditions is whether the explosions can be seen from Las Vegas, sixty-five miles away. The answer is that sometimes enough of a flash is visible to permit a person to say that he has "seen an atomic bomb." But it is not the same as viewing one from relatively close range, which generally is a breathtaking experience.

Our vulgarity [19] Talk of Nero fiddling while Rome burned. . . . We seem to have an unlimited capacity for banalizing, trivializing (and making money from) the most horrible phenomena. Most moderns claim they cannot understand the insensitivity of a Roman public that could view the spectacle of Christians thrown to lions, or the callousness of an 18th century public that would turn out for public hangings. But what is one to say of contemporary insensitivity which would make a tourist attraction of nuclear testing with its implications of racial destruction? It is perhaps worthwhile to recall the obvious fact that restraint and gentleness are not part of man's germ plasm. They are cultivated products of civilization. **Transition** When destruction is made into a public spectacle, becomes a commonplace, that cultivation is endangered.

Changes to question if standard is actually rising [20] In considering the social effects of the rising standard of living, we have, perhaps, been taking the latter too much for granted. To be sure more goods and services *are* available to more people today in America than ever before, but not because they have become cheaper. **Credit deceives** On the contrary. They are available largely because of the extension of mass credit. It is obvious that easy credit terms foster only the illusion of cheapness and availability, while actually increasing the price of all commodities.

Obsolescence [21] There is still another basic reason why commodities that appear cheap are not really so and that is their built-in obsolescence. Consider so useful and commonplace an item as shoes. Virtually everyone in this country now wears shoes. This certainly was not the case 30 years ago. So far, so good. Unfortunately, the matter does no rest there for not only does everyone wear shoes, but shoes wear everyone—out. One seems to be continually buying them: either they never fit, or there are style changes, or they wear out very soon. This is particularly true of women's shoes: the average female supposedly purchases six pairs a year. Multiply the original six dollar purchase price, which *is* undoubtedly cheap, six times and the result is not so very cheap. Style changes somehow shade unobtrusively into shoddy workmanship; function follows form in many of our artefacts. Women's high-heeled shoes, with their turned-out heels is one case in point; nylon stockings, which are apparently designed to run are another; women's handbags, with the clasps that fail to function long before the bag is half worn is yet another. Continual replacement raises the cost of the most commonplace items, yet the quality of commodities is not easily or often measured in cost-of-living computations.

Useless and harmful products [22] There is another unmeasured factor: Quite a few of the commodities that are part of the rising standard are not very useful and may even be pernicious. The automobile is an example of this "shortcoming" and of other generally glossed-over deficiencies of the pretty economic picture. Supposedly we are now on the road to fulfilling that great "utopian" dream of "two cars in every American garage." Does this mean that the auto is getting cheaper? It does not. The price, despite temporary regressions, is steadily rising. Nor is the American auto a well-made, durable commodity: the fashion is to trade in *every* year. The car is flashy—but construction is poor, lasting quality poor, style changes many. The old joke about the fellow who was supporting a car instead of a wife has as much point as ever, except that that fellow today is probably supporting both plus a house and is working night and day to do it.

Automobile used as example

[23] The auto has, in addition, created grave social problems which have, in practice, proven to be insuperable. It is responsible, among other things, for: insoluble traffic problems, enormous highway fatalities and injuries, the transformation of whole cities into mere traffic arteries or adjuncts thereof. It is also responsible for making public transportation, which every car owner indirectly supports whether or not he ever uses it, increasingly unwieldy and uneconomical.

[24] Consider the last point rationally. Does it make sense to have an enormous number of private vehicles capable of carrying only 4 to 6 people in view of the fact that public vehicles can transport many times that number of passengers per unit? This is no brief for public transportation; service on the latter is often shoddy and over-expensive. Nevertheless, in all fairness, it must be recognized that one of the major things wrong with public transportation is the existence of an over-abundance of private autos on the road.

[25] The car symbolizes one thing, preeminently: escape. Theoretically, you can fly away from "it all" in an auto. But, of course, you really can't—as you sorrowfully discover when your auto is part of the line-up waiting to get through the Holland Tunnel and either in or out of New York City on a Sunday evening, or when you're trying to park on a Saturday evening. At such times one is apt to reflect that if every American family *were* to have two cars in the garage the result would, from every reasonable point of view, be a social catastrophe.

[26] We have been trying, ever so gingerly, to indicate two things about our expanding economy: 1. That the increased availability of goods and services is no indication of diminished price. 2. That a rising standard of living is by no means synonymous with an improving standard of living.

Sums up so far

[27] Both of these are among the reasons people are not satisfied though they possess ever so much—for much that they possess is not designed for their satisfaction but simply to sell. And it is by no means the case that the saleable need be either functional or beautiful. So Americans are always in the market for "something else," and the world is confronted by the paradox of the richest nation on earth being, at the same time, the most indebted nation on earth. Both collectively and individually, the U.S.A. is a nation of people in debt.

[28] If the rising standard of living has not yet made commodities cheaper, has it at least made life more comfortable? Some people would

Transition

probably say "yes," a few would say "no." The fact is, however, that before one can even begin to discuss this matter, it is necessary to introduce a commonsense if nonetheless uncommon qualification, without which the discussion makes no sense at all. Comfort, like everything else, is not *in itself* either good or bad. For example, some of the comforts to modern life are the time and work savers. But neither time saved nor work avoided are always good things. Time saved is valuable only *if saved in the execution of monotonous tasks for the execution of interesting or creative work.* Is this actually the case with most modern time savers? This has to be proven in every instance. Frozen, canned or irradiated foods may save time spent in cookery, but cooking, if not a fine art, is at least a useful one, and as such should be as productive of pleasure as any other useful art.

[29] On the other hand, what is the time saved for? One TV executive has estimated that the average American now spends more time watching TV than he spends on any other single activity except for sleeping and working. Yet cooking (real cooking, not package mix cooking) is more apt to be creative than TV viewing. Not that it is impossible to do the latter creatively, e.g., if one watches in a genuinely *critical* fashion—but the whole "charm" and "appeal" of TV lies in the very passivity involved.

[30] At any rate, the reader may say, less energy *is* expended in watching TV than in cooking. Here again it is necessary to interject that the expenditure of smaller amounts of energy is not in and of itself a good thing. Whether or not it *is* valuable depends on the concrete instance. Much fatigue as we now realize, is simple boredom and the best therapy for fatigue is often precisely greater expenditure of energy.

[31] It may perhaps be claimed that all else aside, our jobs are becoming more comfortable. If one analyzes this contention further one usually discovers that what is actually meant is that our jobs are becoming less *arduous.* Unfortunately, the fact that they are less arduous does not guarantee that they will be less alien. Much of the effort involved in lightening labor is misdirected. More often today (not always!) it is not the lightness or heaviness of the work which makes us dislike it, or tires us, but its alien aspect. The receptionist, for example, does not work "very hard" in terms of actual energy expenditure, nevertheless she probably enjoys her work neither more nor less than the coalminer. Experience has shown that it is socially far easier to solve the problem of lightening labor than to solve the problem of making it more meaningful.

[32] For these reasons one must approach the modern claims of "easier living" with more than a little scepticism. Many of the modern comforts are merely frills which divert us from a basically uncomfortable existence. In any case, easier living is not necessarily better living. . . .

[33] . . . Our literature has, in some measure, reflected and reacted to the negative side of American life. Both the reflection and the reaction have been more or less muted either because of psychological considerations (the doctrine of original sin is back in style and this necessarily softens social criticism—for to the extent that man is considered inherently

vicious his social institutions are either above or below criticism) or for material reasons (the critics are not usually independent people but part of the very mechanism, indeed large cogs in the wheels which run over all of us: editors of mass publications, TV producers, etc.). This "literature of protest" has been directed either to our enslavement by commodities (*Surfeit of Honey, Hidden Persuaders* and the more outspoken *Crack in the Picture Window*) or to our enslavement through conformity or security (*The Last Angry Man, Company Manners, The Organization Man, From the Dark Tower*).

> 2 forms
> of our
> problem

[34] As noted before much of the "honey" appears, under scrutiny, to be mere sugar-water, just as the characteristic security of our age is that of an atomic shelter. In a word, the essence in both instances is: spuriousness. Real honey one can only enjoy so much of; real security, too, has its limits. Substitutes for the real thing, *because they do not truly satisfy or nourish*, are always in demand. One recalls that amusing and rather haunting novel of a few years ago *Catcher in the Rye*. It is the story of a sensitive adolescent, Holden Caulfield, so paralyzed by the phoniness of institutions, commodities, and people that he can no longer function socially.

> *Phoniness*
> —why it is all
> unsatisfying

> Example

[35] At least Holden "went through the motions" of living. What are we to say of the chief character of the interesting if less well-known short story "Rock-a-bye Baby"? The "hero" simply won't get out of bed as days stretch into weeks and weeks into months. What for? He is a latter-day Oblomov—only more so. The great Russian classic depicted the paralysis of an outmoded social class. In the two modern works under discussion the paralysis affects two rather ordinary members of the upper and lower middle class respectively, and significantly, both are quite young.

> Example

[36] It seems that the scramble to make an "extra buck" is producing an exactly opposite effect: a rather generalized apathy, cynicism, and disillusionment. Perhaps the most amazing translation of this mood into real life terms in the last decade was the bored, sullen, hostile, and disbelieving attitude of the American public and armed forces toward the Korean "police action."

> Apathy
> and
> boredom

[37] Consider for a moment the matter of our enslavement through "security." Security in our time is equated with conformity: security is supposed to lie in conformity and once we have "achieved" security we must continue to conform in order to remain "secure." Apparently, however, the price is a bit steep and we chafe restlessly under the burden of security. The spate of post-war novels dealing in one way or another with *revolt* in the armed forces (*The Caine Mutiny, From Here to Eternity*, etc.) is one indication of this. On the other hand, there is an organic relation between the surfeit of security and the surfeit of commodities. We are all to have vested interests, to become "capitalists." What safer, surer, more tried and tested way to turn us into conformists. "Unfortunately," this gimmick won't work: because what we are being bribed with isn't really that good, and, more important, not everyone can be bribed.

> The
> problem of
> conformity

Example [38]   The anguished cry of the chief character in *The Last Angry Man* is, "the bastards won't let you live." Who are the bastards?—the phonies, the exploiters, the bureaucrats. But they are human beings too, and, as the "literature of protest" shows, capable of disgust and shame, however qualified, with their roles. The phoney in *The Last Angry Man*, Woody Thrasher, a TV advertising executive, is a pretty nice guy and so are many of the phonies and bureaucrats one meets in the course of things. They victimize but they are victims too. Their dilemma often appears to them as basically psychic. But this deceptiveness too, is a product of the times. Their problem really is that they are human, but they are more or less forced to act inhumanly.

Questioning
of our
freedom [39]   They have their moments, however, lengthening into hours, when the truth forces itself upon them. At such times they are apt to reflect: "We are ourselves, and we are the roles we play in society: we are both and we are neither, and we are never certain which we are, and we are unhappy; we think like men and act like commodities; there seems to be a dichotomy between the "inner" or "free" man and the "outer" or conforming man. Yet how free are we?—if we can, at best, only be free in thought, but hardly ever in action or expression." "I think, therefore I am," is only part of the truth. "I am, therefore I think" is its complementary. Freedom is more than a state of mind.

The suggested
remedy [40]   The issue now is one of proportion, of avoiding being buried under the great pile of material wealth, of making the latter work for us, instead of our always working for it, of producing wealth to satisfy human need, of making need rather than profitability the determinant of what is produced, how it is produced.

Turns briefly
to question
of its
necessity [41]   The above stands in imminent danger of being considered mere empty verbiage unless one is prepared to say at least a word about the stick question of whether or not the present expansion is *necessary* to keep the economy going. It seems fairly obvious that an expanding population requires expanding production. Unfortunately, this formulation is both too gross and too facile to tell us very much. For example, despite expanding population food surpluses grow ever larger and, incidentally, there is no decline in food prices. In a word, the mere fact of increased supply does not tell us very much about supply that will be *used*. Social relations rather than productive deficiencies are at the root of the trouble. Moreover, vast increases in luxury goods production and war production are certainly not related to the *needs* of a rising population. To be plain: The
problem unplanned expansion may be necessary to keep an *unplanned* economy going, but there is no guarantee whatever that it will satisfy human need. Increases in the production of some commodities, e.g., houses, *are* necessary (we are speaking only of the domestic market) to keep up with a rising population, but general expansion is valueless and wasteful.

[42]   Economic activity has become a fetish in the U.S. The apologists for the system are so busy congratulating themselves on the fact that they seem to have found ways and means to beat the cyclical depression (war, destruction and waste of "surplus" goods, permanent consumer indebtedness, the proliferation and sale of useless luxury goods) that they

have quite forgotten what it is that economic activity is engaged in *for*. An economic system is not adjudged humanly adequate just because it "keeps going." Slavery kept going for hundreds of years. Asiatic feudalism for thousands of years.

[43] Nor is the fact that people now have *fairly* steady employment an adequate index of the successful social system. Coolies, peasants, slaves have long enjoyed this same benefit. Neither do men labor to keep an economic system running; the system is supposed to run for them, not they for it. To "keep going" is hardly a human ideal. As ideal, it is more worthy of a vegetable. On the other hand, can we forget that the "keeping going" cannot with surety be extrapolated too far in this atomic age?

The trouble with "keeping going"

[44] To be sure, most of us in the U.S. have pretty full bellies. But the price paid for the full belly is all too often forgotten. It seems a rule of modern life that as the quantity of commodities increases, the quality of life just as surely decreases. One of the major reasons for this is that the quantity increases beyond measure, beyond reason, and we are spiritually enslaved by the surplus. Our personal and social lives are dominated by excess. The "specter" that haunts America is that of surplus. To destroy that "specter" atomic and hydrogen bombs are exploded, food is burned or permitted to rot, war is indulged in, industrial strikes are fomented, and our lives are cluttered up, moronized, by an endless stream of trivia, in the form of useless and pernicious "gadgets," useless and false information.

Final summary

[45] It is time to re-evaluate this "going" concern, this "successful" economy, to weigh its meager benefits against its high costs. In social life "survival of the fittest" means "fittest to live with"—survival of the most harmonious organism. It is just harmony which is lacking in our social order, an order which, though it survives, is predicated upon imbalance and repression. The limits of such survival are more evident today than ever before.

WRITING ASSIGNMENTS

1. Mr. Dutscher's title "Why Are Americans Unhappy?" assumes that we are unhappy. Do you agree or disagree? Whichever side you choose, be sure that your essay refers to specific *symptoms* that indicate this happiness or unhappiness. These symptoms may be events or conditions from your personal experience or from the news of the country at large.

2. Basic to Mr. Dutscher's indictment of our society is our emphasis on possessing more and more *things*. Applying this to your own personal life, do you think that an emphasis on the possession of material goods can produce dangers or benefits for you, or possibly a combination of both?

3. Happiness, of course, is a difficult thing to pin down. What does it consist of? What can someone do to achieve it? In writing your own definition of happiness, set up some specific goals—conditions, occurrences, possessions—that you want to reach and show why attaining each of these goals will produce happiness.

The Great Texas Crash

VOCABULARY STUDY

1. In Par. 1 the word that means *extravagantly and strangely comic* is _____

2. In Par. 1 the word that means *violent and disorderly* is _____

3. In Par. 6 the word that means *old and broken down* is _____

4. In Par. 7 the word that means *bright and showy* is _____

5. In Par. 10 the word that means *the force and speed of forward movement* is _____

6. In Par. 16 the word that means *a steady increase in loudness* is _____

7. In Par. 18 the word that means *tearing violently apart* is _____

8. In Par. 18 the word that means *parallel to the ground* is _____

9. In Par. 20 the word that means *very large* is _____

10. In Par. 25 the word that means *without exaggeration* is _____

UNDERSTANDING THE ARTICLE
There may be more than one correct answer in each exercise.

1. Mr. Crissey tells this story because

   a. He wants to attack the management of the railway.   a. _____

   b. He wants to expose American business practices   b. _____

   c. He finds it a strange and fascinating event.   c. _____

   d. He believes officials have kept it from the public.   d. _____

2. The M. K. & T. Railway staged the great crash to

    a. Test some experimental equipment.   a. _____

    b. Discover the causes of recent crashes.   b. _____

    c. Gain publicity.   c. _____

    d. Make money from ticket sales.   d. _____

3. The great crash

    a. Produced the explosion that was expected. a. _____

    b. Caused much more damage than was expected. b. _____

    c. Was considered a success by the railway.   c. _____

    d. Was the worst railroad catastrophe of the century. d. _____

4. After the crash

    a. Only one car was left of each train.   a. _____

    b. People were deeply shocked by the destruction and
       casualties.   b. _____

    c. People were eager for souvenirs.   c. _____

    d. People threatened the railway officials.   d. _____

5. After the crash, the M. K. & T. officials

    a. Expressed sincere regrets for the damage caused. a. _____

    b. Were proud of themselves and their railroad. b. _____

    c. Took pictures of the dead and wounded.   c. _____

    d. Realized they had made a great mistake.   d. _____

Is Football A Substitute For Motherhood?

VOCABULARY STUDY

1. In Par. 1 the word that means *a fixed method in which something is done* is _____

2. In Par. 1 the word that means *the act of doing away with* is _____

3. In Par. 2 the word that means *a dispute concerning a matter of opinion* is _____

4. In Par. 3 the word that means *relating to the sense of the beautiful* is _____

5. In Par. 4 the word that means *done with great warmth and eagerness* is _____

6. In Par. 5 the word that means *dignified or majestic* is _____

7. In Par. 6 the word that means *not capable of being held or defended* is _____

8. In Par. 7 the word that means *the act of setting apart as sacred or holy* is _____

9. In Par. 7 the word that means *noisy* is _____

10. In Par. 7 the word that means *the practice of doing something for personal pleasure and not money* is _____

11. In Par. 8 the word that means *a statement that has been overused and made empty* is _____

12. In Par. 9 the word that means *what something or someone deserves to have* is _____

13. In Par. 9 the word that means *the act of showing something to be right* is _____

14. In Par. 11 the word that means *a foolish, silly show* is _____

15. In Par. 11 the word that means *done with seriousness* is _____

UNDERSTANDING THE ARTICLE
There may be more than one correct answer in each exercise.

1. *Sports Illustrated*'s article reveals that the magazine published it because

    a. It agrees with Thompson.   a. _____

    b. It agrees with Athletic Director MacKesey.   b. _____

    c. It believes that the incident was humorous and interesting.   c. _____

    d. It believes that Thompson should be fired.   d. _____

2. Although Thompson did not explain the purpose of his advertisement, his statements indicate that

    a. He is opposed to all sports.   a. _____

    b. He wants to abolish football.   b. _____

    c. He believes football is considered too sacred.   c. _____

    d. He wanted to start a controversy over football.   d. _____

3. "Motherhood" is used in the title and in Thompson's speech because

    a. It is a subject that is considered sacred.   a. _____

    b. It should be stressed in college instead of football.   b. _____

    c. It helps him illustrate people's exaggerated feelings about football.   c. _____

    d. It is something that we do not pay enough attention to.   d. _____

4. Athletic Director MacKesey believes that

    a. Football is the most important sport.   a. _____

    b. Sports are more important in today's world than scholarship.   b. _____

    c. Football players are prepared for the whole of life.   c. _____

    d. Scholarship is not enough to prepare a student for life.   d. _____

5. After the debate was over

   a. Thompson conceded that his opponent had won.   a. _____

   b. Thompson had convinced the audience that he had been
      right.   b. _____

   c. Thompson hoped that the students would actually abolish
      football.   c. _____

   d. Thompson decided to stop his campaign.   d. _____

6. Thompson claimed that the uproar that resulted from his
   advertisement showed that

   a. He had been right.   a. _____

   b. Students were immature and foolish.   b. _____

   c. People get too excited over anything pertaining to football. c. _____

   d. His adversaries would not let the matter drop.   d. _____

7. The petition mentioned in Thompson's advertisement was

   a. Signed by 400 students and faculty members.   a. _____

   b. Outlawed from the Brown University campus.   b. _____

   c. Found to be nonexistent.   c. _____

   d. Distributed by anti-football students.   d. _____

8. The article that appeared in the student newspaper

   a. Insulted Thompson.   a. _____

   b. Cheered his brave stand.   b. _____

   c. Called people's attention to his advertisement.   c. _____

   d. Started the campaign to abolish football.   d. _____

9. The fact that Thompson organized the Radio City Music
   Hall Rockettes into a labor union is used to show that

   a. He is a man of varied interests.   a. _____

   b. He has been a professional dancer.   b. _____

   c. He has always done unusual things.   c. _____

   d. He is a dangerous man to have around.   d. _____

10. The Brown University football captain

    a. Threatened to attack Thompson.   a. _____

    b. Agreed that Thompson was right.   b. _____

    c. Offered to protect Thompson if necessary.   c. _____

    d. Debated against Thompson's ideas.   d. _____

Concerning A Rumor In August

VOCABULARY STUDY

1. In Par. 1 the word that means *about to happen* is _____

2. In Par. 2 the word that means *happening by chance* is _____

3. In Par. 4 the word that means *wandering from a proper course* is _____

4. In Par. 5 the word that means *moving force* is _____

5. In Par. 5 the word that means *the withdrawal of people* is _____

6. In Par. 6 the word that means *open to various interpretations* is _____

7. In Par. 7 the word that means *a proof of the truth of something* is _____

8. In Par. 8 the word that means *a loud outcry* is _____

9. In Par. 10 the word that means *occurring at regular intervals* is _____

10. In Par. 11 the word that means *uneasiness of conscience* is _____

11. In Par. 16 the word that means *the departure of a large number of people* is _____

12. In Par. 16 the word that means *an uproar* is _____

13. In Par. 18 the word that means *the people of a community* is _____

14. In Par. 19 the word that means *coming to rest* is _____

15. In Par. 22 the word that means *confined within limits* is _____

UNDERSTANDING THE ARTICLE

There may be more than one correct answer in each exercise.

1. This article was written for the purpose of

   a. Revealing the dangers of floods.   a. _____

   b. Revealing the dangerous results of a rumor.   b. _____

   c. Revealing the way in which a rumor spreads.   c. _____

   d. Revealing the inadequacy of our Civil Defense organizations.   d. _____

2. Within an hour and a half the rumor had caused

   a. A mass evacuation in Matamoras.   a. _____

   b. Three heart attacks.   b. _____

   c. Evacuation of a third of the people of Port Jervis.   c. _____

   d. The mobilization of the State Militia.   d. _____

3. The rumor got started in Port Jervis because

   a. The Port Jervis Fire Chief acted hysterically.   a. _____

   b. A stranger misinterpreted the intentional opening of the Dam gates.   b. _____

   c. A stranger told a restaurant owner the Dam had broken.   c. _____

   d. The Sparrowbush Fire Captain spread the news without first checking.   d. _____

4. Several Port Jervis fire trucks

   a. Helped spread the rumor.   a. _____

   b. Had been given orders to announce the news.   b. _____

   c. Were reprimanded by the chief radio operator.   c. _____

   d. Sounded their sirens.   d. _____

5. The blowing of the fire siren in Matamoras

   a. Helped to calm down the frightened people.   a. _____

   b. Caused an evacuation of Matamoras.   b. _____

   c. Was originally caused by the panic in Port Jervis.   c. _____

   d. Helped to increase the panic in Port Jervis.   d. _____

6. The first person to learn definitely that the announcement was a rumor was

   a. The Civil Defense Chief in Port Jervis.   a. _____

   b. The Port Jervis police radio operator.   b. _____

   c. The radio "ham" operator.   c. _____

   d. The Port Jervis Fire Chief.   d. _____

7. As a result of the frightening news

   a. All the people who fled acted selfishly.   a. _____

   b. Some people acted without thinking.   b. _____

   c. Some people acted considerately.   c. _____

   d. People volunteered their assistance in fighting the flood.   d. _____

8. When he heard that the rumor was definitely false, the Port Jervis Fire Chief

   a. Had the fire department broadcast the news to the people.   a. _____

   b. Had the radio station broadcast the news.   b. _____

   c. Told the people in front of the fire department to go home.   c. _____

   d. Stopped the fire trucks that were coming to the aid of the town.   d. _____

9. When it went back on the air to broadcast the news, the radio station

   a. Stressed that the Dam was not broken.   a. _____

   b. Avoided any direct mention of the Dam.   b. _____

   c. Was careful not to frighten anyone who was not listening carefully.   c. _____

   d. Blamed the Dam Superintendent for the panic.   d. _____

10. The man who acted most wisely through the confusion was

   a. The Police Chief.   a. _____

   b. The railroad station clerk.   b. _____

   c. The Sparrowbush Fire Captain.   c. _____

   d. The Port Jervis Fire Chief.   d. _____

The Jet That Crashed Before Take-off

VOCABULARY STUDY

1. In Par. 2 the word that means *more than enough* is _____

2. In Par. 4 the word that means *without a chance to take back* is _____

3. In Par. 4 the word that means *harsh and absolute* is _____

4. In Par. 9 the word that means *to be directly faced* is _____

5. In Par. 11 the word that means *lengthened in amount of time* is _____

6. In Par. 11 the word that means *that may be disregarded* is _____

7. In Par. 12 the word that means *hardly noticeable* is _____

8. In Par. 13 the word that means *appropriate to the subject* is _____

9. In Par. 14 the word that means *gay and festive* is _____

10. In Par. 16 the word that means *used as a reserve* is _____

11. In Par. 16 the word that means *without noticing* is _____

12. In Par. 17 the word that means *a faithful and careful attitude* is _____

13. In Par. 19 the word that means *last-minute release from death* is _____

14. In Par. 19 the word that means *to drop away* is _____

15. In Par. 19 the word that means *leaving something out* is _____

UNDERSTANDING THE ARTICLE

There may be more than one correct answer in each exercise.

1. In this story Mr. Lay means to show

    a. How airport safety regulations are inadequate.   a. _____

    b. How small errors can add up to disaster.   b. _____

    c. How every take-off of a jet plane is a crisis.   c. _____

    d. How every take-off of a jet plane is merely routine.   d. _____

2. Mr. Lay organizes the details of his story

    a. In exact sequence of the passage of time.   a. _____

    b. In reversed time order.   b. _____

    c. Around the character traits of the pilot.   c. _____

    d. Around the four basic causes of the crash.   d. _____

3. The four thefts and two additional circumstances mentioned show

    a. Why the plane this time needed an 8100 foot runway.   a. _____

    b. Why the 1300 foot surplus was not enough.   b. _____

    c. Why the plane had to take more than 6700 feet to get into the air.   c. _____

    d. Why the crash occurred.   d. _____

4. Theft number one

    a. Was caused by negligence in the control tower.   a. _____

    b. Was caused by a sudden slight rise in the wind.   b. _____

    c. Was caused by the pilot's delay in taking off.   c. _____

    d. Was caused by the pilot's negligence.   d. _____

5. The rise of the temperature—theft number two—

    a. Lessened the thrust of the engine.   a. _____

    b. Occurred during an unavoidable delay.   b. _____

    c. Was not taken into account by the drawing of a new flight plan.   c. _____

    d. Thinned the air.   d. _____

6. The third theft cost the pilot 550 feet of runway because

   a. The runway slanted uphill.   a. _____

   b. The pilot couldn't tell the runway slanted.   b. _____

   c. The pilot was concentrating on the mountains beyond the runway.   c. _____

   d. The runway slanted downhill.   d. _____

7. The pilot's lack of adequate rest—theft number four—

   a. Caused him to react more slowly at the controls.   a. _____

   b. Caused him to miss an error relating to the weight of the plane.   b. _____

   c. Caused him to arrive late for his take-off.   c. _____

   d. Caused him to fill out his flight papers incorrectly.   d. _____

8. The two things that might have saved the pilot were

   a. Dropping the extra fuel.   a. _____

   b. Gunning the engine.   b. _____

   c. Slowing the engine.   c. _____

   d. Pulling back on the stick.   d. _____

9. The pilot's first chance at a reprieve failed because

   a. The addition to the runway was not yet completed.   a. _____

   b. The runway markers had not been moved.   b. _____

   c. The runway markers had been moved.   c. _____

   d. He was always 400 feet further along the runway than he thought.   d. _____

10. The pilot's last chance at a reprieve failed because

    a. He dropped the fuel tanks.   a. _____

    b. He didn't release the tanks with the hand lever provided.   b. _____

    c. The tanks dropped clear too late.   c. _____

    d. The tanks were over-full.   d. _____

The Civil War

VOCABULARY STUDY

1. In Par. 2 the word that means *a mental disorder* is   _____

2. In Par. 6 the word that means *shame and dishonor* is   _____

3. In Par. 11 the word that means *memorial burnings of a pile of wood* is   _____

4. In Par. 15 the word that means *lying* is   _____

5. In Par. 15 the word that means *an economy based on farming* is   _____

6. In Par. 16 the word that means *the withdrawal from a government* is   _____

7. In Par. 34 the word that means *that cannot be held* is   _____

8. In Par. 42 the word that means *responsibility* is   _____

9. In Par. 54 the word that means *stupid people* is   _____

10. In Par. 55 the word that means *plundering* is   _____

11. In Par. 60 the word that means *fireside of a home* is   _____

12. In Par. 77 the word that means *the one that comes before* is   _____

13. In Par. 97 the word that means *warnings or hints of what is to come* is   _____

14. In Par. 104 the word that means *pulled together and strengthened* is   _____

15. In Par. 113 the word that means *to wane or decline* is   _____

UNDERSTANDING THE ARTICLE

There may be more than one correct answer in each exercise.

1. In telling the story of the Civil War, James Street

   a. Sees it as a romantic and glorious event.   a. _____

   b. Is sympathetic toward the South.   b. _____

   c. Vents many opinions about the war.   c. _____

   d. Sees the stupidity and horror of it.   d. _____

2. In interpreting the causes of the war, more and more historians, Mr. Street believes, tend to stress

   a. The moral issue of slavery.   a. _____

   b. The need for foreign trade.   b. _____

   c. The arrogance of the South.   c. _____

   d. The need for higher tariffs.   d. _____

3. In his own analysis of what really started the conflict, Street claims

   a. Economic interests came first, slavery followed.   a. _____

   b. The Abolitionists caused the whole thing.   b. _____

   c. Lincoln's stubbornness was the chief cause.   c. _____

   d. The South's opposition to Lincoln set off the spark. d. _____

4. Street points out that Lincoln's position at the start of the war

   a. Stressed the abolition of slavery at any cost.   a. _____

   b. Stressed economic issues above all.   b. _____

   c. Stressed the need for preserving the Union.   c. _____

   d. Stressed the danger of the abolition of slavery.   d. _____

5. Events at the start of the war followed this sequence:

   a. A Union attack, secession, the firing on Ft. Sumter.   a. _____

   b. The firing on Ft. Sumter, secession, a Union attack.   b. _____

c. Secession, the firing on Ft. Sumter, a Union attack.   c. _____

d. Secession, a Union attack, the firing on Ft. Sumter.   d. _____

6. Mr. Street believes the South held out for as long as it did because of

   a. The aid of European nations.   a. _____

   b. The uncertainty of the North.   b. _____

   c. The poor military leadership of the North.   c. _____

   d. The battleground on which the war was fought.   d. _____

7. Mr. Street sees General Grant

   a. As the reason it took the North so long to win.   a. _____

   b. As the best General the North had.   b. _____

   c. As a far better General than Robert E. Lee.   c. _____

   d. As a General who couldn't make up his mind.   d. _____

8. The Northern strategy that finally proved successful

   a. Attacked the South from the West.   a. _____

   b. Struck immediately at the Southern capital of Richmond.   b. _____

   c. Was the work of Gen. McClellan.   c. _____

   d. Struck at the South's sources of supply.   d. _____

9. The last great Southern victory described in the article occurred

   a. At Gettysburg.   a. _____

   b. At Bull Run.   b. _____

   c. At Chancellorsville.   c. _____

   d. At Shiloh.   d. _____

10. The beginning of the end for the South occurred

    a. When Grant took Vicksburg and Lee lost at Gettysburg.   a. _____

    b. When Grant defeated Lee at Gettysburg.   b. _____

    c. At about the same time in both the West and the East.   c. _____

    d. When McClellan resumed control of the Union Army.   d. _____

Too Early Spring

VOCABULARY STUDY

Note that since the story is told in the words of Chuck Peters,
the exercises refer to the slang terms that he uses.

1. In Par. 1 the slang term that means *a stupid person* is   _____

2. In Par. 7 the word that shows *just how fast Sheila can swim* is   _____

3. In Par. 8 the word that describes *a hair style* is   _____

4. In Par. 9 the word that means *threw* is   _____

5. In Par. 13 the word that means *very fine* is   _____

6. In Par. 24 the word that means *liking* is   _____

7. In Par. 31 the word that means *raincoat* is   _____

8. In Par. 32 the word that means *overly sentimental* is   _____

9. In Par. 37 the word that suggests *the cool feeling of Helen's kiss* is   _____

10. In Par. 46 the word that suggests *Mrs. Sharon's bad moods* is   _____

11. In Par. 89 the word that suggests *Chuck's feeling of love* is   _____

12. In Par. 99 the word that means *dinner* is   _____

13. In Par. 101 the word that means *party* is   _____

14. In Par. 112 the word that suggests *Chuck's disillusionment* is   _____

15. In Par. 118 the word that means *cocky and rude* is   _____

UNDERSTANDING THE STORY

There may be more than one correct answer in each exercise.

1. This story may be interpreted as illustrating the author's view that

   a. Innocence can be destroyed by suspicion.   a. _____

   b. Teenagers are foolish and wild.   b. _____

   c. Parents don't understand their children.   c. _____

   d. Youthful and adult worlds sometimes clash.   d. _____

2. At the end of the story, Chuck Peters

   a. Sees the world differently.   a. _____

   b. Accepts the decision of the adults.   b. _____

   c. Hopes he and Helen can someday re-establish their
   previous relationship.   c. _____

   d. Realizes it will never be the same with Helen again. d. _____

3. Helen's parents

   a. Misinterpreted the scene in the dark living room. a. _____

   b. Saw Helen and Chuck going to the house in the country. b. _____

   c. Did not understand as Chuck's parents did.   c. _____

   d. Forced Chuck to quit school.   d. _____

4. Their actions at the house in the country reveal

   a. Their desire to be adults.   a. _____

   b. Their ease with one another.   b. _____

   c. Their foolishness.   c. _____

   d. Their innocence.   d. _____

5. Chuck Peters is telling this story

   a. Many years after the event.   a. _____

   b. The day after Helen was sent to a convent.   b. _____

   c. Shortly after being sent to school in the East.   c. _____

   d. While his emotional reaction is still immediate and
   intense.   d. _____

My Average Uncle

VOCABULARY STUDY

1. In Par. 1 the word that means *an outstanding characteristic* is   _____

2. In Par. 3 the word that means *pants* is   _____

3. In Par. 4 the word that that means *varied collections* is   _____

4. In Par. 4 the word that means *to rise into view* is   _____

5. In Par. 5 the word that means *marriage* is   _____

6. In Par. 7 the word that means *elaborate displays* is   _____

7. In Par. 7 the word that means *cautious or moderate* is   _____

8. In Par. 11 the word that means *suspenders* is   _____

9. In Par. 11 the word that means *longed for* is   _____

10. In Par. 13 the word that means *ill-temper* is   _____

UNDERSTANDING THE ARTICLE
There may be more than one correct answer in each exercise.

1. In this essay Mr. Coffin intends
   a. To criticize his uncle for being so ordinary.   a. _____
   b. To praise his uncle for being so ordinary.   b. _____
   c. To amuse the reader with details of his uncle's life.   c. _____
   d. To merely sum up his uncle's personality.   d. _____

2. Uncle Amos is summed up as the kind of a man who
   a. Was always striving for happiness.   a. _____
   b. Was always moderate in what he did.   b. _____
   c. Was always content with his lot.   c. _____
   d. Was always telling funny stories.   d. _____

165

3. The average quality of Uncle Amos was illustrated

    a. By his house burning down.   a. _____

    b. By his interest in books.   b. _____

    c. By his appearance.   c. _____

    d. By his conversation.   d. _____

4. Uncle Amos was nicer to be with than some of Coffin's other uncles because

    a. He made no demands upon anybody.   a. _____

    b. He told such amusing stories.   b. _____

    c. He took life easy.   c. _____

    d. He had several tricks and specialties.   d. _____

5. When he was at home, Uncle Amos

    a. Always ordered his wives around.   a. _____

    b. Was always ordered around by his wives.   b. _____

    c. Was always content.   c. _____

    d. Was always drinking ale.   d. _____

New York

VOCABULARY STUDY

1. In Par. 1 the word that means *one can see things beyond powers of ordinary vision* is _____

2. In Par. 2 the word that means *those who are unusual or odd* is _____

3. In Par. 5 the word that means *large crowds* is _____

4. In Par. 6 the word that means *people who can't sleep* is _____

5. In Par. 11 the word that means *reddish-complexioned* is _____

6. In Par. 12 the word that means *able to talk easily* is _____

7. In Par. 13 the word that means *down-and-out people* is _____

8. In Par. 14 the word that means *without a fault* is _____

9. In Par. 15 the word that means *to live easily and healthily* is _____

10. In Par. 16 the word that means *shadowy, not easily seen* is _____

11. In Par. 17 the word that means *shabby* is _____

12. In Par. 17 the word that means *a kind of sail* is _____

13. In Par. 19 the word that means *one who lures or tempts* is _____

14. In Par. 20 the word that means *active by night* is _____

15. In Par. 21 the word that means *wandering* is _____

UNDERSTANDING THE ARTICLE

There may be more than one correct answer in each exercise.

1. According to Mr. Talese, the distinctive quality of New York City is that

 a. People are not very friendly.   a. _____

 b. People will only pay attention to odd things. b. _____

 c. Many odd things occur but are not really noticed. c. _____

 d. People never notice celebrities.   d. _____

2. Talese's judgment of this quality of New York is one of

 a. Complete disapproval.   a. _____

 b. Fascinated affection.   b. _____

 c. Mixed approval and disapproval. c. _____

 d. Bored disinterest.   d. _____

3. In his description of New York City Talese stresses

 a. Its political leaders.   a. _____

 b. Its skyscrapers and monuments. b. _____

 c. Its strange characters.   c. _____

 d. Its unimportant but odd statistics. d. _____

4. By describing the actions of such non-humans as ants, hawks, cats, etc. in the midst of descriptions of humans, Talese wants to show

 a. That New York has more animals than any other city. a. _____

 b. That New Yorkers know as little about the people as they do about the animals. b. _____

 c. That it is difficult for animals to live in New York. c. _____

 d. That New Yorkers are not fond of animals. d. _____

5. Talese's method of writing places greatest stress on

 a. Judgments by the author.   a. _____

 b. Brief anecdotes or stories.   b. _____

 c. Concrete details of actions and appearances. c. _____

 d. Historical summaries of the city's landmarks. d. _____

Miami—Florida's Gold Coast

VOCABULARY STUDY

1. In Par. 2 the word that means *groups moving from one place to another* is   _____

2. In Par. 3 the word that means *a fleet (like warships)* is   _____

3. In Par. 4 the word that means *the quality of always being the same* is   _____

4. In Par. 4 the word that means *made to conform to a certain manner or style* is   _____

5. In Par. 4 the word that means *wasteful, extravagant, careless with money* is   _____

6. In Par. 4 the word that means *common people* is   _____

7. In Par. 4 the word that means *an unreal, false belief* is   _____

8. In Par. 5 the word that means *overly refined and polite* is   _____

9. In Par. 5 the word that means *forgetful, unnoticing* is   _____

10. In Par. 6 the word that means *lazy* is   _____

11. In Par. 6 the word that means *with great effort or energy* is   _____

12. In Par. 9 the word that means *having religious devotion* is   _____

13. In Par. 11 the word that means *the place people most yearn to go to* is   _____

14. In Par. 12 the word that means *deserted, wasted* is   _____

15. In Par. 13 the word that means *having fantastic schemes* is   _____

Miami

VOCABULARY STUDY

1. In Par. 1 the word that means *horrified or sickened* is _____

2. In Par. 1 the word that means *emergency needs* is _____

3. In Par. 1 the word that means *paled and sickly* is _____

4. In Par. 1 the word that means *dull and lifeless* is _____

5. In Par. 2 the word that means *uninteresting, lifeless* is _____

6. In Par. 3 the word that means *softened, lowered* is _____

7. In Par. 3 the word that means *things that come away from the main surface* is _____

8. In Par. 4 the word that means *faked, devised dishonestly* is _____

9. In Par. 4 the word that means *headlong and sudden* is _____

10. In Par. 4 the word that means *inactive and dull* is _____

11. In Par. 4 the word that means *trite, unoriginal* is _____

12. In Par. 5 the word that means *to become lowered in efficiency and quality* is _____

13. In Par. 5 the word that means *quick and easy of movement* is _____

14. In Par. 7 the word that means *non-living* is _____

15. In Par. 7 the word that means *varied or different* is _____

UNDERSTANDING THE ARTICLES

There may be more than one correct answer in each exercise.

MIAMI—FLORIDA'S GOLD COAST and MIAMI

1. The interpretations or impressions of Miami presented by these two articles

   a. Are exactly the same.   a. _____

   b. Are quite similar, though differing slightly.   b. _____

   c. Are very different.   c. _____

   d. Are slightly different, though basically the same.   d. _____

2. Mr. Schulberg finds that Miami

   a. Is very impressive.   a. _____

   b. Is very exciting.   b. _____

   c. Has many contrasts.   c. _____

   d. Has a strong deadening effect.   d. _____

3. Mr. Wilson finds that Miami

   a. Is very exciting.   a. _____

   b. Is artificial and empty.   b. _____

   c. Is the most impressive vacation spot in America.   c. _____

   d. Is an example of much that is wrong with our life today. d. _____

4. According to Schulberg, the average Miami vacationer

   a. Is very wealthy.   c. _____

   b. Continually takes part in sports.   d. _____

   c. Sits around a lot.   a. _____

   d. Is deadened, lifeless, unnatural.   b. _____

5. According to Schulberg, the hotels of Miami Beach

   a. Indicate God's blessing to us.   a. _____

   b. Indicate an amazing human accomplishment.   b. _____

   c. Indicate the artificial quality of our society.   c. _____

   d. Have all been built by Mr. Collins.   d. _____

6. Wilson thinks the Miami palm trees

   a. Are beautiful and exotic.   a. _____

   b. Are as dull and lifeless as the rest of the place.   b. _____

   c. Go beautifully with the hotels.   c. _____

   d. Are more beautiful than the hotels.   d. _____

7. Wilson finds the movie theater is

   a. The most exciting place in Miami.   a. _____

   b. Typical of the artificial and lifeless atmosphere of Miami.   b. _____

   c. Unable to lure the tourists away from the outdoors.   c. _____

   d. Full of as much false glamour as the movie showing there.   d. _____

8. Wilson believes Americans love to watch animal movies because

   a. They are usually outdoorsmen.   a. _____

   b. They are so deadened and unnatural themselves.   b. _____

   c. They feel sorry for the animals.   c. _____

   d. They envy the animals.   d. _____

9. Wilson decides that the cartoons of Walt Disney and the airplane

   a. Both capture some of the power and beauty of nature.   a. _____

   b. Are examples of the worst elements of our society.   b. _____

   c. Are examples of the worthy accomplishments of mankind.   c. _____

   d. Both reveal nature's superiority to mankind.   d. _____

10. The only time Wilson feels some pride for his country occurs when

   a. He goes to the movie theater.   a. _____

   b. He removes the cellophane from the toilet seat.   b. _____

   c. He watches the animal short subjects.   c. _____

   d. He sees some airplanes.   d. _____

The Innocence of Marilyn Monroe

VOCABULARY STUDY

1. In Par. 1 the word that means *call forth, produce in the mind* is _____

2. In Par. 1 the word that means *definite, understandable, actual* is _____

3. In Par. 1 the word that means *a fictional, goddess-like story or legend* is _____

4. In Par. 3 the word that means *a pitiful, homeless child* is _____

5. In Par. 3 the word that means *near-sighted* is _____

6. In Par. 4 the word that means *direct opposite* is _____

7. In Par. 4 the word that means *lack of intentional skill* and *strategy* is _____

8. In Par. 5 the word that means *made distinct, different or unique* is _____

9. In Par. 5 the word that means *glorification, the act of making a god of a person* is _____

10. In Par. 5 the word that means *revealed, made evident* is _____

11. In Par. 7 the word that means *original, basic model* is _____

12. In Par. 9 the word that means *a clownish person* is _____

13. In Par. 10 the word that means *non-human objects of sexual feelings* is _____

14. In Par. 13 the word that means *produces* is _____

15. In Par. 14 the word that means *clear and shining, transparent* is _____

UNDERSTANDING THE ARTICLE
There may be more than one correct answer in each exercise.

1. In this article Mr. Sylvester
   a. Exposes some of the facts in the personal life of a star.   a. _____
   b. Relates a star's movie roles to her personal life.   b. _____
   c. Interprets the public screen personality of a star.   c. _____
   d. Interprets an interview with a star.   d. _____

2. To begin with, Sylvester explains that a famous movie star
   a. Develops a definite, unchanging screen personality.   a. _____
   b. Needs to change her personality with each new role.   b. _____
   c. Brings to life certain ideals of the audience.   c. _____
   d. Is always the same on and off the screen.   d. _____

3. Sylvester's thesis about Marilyn Monroe is that
   a. Like all other stars she embodies a clear-cut personality.   a. _____
   b. She is the sexiest star the movies have produced.   b. _____
   c. She is the worst actress in Hollywood.   c. _____
   d. She presents a split-screen personality that is hard to pin
      down.   d. _____

4. According to Sylvester, Marilyn's screen personality
   a. Presents an image of dangerous sexiness.   a. _____
   b. Mixes innocence and sexiness.   b. _____
   c. Mixes the image of a gold-digger and a pitiful child.   c. _____
   d. Mixes the evils and glories of sex.   d. _____

5. Marilyn's serious and comic parts reveal
   a. A single unified personality to the public.   a. _____
   b. Her amazing acting talents.   b. _____
   c. Different aspects of her screen personality.   c. _____
   d. One character trait that is unchanging, although not al-
      ways noticeable.   d. _____

6. Marilyn's innocence is revealed

    a. By her surprise at her own sexiness.   a. _____

    b. As the unifying trait of her screen personality.   b. _____

    c. By the usual lack of real passion in her films.   c. _____

    d. By her lack of complete commitment to sex.   d. _____

7. As the gold-digger in several comedy films, Marilyn

    a. Was completely a calculating hussy.   a. _____

    b. Was still concerned with being nice.   b. _____

    c. Was still worried about being too sexy.   c. _____

    d. Was not a very passionate lover.   d. _____

8. Marilyn's attempt to be seriously sexy in *Niagara*

    a. Proved she could convey a clear-cut image of pure sex   a. _____

    b. Produced the most passionate love scenes in years.   b. _____

    c. Produced some unintentional comedy.   c. _____

    d. Illustrated the problem of her screen personality.   d. _____

9. Marilyn's screen romances quite often

    a. Make a joke of sex.   a. _____

    b. Turn out very tragically.   b. _____

    c. Bewilder her.   c. _____

    d. Make love a purely business proposition.   d. _____

10. Marilyn's voice

    a. Matches her usual pin-up picture personality.   a. _____

    b. Gives away her basic little girl's innocence.   b. _____

    c. Matches her lack of understanding of her own sexiness. c. _____

    d. Changes greatly from picture to picture.   d. _____

Marlon Brando: The Gilded Image

VOCABULARY STUDY

1. In Par. 4 the word that means *an extraordinary occurrence or person* is

2. In Par. 4 the word that means *coarseness, vulgarity* is

3. In Par. 5 the word that means *quality of being true or real* is

4. In Par. 11 the word that means *to meaningfully make a connection in a psychological, human way* is

5. In Par. 12 the word that means *giving free rein to one's own desires* is

6. In Par. 13 the word that means *exaggerated, showy greatness* is

7. In Par. 13 the word that means *slavish surrender, submissiveness* is

8. In Par. 15 the word that means *honesty, sincerity, loyalty to ideals* is

9. In Par. 16 the word that means *makes itself visible* is

10. In Par. 21 the word that means *the quality of naturalness, freedom, impulsiveness* is

11. In Par. 21 the word that means *the central character of a story* is

12. In Par. 24 the word that means *unable to express oneself* is

13. In Par. 24 the word that means *massive, stonelike form* is

14. In Par. 24 the word that means *apparent* is

15. In Par. 25 the word that means *devouring jaws* is

UNDERSTANDING THE ARTICLE
There may be more than one correct answer in each exercise.

1. Mr. Tallmer wrote this article to

    a. Criticize the personal life of Brando.   a. _____

    b. Capture a change that has occurred in Brando.   b. _____

    c. Trace the growth of Brando.   c. _____

    d. Lament the destruction of Brando's greatest qualities.   d. _____

2. Tallmer characterizes Brando's performances today as

    a. Dishonest.   a. _____

    b. Self-indulgent.   b. _____

    c. Mature.   c. _____

    d. Improving.   d. _____

3. The causes of the change in Brando are

    a. Hollywood.   a. _____

    b. Fame.   b. _____

    c. Egotism.   c. _____

    d. Lack of ability.   d. _____

4. Tallmer's and the director's comments on Brando's early performances indicate

    a. The reasons for his failure.   a. _____

    b. The greatness and power he once had.   b. _____

    c. The dishonesty of his career from the beginning.   c. _____

    d. The reasons critics tended to over-estimate him.   d. _____

5. Tallmer characterizes Brando's earlier qualities as

    a. Powerful masculinity.   a. _____

    b. Complete truthfulness.   b. _____

    c. Grandiosity.   c. _____

    d. Self-reliant freedom.   d. _____

6. Tallmer quotes the director to illustrate

   a. How wrong people can be about Brando.   a. _____

   b. What Brando's greatness was like.   b. _____

   c. What Brando's fall has been like.   c. _____

   d. Why Brando may still improve.   d. _____

7. As the marginal notes indicate, Tallmer states his central thesis in

   a. Paragraph One.   a. _____

   b. Paragraph Fifteen.   b. _____

   c. Paragraph Two.   c. _____

   d. Paragraph Five.   d. _____

8. Both Tallmer and the Director comment that in *Streetcar* and *On the Waterfront* Brando captured a human being's

   a. Deep response to people and things around him.   a. _____

   b. Urge to kill.   b. _____

   c. Need to make a meaningful connection to others.   c. _____

   d. Need to dominate others.   d. _____

9. Brando's performance in *Viva Zapata* illustrated

   a. His loss of integrity.   a. _____

   b. The beginning of his decline.   b. _____

   c. His imitation of himself.   c. _____

   d. The high point of his career.   d. _____

10. Brando's performance in *On the Waterfront*

   a. Revealed the final emptiness of his talent.   a. _____

   b. Captured a human being in all of his truth and complexity.   b. _____

   c. Marked the beginning of his comeback.   c. _____

   d. Illustrated the great qualities of his talent.   d. _____

Disneyland and Las Vegas

VOCABULARY STUDY

1. In Par. 2 the word that means *violent reaction of disgust* is _____

2. In Par. 8 the word that means *wise* is _____

3. In Par. 9 the word that means *control, rule* is _____

4. In Par. 9 the word that means the *basic legend of a way of life* is _____

5. In Par. 9 the word that means *engages in dishonest trade* is _____

6. In Par. 10 the word that means *cheap and trivial, showy in a phony way* is _____

7. In Par. 10 the word that means *a valid accusation* is _____

8. In Par. 10 the word that means *a fake, a counterfeit* is _____

9. In Par. 11 the word that means *deep and serious* is _____

10. In Par. 11 the word that means *drugs, numbs, deadens* is _____

11. In Par. 15 the word that means *all-powerful* is _____

12. In Par. 24 the word that means *comparisons* is _____

13. In Par. 25 the word that means *those who are sorry for having done wrong* is _____

14. In Par. 29 the word that means *a sign, an indication* is _____

15. In Par. 30 the word that means *satisfied in a false, phony manner* is _____

UNDERSTANDING THE ARTICLE

There may be more than one correct answer in each exercise.

1. Mr. Halevy's article

   a. Presents a balanced, objective view of two places of entertainment.   a. _____

   b. Presents his own emotional reactions to the two places.   b. _____

   c. Presents his interpretation of their significance and meaning in our society.   c. _____

   d. Presents all the facts necessary for a judgment.   d. _____

2. Halevy's thesis is that both Disneyland and Las Vegas

   a. Represent a running away from real life.   a. _____

   b. Provide a false excitement for people with feeble, empty
lives.   b. _____

   c. Do not seem to fit the rest of American life.   c. _____

   d. Provide valuable outlets for people's energies.   d. _____

3. Disneyland, according to Halevy,

   a. Is valuable because it gives pleasure to children.   a. _____

   b. Can provide the satisfactions of adventure with no risk of
danger.   b. _____

   c. Reduces the real challenge of adventure of life to a series
of phony gimmicks.   c. _____

   d. Needs more rides for adults.   d. _____

4. Las Vegas, according to Halevy,

   a. Is not as completely empty and phony as Disneyland.   a. _____

   b. Allows people to escape from the economic pressures of
their lives.   b. _____

   c. Allows people to treat money as if they didn't care about
it.   c. _____

   d. Is filled with people who don't really expect to or care
to win.   d. _____

5. Halevy uses the episode on the river launch at Disneyland

    a. To illustrate one of the few interesting rides there.   a. _____

    b. To illustrate the amazing skill of the pilot.   b. _____

    c. To illustrate the imagination of Disney's designers.   c. _____

    d. To illustrate the phony gimmicks employed.   d. _____

6. The exhibits sponsored by big corporations are mentioned

    a. To show the educational displays available.   a. _____

    b. To stress the widespread interest in and support of Disneyland.   b. _____

    c. To emphasize the commercialism involved in the whole enterprise.   c. _____

    d. To suggest the falseness of the amusements.   d. _____

7. For Halevy, the most amazing aspect of Las Vegas was that

    a. Some of the card players showed great skill and courage.   a. _____

    b. Only the big plungers really wanted to win.   b. _____

    c. Most of the gamblers weren't there because they thought they could win.   c. _____

    d. People were gaining satisfaction from being able to throw money away.   d. _____

8. The thing that Halevy liked best about Las Vegas

    a. Was the luxuries of the big hotels.   a. _____

    b. Was the carefree attitude of most of the gamblers.   b. _____

    c. Was the old-style card games downtown.   c. _____

    d. Was the legalizing of gambling.   d. _____

9. The old gamblers downtown seemed to Halevy to be

    a. More pathetic than the people at the big hotels.   a. _____

    b. More honest and realistic than the people at the hotels.   b. _____

    c. More truly adventurous than the people at the hotels.   c. _____

    d. More courageous than most people he has met lately.   d. _____

10. Halevy refers to the Mexicans and Indians

    a. To show that we are not very civilized.   a. _____

    b. To suggest the possible psychology behind throwing money away.   b. _____

    c. To illustrate the realism of Las Vegas gamblers.   c. _____

    d. To suggest that, without really knowing or admitting it, Americans have very mixed emotions about money.   d. _____

What Is History?

VOCABULARY STUDY

1. In Par. 1, the word that means *having a general likeness, not identical* is _____

2. In Par. 2, the word that means *completely* is _____

3. In Par. 2 the word that means *physical powers or functions* is _____

4. In Par. 2, the word that means *go about aimlessly* is _____

5. In Par. 2, the word that means *to find again your place in the existing situation* is _____

6. In Par. 2, the word that means *stopped* is _____

7. In Par. 2, the word that means *dealings with other people* is _____

8. In Par. 3, the word that means *leave out* is _____

9. In Par. 3, the word that means *expect, or look forward to* is _____

10. In Par. 3, the word that means *to state exactly what will happen* is _____

UNDERSTANDING THE CHAPTER
There may be more than one correct answer in each exercise.

1. In this brief piece, Mr. Becker's purpose is to tell the reader

   a. What history is.   a. _____

   b. Why history is important.   b. _____

   c. Why Gibbon's *Decline and Fall of the Roman Empire* is a great book.   c. _____

   d. Why memory is important.   d. _____

2. Becker *defines* historical knowledge as

    a. The most important goal of education.   a. _____

    b. The memory of things said and done in the past.   b. _____

    c. The understanding of the causes of past events.   c. _____

    d. The greatest problem of college students.   d. _____

3. According to Becker, a knowledge of history

    a. Allows us to anticipate what may happen.   a. _____

    b. Allows us to predict what will happen.   b. _____

    c. Allows us to manage our present affairs.   c. _____

    d. Allows us to prepare for what may happen.   d. _____

4. To live intelligently, according to Becker,

    a. You must constantly "re-orient" yourself and get a new
start.   a. _____

    b. You must read the best historical books.   b. _____

    c. You must remember a great deal of the past.   c. _____

    d. You must apply what you know of the past to the present
and future.   d. _____

5. By explaining the value of a knowledge of your personal
history, Becker wants to show that your personal history

    a. Is the most important kind of history.   a. _____

    b. Is one kind of history.   b. _____

    c. Involves the same process of memory as general history.   c. _____

    d. Is not really a part of what is meant by history.   d. _____

The Individual and the Group

1. In Par. 1 the word that means *the system of names and terms used* is   _____

2. In Par. 1 the word that means *two-way, on both sides, done in return* is   _____

3. In Par. 1 the word that means *contact via some kind of language* is   _____

4. In Par. 2 the word that means *totals of two or more* is   _____

5. In Par. 3 the word that means *contact with one another* is   _____

6. In Par. 5 the word that means *spread* is   _____

7. In Par. 6 the word that means *received organically from parents* is   _____

8. In Par. 6 the word that means being *shaped by living in groups* is   _____

9. In Par. 7 the word that means *varying, different* is   _____

10. In Par. 7 the word that means *an illustration or something that clearly reveals an idea* is   _____

UNDERSTANDING THE CHAPTER
There may be more than one correct answer in each exercise.

1. The purpose of this piece is

   a. To prove groups restrict the growth of humans.   a. _____

   b. To explain our natural instincts toward group living.   b. _____

   c. To pin down a special meaning of the word "group."   c. _____

   d. To explain why we live in groups.   d. _____

2. According to Cuber's *definition*, the word "group" refers only

    a. To those who have physical contact with one another.   a. ____

    b. To those who know each other personally.   b. ____

    c. To those who have no direct contact with one another.   c. ____

    d. To those who have some kind of two-way contact with one another through language.   d. ____

3. Cuber's *comparison* shows a "group" is different than an "aggregation" and a "category" because

    a. An aggregation is not physically or geographically connected.   a. ____

    b. A category merely refers to people who are classified as being similar.   b. ____

    c. An aggregation and a category do not always involve intercommunication.   c. ____

    d. A group is based on intercommunication.   d. ____

4. Our inherited urge toward group living (one theory he *compares* to his own)

    a. Is supported by much experimental evidence.   a. ____

    b. Is a mistaken explanation of the reason for groups.   b. ____

    c. Is even less true than the false notion of common interest.   c. ____

    d. Accounts for the existence of *some* groups.   d. ____

5. Cuber's thesis is that groups exist because

    a. A human has an instinct toward group living.   a. ____

    b. A human realizes he needs others to help him.   b. ____

    c. A human becomes accustomed to the advantages of group living.   c. ____

    d. Over-all, it is easier to live within a group.   d. ____

Thinking Machines Are Getting Smarter

VOCABULARY STUDY

1. In Par. 1 the word that means *things that are changeable* is   _____

2. In Par. 4 the word that means *having the power to retain well* is   _____

3. In Par. 8 the word that means *changed from a usual order* is   _____

4. In Par. 11 the word that means *shares of profits* is   _____

5. In Par. 12 the word that means *to change* is   _____

6. In Par. 13 the word that means *amazingly clever* is   _____

7. In Par. 14 the word that means *a complex network* is   _____

8. In Par. 16 the word that means *a list that lists the location and context of words in a book* is   _____

9. In Par. 17 the word that means *coming before* is   _____

10. In Par. 19 the word that means *something that serves. as a rule for later decisions* is   _____

11. In Par. 21 the word that means *the ability to adjust or change* is   _____

12. In Par. 24 the word that means *so good as to be frightening* is   _____

13. In Par. 24 the word that means *a stock of available items* is   _____

14. In Par. 25 the word that means *sciences of industrial machinery* is   _____

15. In Par. 26 the word that means *elaborately complicated* is   _____

UNDERSTANDING THE ARTICLE
There may be more than one correct answer in each exercise.

1. In this article Mr. Strother

   a. *Summarizes* some of the material available about computers.   a. _____

   b. *Divides* the subject into the many marvels computers can perform.   b. _____

   c. Shows the possible dangers of overuse of computers.   c. _____

   d. Explains the electronic theories that underlie all computer work.   d. _____

2. Strother's thesis is that the computer's chief value is

   a. Its ability to create new ideas and theories.   a. _____

   b. Its ability to manage complex problems at great speed.   b. _____

   c. Its ability to win at checkers.   c. _____

   d. Its ability to solve the problems of human nature and conduct.   d. _____

3. Computers are necessary in conducting missile flights because

   a. They are the basis of all radar operations.   a. _____

   b. They can learn from experience better than men can.   b. _____

   c. Men are too emotionally involved to be reliable.   c. _____

   d. Men cannot figure fast enough.   d. _____

4. The computer at the John Hancock Insurance Company

   a. Learns from experience.   a. _____

   b. Has replaced all clerical personnel.   b. _____

   c. Keeps all records except those on compounded interest.   c. _____

   d. Furnishes all statements, premium notices and paychecks.   d. _____

5. A computer's "memory"

   a. Consists of millions of IBM cards.   a. _____

b. Tells it what to do with its new information.   b. _____

c. Stores electrical signals, which represent information.   c. _____

d. Consists of its stock of electrical tape.   d. _____

6. The computer used to compile a Concordance of the Bible

   a. Discovered several textual inaccuracies.   a. _____

   b. Completed numerous half-known words.   b. _____

   c. Required 30 years of preparation before it could do the
      job.   c. _____

   d. Required a few hours to do the job after all coding was
      finished.   d. _____

7. The quotation of a computer's translation: "Invisible and
insane" is used to illustrate

   a. Its poetic possibilities.   a. _____

   b. Its difficulty with the complexities of language.   b. _____

   c. Its amazing grasp of Russian.   c. _____

   d. Its value in the Cold War conflicts with the Russians.   d. _____

8. One striking advantage computers have over men is that

   a. Each new set of computers work faster than their prede-
      cessors.   a. _____

   b. Each new set of computers can be taught all over again
      to solve a problem.   b. _____

   c. Each new set of computers can apply what previous com-
      puters have learned.   c. _____

   d. Each new set of computers learn more by experience.   d. _____

9. One of the key problems *analyzed* as requiring solution is
that involving

   a. A computer's ability to discover its wrong answers.   a. _____

   b. A computer's difficulty in handling moral problems.   b. _____

   c. A computer's costly maintenance.   c. _____

   d. A computer's ability to learn from its own experience.   d. _____

10. When a computer marks a play in checkers that led to a defeat, it shows

    a. Its ability to create new ideas.   a. _____

    b. Its ability to learn from its past experience.   b. _____

    c. Its failure to learn from its past experience.   c. _____

    d. Its inability to create new ideas.   d. _____

Why They Race With Fate

VOCABULARY STUDY

1. In Par. 1 the word that means *in a gay and swaggering manner* is   _____

2. In Par. 3 the word that means *without change* is   _____

3. In Par. 4 the word that means *out of date* is   _____

4. In Par. 5 the word that means *the existence of death* is   _____

5. In Par. 5 the word that means *obviously* is   _____

6. In Par. 6 the word that means *speak clearly* is   _____

7. In Par. 7 the word that means *an endless number* is   _____

8. In Par. 7 the word that means *error or lapse* is   _____

9. In Par. 7 the word that means *speaking with few words* is   _____

10. In Par. 8 the word that means *similar to* is   _____

11. In Par. 8 the word that means an *often-used saying* is   _____

12. In Par. 8 the word that means a *mysterious goal* is   _____

13. In Par. 9 the word that means *of small importance* is   _____

14. In Par. 20 the word that means *an official substitute* is   _____

15. In Par. 23 the word that means *undisturbed calmness of manner* is   _____

UNDERSTANDING THE ARTICLE
There may be more than one correct answer in each exercise.

1. Gilbert Millstein wrote this article

    a. To criticize the dangers of auto racing.   a. _____

    b. To present his own thesis about why men race.   b. _____

    c. To *summarize* the theories of several men in the profession.   c. _____

    d. To *explain* a kind of process: the life of an auto racer.   d. _____

2. From his own remarks, it is clear that Eddie Sachs

    a. Races only for the money it might bring him.   a. _____

    b. Races to run away from thoughts of death.   b. _____

    c. Races for the success it might bring him.   c. _____

    d. Races for the thrill and satisfaction the race itself gives
    him.   d. _____

3. Dr. Carlyle Bohner believes that the biggest motivation of
   drivers

    a. Is the glory and publicity they gain.   a. _____

    b. Is the financial rewards that await them.   b. _____

    c. Is their unique need to succeed.   c. _____

    d. Is their love of racing.   d. _____

4. Bob Stroud and Tony Bettenhausen agree that racing

    a. Can bring them more money than anything else.   a. _____

    b. Is no more dangerous than any other job.   b. _____

    c. Is something you get addicted to and can't let go.   c. _____

    d. Requires a rare kind of courage.   d. _____

5. As a person, Eddie Sachs is characterized as

    a. Cynical.   a. _____

    b. Dedicated.   b. _____

    c. Confident.   c. _____

    d. Talkative.   d. _____

6. Eddie Sachs' one year earnings of $38,244

   a. Are about average for all race drivers.   a. _____

   b. Occurred only after many years of small incomes.   b. _____

   c. Must be shared with the owner and mechanic.   c. _____

   d. Represent his full take-home pay.   d. _____

7. The share of the race car owner

   a. Totals 50% of the total earnings.   a. _____

   b. Is resented by all racing drivers.   b. _____

   c. Only applies for beginning drivers.   c. _____

   d. Compensates for the owner's many expenses.   d. _____

8. The death rate of auto racers

   a. Is about equal to that of football players.   a. _____

   b. Has been rising swiftly the last few years.   b. _____

   c. Doesn't really apply to championship drivers.   c. _____

   d. Is about eight per cent a year.   d. _____

9. Sachs' attitude toward death

   a. Is different than most racing drivers'.   a. _____

   b. Is cold and business-like.   b. _____

   c. Shows his usual loud bravado.   c. _____

   d. Shows his adjustment to this fact of his life.   d. _____

10. That racing cars contribute to advances in automotive engineering

   a. Is seen by Mr. Millstein as the chief reason for auto racing.   a. _____

   b. Is a claim that is often disputed.   b. _____

   c. Makes the cars valuable and useful for many years.   c. _____

   d. Is the main reason for the big crowds at the Memorial Day race.   d. _____

The Place of Jazz

VOCABULARY STUDY

1. In Par. 4 the words that mean *the particular field of action of something* are _____

2. In Par. 4 the word that means *based on inner personal thoughts or emotions* is _____

3. In Par. 4 the word that means *calls forth or suggests* is _____

4. In Par. 5 the word that means *with emphasis on intellectual matters* is _____

5. In Par. 5 the word that means *tending to relate or unite one thing with another* is _____

6. In Par. 5 the word that means *sentimentally, drippingly sad* is _____

7. In Par. 5 the word that means *knowing by natural insight* is _____

8. In Par. 5 the word that means *an ability or power* is _____

9. In Par. 8 the word that means *appropriate* is _____

10. In Par. 10 the word that means *utter confusion* is _____

11. In Par. 10 the word that means *strikingly moving or touching* is _____

12. In Par. 11 the word that means *great secrets* is _____

13. In Par. 11 the word that means *to examine carefully* is _____

14. In Par. 11 the word that means *the loftiest, awe-inspiring things* is _____

15. In Par. 11 the word that means a *feeling of the highest, purest kind of joy* is _____

UNDERSTANDING THE ARTICLE
There may be more than one correct answer in each exercise.

1. In *classifying* the kind of art Jazz is, Mr. Ulanov's thesis is that

   a. It is as major an art as the classical symphony.   a. _____

   b. It is a major phase of what may be a minor civilization.   b. _____

   c. It is as minor an art as petit point.   c. _____

   d. It is certainly more important than petit point.   d. _____

2. In the first few paragraphs Ulanov makes a *comparison* to stress

   a. How jazz is like other music.   a. _____

   b. How jazz is different than other music.   b. _____

   c. Why jazz is more difficult than other music.   c. _____

   d. Why jazz is simpler than other music.   d. _____

3. Beginning with Paragraph 6 he attempts to *define*

   a. Just what jazz communicates that no other art does.   a. _____

   b. What kind of responses jazz calls forth.   b. _____

   c. How jazz is based on classical forms.   c. _____

   d. Why jazz breaks all the musical rules.   d. _____

4. Jazz, he says, can communicate

   a. The feeling of good times.   a. _____

   b. The awareness of what it means to live in the twentieth century.   b. _____

   c. The sense of the reality of life.   c. _____

   d. The sense of what it means to be a human being.   d. _____

5. He emphasizes that Jazz most particularly reflects

   a. Life in the South.   a. _____

   b. Life among the rich.   b. _____

    c. Life in the small town.   c. _____

    d. Life in a big city.   d. _____

6. Ulanov believes that being limited to one kind of environment

    a. Keeps jazz from becoming an art.   a. _____

    b. Helps jazz establish communication with its audience.   b. _____

    c. Can contribute to its becoming an art.   c. _____

    d. Damages the reputation of jazz.   d. _____

7. Ulanov finds that the reflections on life made by jazzmen

    a. Often show the very heights of human emotion and experience.   a. _____

    b. Seldom show the very heights of human emotion and experience.   b. _____

    c. Speak truly of the kind of emotion and experience jazz does deal with.   c. _____

    d. Distort the life jazz deals with.   d. _____

8. In another *comparison* Ulanov uses petit point as an example of

    a. A trivial kind of art.   a. _____

    b. A difficult kind of art.   b. _____

    c. A modern kind of art.   c. _____

    d. A major art of the past.   d. _____

9. Jazz admirers, according to Ulanov's *summary*, believe jazz is important because

    a. It is a clear expression of real parts of their lives.   a. _____

    b. It is more honest than classical music.   b. _____

    c. It produces more exaltation than classical music.   c. _____

    d. It is an advancement in musical form.   d. _____

10. Jazz is like other forms of music in that

    a. It never narrates a story.   a. _____

b. It sometimes conveys a picture.   b. _____

c. It appeals to stock emotional responses.   c. _____

d. Its form is always more important than its content.   d. _____

The Science of Dreams

VOCABULARY STUDY

1. In Par. 1 the word that means *quiet and inactive* is ⎯⎯⎯⎯⎯⎯⎯

2. In Par. 2 the word that means *of the night* is ⎯⎯⎯⎯⎯⎯⎯

3. In Par. 8 the word that means *secluded, hidden places* is ⎯⎯⎯⎯⎯⎯⎯

4. In Par. 10 the word that means *kept from being known* is ⎯⎯⎯⎯⎯⎯⎯

5. In Par. 14 the word that means *a close or mutual connection* is ⎯⎯⎯⎯⎯⎯⎯

6. In Par. 15 the word that means *clearly marked off and different* is ⎯⎯⎯⎯⎯⎯⎯

7. In Par. 16 the word that means *continued for a long time* is ⎯⎯⎯⎯⎯⎯⎯

8. In Par. 17 the word that means *to make up for* is ⎯⎯⎯⎯⎯⎯⎯

9. In Par. 17 the word that means *seriously mentally disordered* is ⎯⎯⎯⎯⎯⎯⎯

10. In Par. 19 the word that means *seemingly true* is ⎯⎯⎯⎯⎯⎯⎯

11. In Par. 22 the word that means *unintentional* is ⎯⎯⎯⎯⎯⎯⎯

12. In Par. 27 the word that means *very talkative* is ⎯⎯⎯⎯⎯⎯⎯

13. In Par. 31 the word that means *as a result of birth* is ⎯⎯⎯⎯⎯⎯⎯

14. In Par. 33 the word that means *extreme confusion* is ⎯⎯⎯⎯⎯⎯⎯

15. In Par. 35 the word that means *tending to disappear* is ⎯⎯⎯⎯⎯⎯⎯

UNDERSTANDING THE ARTICLE

There may be more than one correct answer in each exercise.

1. Mr. Diamond's article *summarizes* new scientific findings to show that

   a. A new method has been developed to detect dreams.   a. _____

   b. Just about everyone dreams.   b. _____

   c. A person's eyes often move when he dreams.   c. _____

   d. Dreams are harmful to mental health.   d. _____

2. In Paragraphs 22-32 Diamond *explains a process* by telling a story. This story explains

   a. How the new method of detecting dreams was begun.   a. _____

   b. How learning occurs during dreams.   b. _____

   c. How REM's and dreams are related.   c. _____

   d. How body movements and dreams are related.   d. _____

3. Dr. Sigmund Freud discovered that

   a. Dreamers move their eyes.   a. _____

   b. All dreamers are neurotic.   b. _____

   c. Dreams are a complicated kind of fulfillment of unconscious desires.   c. _____

   d. Dreams are useful in treating mental illness.   d. _____

4. Dr. Nathan Kleitman and his associates discovered that

   a. People can learn complicated subjects while asleep.   a. _____

   b. Eye movements increase during dreaming periods.   b. _____

   c. Brain waves form a specific pattern when dreaming occurs.   c. _____

   d. People's dream patterns vary a great deal.   d. _____

5. Medical doctors believe that

   a. Certain illnesses may be aggravated by dreaming.   a. _____

   b. Dreaming can cure certain illnesses.   b. _____

   c. Certain illnesses can be treated by preventing dreams.   c. _____

   d. Dreams occur most frequently during physical illness.   d. _____

6. Experiments have indicated that

   a. People can be trained not to dream.   a. _____

   b. People do not dream after long periods without sleep. b. _____

   c. After long periods without sleep people tend to daydream. c. _____

   d. Lack of opportunity to dream may cause mental illness. d. _____

7. The belief that problems can be solved during sleep

   a. Has been proved false by recent experiments.   a. _____

   b. Has been given some support by recent experiments. b. _____

   c. Has been the chief assumption behind all new experiments on dreams. c. _____

   d. Has been fully proved by recent experiments.   d. _____

8. Rapid eye movements (REM's) were shown to occur

   a. Immediately following a dream.   a. _____

   b. After a person was awakened from a dream.   b. _____

   c. While dreams were in progress.   c. _____

   d. Just before body movements occur.   d. _____

9. It was decided that body movements seem to occur

   a. When the person is about to awaken.   a. _____

   b. When a person is upset by his dream.   b. _____

   c. Before the dreams begin.   c. _____

   d. Between separate scenes of a dream.   d. _____

10. By tracing brain-wave signals on a graph, doctors have concluded that

   a. Dreams usually begin after about 90 minutes of sleep. a. _____

   b. Dreams increase in length during the night.   b. _____

   c. Dreams are experienced an average of four times a night. c. _____

   d. Dreams increase in frequency toward morning.   d. _____

The Push into Space

VOCABULARY STUDY

1. In Par. 1 the word that refers to *the force by which masses attract matter to them* is   _____

2. In Par. 2 the word that means *an elf or fairy* is   _____

3. In Par. 3 the word that means *to form a systematic statement of laws and principles* is   _____

4. In Par. 4 the word that means *of an equal relationship as to size, quantity, etc.* is   _____

5. In Par. 4 the word that means *completely reversed or opposite* is   _____

6. In Par. 5 the word that means *able to be travelled on or through* is   _____

7. In Par. 7 the word that means *forward-moving impulse* is   _____

8. In Par. 8 the word that means *the air surrounding the earth* is   _____

9. In Par. 9 the word that means *bent or turned to one side* is   _____

10. In Par. 13 the word that means *arrangements of colored bands or waves of lights* is   _____

11. In Par. 14 the word that means *a solid body passing through space* is   _____

12. In Par. 14 the word that means *calm and quiet* is   _____

13. In Par. 16 the word that means *made liquid by heat* is   _____

14. In Par. 20 the word that means *powerful rays from outer space* is   _____

15. In Par. 30 the word that means *a group of primitive moss-like plants* is   _____

UNDERSTANDING THE ARTICLE
There may be more than one correct answer in each exercise.

1. In this article the *Time* magazine writer
   a. Explains why the Russians are ahead of the U.S. in space flights.   a. _____
   b. *Summarizes* the basic laws and techniques of space flight.   b. _____
   c. Explains why space flights are necessary in the Cold War.   c. _____
   d. *Summarizes* some theories about planets that space flight may explore.   d. _____

2. The article groups its details into major sections on
   a. How Isaac Newton's laws are related to space flight.   a. _____
   b. How space flights work.   b. _____
   c. What spacemen will do to stay alive.   c. _____
   d. What questions about the planets space flight may answer.   d. _____

3. Sir Isaac Newton's laws of motion
   a. Have all been proved false by space experiments.   a. _____
   b. Have been used as a basis for space experiments.   b. _____
   c. Have had to be revised because of space experiments.   c. _____
   d. Have all but one been proved by space experiments.   d. _____

4. The gravitational fields that surround stars and planets
   a. Are not strong enough to bother rockets.   a. _____
   b. Are like whirlpools in the smooth surface of a pond.   b. _____
   c. Are the biggest problem in space flight.   c. _____
   d. Are heavily radioactive.   d. _____

5. Escape from a particular gravitational field
   a. Is never possible.   a. _____
   b. Is possible if certain required speeds are maintained.   b. _____

    c. Is easier than the actual long-distance travel through space.

c. _____

    d. Is more difficult than the actual long-distance travel through space.

d. _____

6. Full escape from the gravitational pull of the sun

    a. Would demand greater speed than it is possible to obtain.

a. _____

    b. Would release a ship from our solar system.

b. _____

    c. Would not be profitable.

c. _____

    d. Would begin a voyage that would take too long for man's life.

d. _____

7. Gerard Kuiper's theory of the moon (one of several *compared* in the article) asserts

    a. The moon's craters were caused by its crashing into lesser satellites.

a. _____

    b. Lava on the moon's surface came from inside the moon.

b. _____

    c. Lava on the moon's surface was produced by crashing meteors.

c. _____

    d. Lava does not exist on the surface of the moon.

d. _____

8. Thomas Gold believes that the "seas" of the moon

    a. Will prevent landings on the moon.

a. _____

    b. Are full of fine dust, a mile deep in some places.

b. _____

    c. Contain dust that has been eroded from the moon's rocks by radiation.

c. _____

    d. Contain meteorites that have crashed on the moon.

d. _____

9. The abundance of carbon dioxide in the atmosphere of Venus

    a. Proves that the planet supports earthlike plants.

a. _____

    b. Proves that the planet does not support earthlike plants.

b. _____

    c. Contributes to the thick yellowish cloud around the planet.

c. _____

    d. Allows perfect visibility of the surface of the planet.

d. _____

10. The latest theories about life on Mars

    a. Deny the existence of irrigation canals built by intelligent creatures.   a. _____

    b. Maintain earth-like animals exist there.   b. _____

    c. Support the existence of irrigation canals.   c. _____

    d. Suggest the existence of some kind of primitive vegetation.   d. _____

Civil Defense Is a Farce

VOCABULARY STUDY

1. In Par. 2 the word that means *with much careful detail* is _____

2. In Par. 3 the word that means *ordered by law* is _____

3. In Par. 3 the word that means *imitation* is _____

4. In Par. 4 the word that means *the time that came between* is _____

5. In Par. 4 the word that means *odd and old-fashioned* is _____

6. In Par. 5 the word that means *causing horror* is _____

7. In Par. 5 the word that means *calmly* is _____

8. In Par. 6 the word that means *suited to the situation* is _____

9. In Par. 8 the word that means *a terrible failure* is _____

10. In Par. 10 the word that means *dismally dull* is _____

UNDERSTANDING THE ARTICLE
There may be more than one correct answer in each exercise.

1. Miss Robb attempts to prove that

    a. Civil Defense drills are unnecessary. a. _____

    b. Civil Defense drills interfere with the business of a city. b. _____

    c. Civil Defense drills are conducted foolishly. c. _____

    d. Civil Defense drills have not improved. d. _____

2. Civil Defense drills are said to be a "farce" because

    a. They assume a cleared street means safety. a. _____

    b. The sirens are not loud enough. b. _____

    c. The people do not get off the streets quickly enough.   c. _____

    d. The people are not made to take adequate cover.   d. _____

3. The drill Miss Robb just participated in proved that

    a. Civil Defense authorities were repeating the same errors they had made in 1951.   a. _____

    b. People will not stop their daily chores for a drill.   b. _____

    c. Civil Defense authorities did not act quickly enough.   c. _____

    d. People can be quickly cleared from the streets.   d. _____

4. Miss Robb speaks as an expert on such matters because

    a. She is a high Civil Defense official.   a. _____

    b. She witnessed the first Atomic explosion.   b. _____

    c. She has studied methods of Civil Defense.   c. _____

    d. She witnessed real bombings during World War II.   d. _____

5. Miss Robb's criticism

    a. Is a sarcastic emotional argument.   a. _____

    b. Offers alternate methods.   b. _____

    c. Presents the authorities' reasons for their type of drill.   c. _____

    d. Focuses on a minor point of the whole drill.   d. _____

Good Grief, More Peanuts!

VOCABULARY STUDY

1. In Par. 3, the word that means *surprising unsuitability, inappropriateness* is

2. In Par. 4, the word that means *active opposition or resistance* is

3. In Par. 4, the word that means *with kindness and consideration* is

4. In Par. 4, the word that means *overly sweet* is

5. In Par. 5, the word that means *intensely interesting* is

6. In Par. 5, the word that means *imaginative fantasy* is

7. In Par. 5, the word that means *excited and fanatic* is

8. In Par. 6, the word that means *not in an obvious manner* is

9. In Par. 6, the word that means *physical and verbal surroundings* is

10. In Par. 7, the word that means *behavior that merely tolerates one's inferiors* is

11. In Par. 7, the word that means *fighting attitude* is

12. In Par. 8, the word that means *pretentiously learned person* is

13. In Par. 8, the word that means *opposed to and without culture* is

14. In Par. 8, the word that means *superstition or fixation* is

15. In Par. 10, the word that means *weaken* is

UNDERSTANDING THE ARTICLE

There may be more than one correct answer in each exercise.

1. Mr. Weales has written this *criticism* to prove that

    a. We live in a female-dominated society.   a. _____

    b. A comic strip can be a work of the imagination.   b. _____

    c. A comic strip like *Peanuts* comments significantly about life.   c. _____

    d. *Peanuts* is too serious to be funny.   d. _____

2. What makes this comic strip particularly effective is that

    a. The problems presented are those of real children and adults.   a. _____

    b. It is not at all repetitious.   b. _____

    c. Charles M. Schulz uses comic overstatement.   c. _____

    d. Schulz is never serious.   d. _____

3. Schulz is original because

    a. He has omitted parents from this strip about children.   a. _____

    b. His animal characters are the most improbable ever.   b. _____

    c. His children are in violent conflict with adults.   c. _____

    d. Everything he writes is funny, never sad.   d. _____

4. This comic strip is seen as a consistent mixture of

    a. Realism and fantasy.   a. _____

    b. Humor and sadness.   b. _____

    c. Stock comic types and real, individualized characters.   c. _____

    d. Repetition and surprise.   d. _____

5. In achieving his humor, Schulz relies heavily on

    a. Physical violence.   a. _____

    b. Unusual language.   b. _____

c. Strange costumes.　　　　　　　　　　c. _____

d. Personality traits.　　　　　　　　　d. _____

6. Charlie Brown is the kind of person

   a. Who is cruel to small animals.　　　a. _____

   b. Who is always being defeated.　　　b. _____

   c. Who is always late to parties.　　　c. _____

   d. Who is not liked because he is too aggressive.　d. _____

7. From the description of Lucy you can tell that she is likely to

   a. Try to boss people around.　　　　a. _____

   b. Think she knows everything about everything.　b. _____

   c. Play tricks on Charlie Brown.　　　c. _____

   d. Follow other people's advice.　　　d. _____

8. The strip that ends with Charlie Brown saying he will be "lonely" is

   a. Not at all funny.　　　　　　　　a. _____

   b. An example of Schulz' speaking directly to the reader.　b. _____

   c. An indication of the serious side of the comic strip.　c. _____

   d. Typical of the life of Charlie Brown.　d. _____

9. George Herriman's comic strip *Krazy Kat*

   a. Is another new and unique comic strip.　a. _____

   b. Is funnier than *Peanuts.*　　　　　b. _____

   c. Is a comic strip that started many years ago.　c. _____

   d. Is more similar to *Pogo* than to *Peanuts.*　d. _____

10. The career of *Peanuts* has shown that

   a. Comic strips are a waste of time.　a. _____

   b. An intelligent comic strip hasn't a chance.　b. _____

   c. Comic strips can be both adult and successful.　c. _____

   d. Schulz' invention has begun to flag.　d. _____

The Egghead Vs. the Muttonhead

VOCABULARY STUDY

1. In Par. 1 the word that means *a slight trace* is _____

2. In Par. 1 the word that means *a feeling of looking down on, scornful* is _____

3. In Par. 2 the word that means *making fun of, scorn* is _____

4. In Par. 3 the word that means *deserving of severe blame* is _____

5. In Par. 4 the word that means *to describe the particular qualities of* is _____

6. In Par. 5 the word that means *origins, original causes* is _____

7. In Par. 6 the word that means *to have been at the peak of activity and influence* is _____

8. In Par. 8 the word that means *unable to believe* is _____

9. In Par. 10 the word that means to *criticize with regret* is _____

10. In Par. 11 the word that means *very typical* is _____

11. In Par. 16 the word that means *suppliers* is _____

12. In Par. 16 the word that means *to help to develop* is _____

13. In Par. 17 the word that means *growing smaller, decreasing* is _____

14. In Par. 18 the word that means *the act of lowering oneself to reach another's level* is _____

15. In Par. 18 the word that means *possibilities of development and improvement* is _____

UNDERSTANDING THE ARTICLE
There may be more than one correct answer in each exercise.

1. In this article Mr. J. Donald Adams wants to prove that

    a. In America intellectuals consider themselves superior to
    others.   a. _____

    b. In America intelligence and things of the mind are re-
    sented, not valued and respected.   b. _____

    c. In America people are afraid of being considered superior.   c. _____

    d. In America intelligent people are always condescending.   d. _____

2. Mr. Adams defines the muttonhead as

    a. One who resents people who are more intelligent than
    he is.   a. _____

    b. One who has no respect for learning.   b. _____

    c. One who is too stupid to learn.   c. _____

    d. One who makes a point of being careless about his speech.   d. _____

3. According to Mr. Adams, the American frontier spirit

    a. Was always a harmful thing.   a. _____

    b. Developed a strong sense of equality.   b. _____

    c. Stressed practical and material skills.   c. _____

    d. Has contributed to current anti-intellectual attitudes.   d. _____

4. In Russia the egghead

    a. Is scorned by the peasant class.   a. _____

    b. Is respected more than in the United States.   b. _____

    c. Is restricted by the state.   c. _____

    d. Is held in contempt by the state.   d. _____

5. In a recent novel, the writer James Jones

    a. Attacked the arrogance of muttonheads.   a. _____

    b. Demanded better treatment for intellectuals.   b. _____

c. Supported the attitude of the muttonhead.   c. _____

d. Showed a contempt for literate speech.   d. _____

6. The fact that colleges are now over-crowded

a. Proves that Americans respect learning and intelligence.   a. _____

b. Proves that Americans do not respect learning and intelligence.   b. _____

c. Can be traced to a love of money, not learning.   c. _____

d. Will soon end the war between eggheads and muttonheads.   d. _____

7. Popular entertainment

a. Tries to find the lowest common denominator.   a. _____

b. Underestimates the tastes of the audience.   b. _____

c. Furthers the muttonhead attitude.   c. _____

d. Is guided by the profit motive.   d. _____

8. Adams advocates that

a. People should admit they are inferior.   a. _____

b. People should be guided by college professors.   b. _____

c. People should not be afraid of what the other fellow thinks.   c. _____

d. People should be more tolerant of each other's differences.   d. _____

9. Franklin Roosevelt was shrewd because

a. He was careful to speak in simple language to the public.   a. _____

b. He never let the public know what he was thinking.   b. _____

c. He did not try to be a "regular" guy.   c. _____

d. He never talked down to the public.   d. _____

10. The term "highbrow"

a. Has the same meaning as the term egghead.   a. _____

b. Has the same meaning as the term muttonhead.   b. _____

c. Today shows a great deal of respect.   c. _____

d. Showed a great deal of respect when it was first used.   d. _____

Why Not Let Pay TV Have a Trial Run?

VOCABULARY STUDY

1. In Par. 2 the word that means *detailed explanations* is _____

2. In Par. 2 the word that means *meant for a select few* is _____

3. In Par. 3 the word that means *those who want to change, make better* is _____

4. In Par. 5 the word that means *including many different kinds* is _____

5. In Par. 5 the word that means *those who argue for* is _____

6. In Par. 5 another word that means *those who argue for* is _____

7. In Par. 6 the word that means *a period of perfect happiness* is _____

8. In Par. 6 the word that means *without reference to real or natural things or objects* is _____

9. In Par. 7 the word that means *to prosper or grow vigorously* is _____

10. In Par. 10 the word that means *legally establish* is _____

11. In Par. 11 the word that means *an attitude of strong doubt* is _____

12. In Par. 11 the word that means *in a way to produce an effect and not to draw an answer* is _____

13. In Par. 11 the word that means *voters of a district* is _____

14. In Par. 13 the word that means *optimistic or bright* is _____

15. In Par. 13 the word that means *to insert between other things or parts* is _____

UNDERSTANDING THE ARTICLE
There may be more than one correct answer in each exercise.

1. The *Saturday Evening Post* wants to prove that

    a. Pay TV has many drawbacks.   a. _____

    b. Pay TV should be given a trial.   b. _____

    c. Pay TV presents no problems.   c. _____

    d. Pay TV will kill commercially-sponsored TV.   d. _____

2. As the margin notes indicate, in the first two paragraphs of the editorial the *Post* shows

    a. Why commercial television is faced with problems.   a. _____

    b. Why Pay TV should be adopted.   b. _____

    c. Why Pay TV should be blocked.   c. _____

    d. Why people suggest Pay TV.   d. _____

3. As the margin notes indicate, paragraphs 3 through 12 present

    a. The *Post's* arguments against Pay TV.   a. _____

    b. The *Post's* arguments for Pay TV.   b. _____

    c. Arguments of others against Pay TV.   c. _____

    d. Arguments of others for Pay TV.   d. _____

4. As the margin notes indicate, the last Paragraph presents

    a. Mr. Sarnoff's opposition to Pay TV.   a. _____

    b. Rep. Harris' opposition to Pay TV.   b. _____

    c. The consensus of opinion about Pay TV.   c. _____

    d. The *Post's* opinion of Pay TV.   d. _____

5. The *Post's* decision to support a trial for Pay TV is based on its belief that

    a. Commercial TV has been dishonest with the public.   a. _____

    b. Pay TV has proved its superiority in recent tests.   b. _____

    c. Pay TV can only be judged if a trial is allowed.   c. _____

    d. Pay TV should be allowed to try to fulfill people's desires   d. _____
       for other shows.

6. In defending Pay TV, John Crosby argues that

    a. Pay TV has guaranteed more public service programs.   a. _____

    b. More creative shows are possible if advertisers are not   b. _____
       involved.

    c. More educational shows are possible if advertisers are not
       involved.   c. _____

    d. More commercials will soon be allowed on regular TV.   d. _____

7. David Sarnoff, a network executive, argues that

    a. Pay TV will seek the largest audience too.   a. _____

    b. Pay TV will drive public service programs off commer-
       cial TV.   b. _____

    c. Pay TV will kill commercial TV.   c. _____

    d. Pay TV will not last more than a few years.   d. _____

8. Representative Oren Harris

    a. Believes Pay TV will kill commercial TV.   a. _____

    b. Believes Pay TV is not practical.   b. _____

    c. Believes Pay TV will be unfair to the public.   c. _____

    d. Believes the FCC should not allow Pay TV a trial.   d. _____

9. In answer to the fears that Pay TV will harm commercial TV,
   the *Post*

    a. Proves why Pay TV will not harm commercial TV.   a. _____

    b. Proves why we will just have to accept that harm.   b. _____

    c. Does not prove that Pay TV will harm or will not harm
       commercial TV.   c. _____

    d. Does not admit that the fears really exist.   d. _____

10. In answer to the fears that Pay TV will force a reduction
    in the amount of public service programs offered, the *Post*

    a. Proves why no such reduction will be forced.   a. _____

b. Argues that the FCC can demand that Pay TV carry public service programs.   b. _____

c. Argues that commercial TV doesn't carry enough public service programs anyway.   c. _____

d. Claims that these fears have merely been spread by commercial TV executives.   d. _____

The Case Against Pay TV

VOCABULARY STUDY

1. In Par. 1 the word that means *formal public statement* is _____

2. In Par. 2 the word that means *small amount* is _____

3. In Par. 2 the word that means *definite and observable* is _____

4. In Par. 3 the word that means *reactions or after-effects* is _____

5. In Par. 3 the word that means *great importance* is _____

6. In Par. 4 the word that means *penniless, broke* is _____

7. In Par. 5 the word that means *rebirth or re-awakening* is _____

8. In Par. 6 the word that means *personal preferences* is _____

9. In Par. 8 the word that means *all together, in a group* is _____

10. In Par. 8 the word that means *very clever* is _____

11. In Par. 10 the word that means *having to do with the degree of excellence involved* is _____

12. In Par. 11 the word that means *special, designed for a few* is _____

13. In Par. 12 the word that means *large scale, extravagant* is _____

14. In Par. 13 the word that means *supports or justifies* is _____

15. In Par. 14 the word that means *those who believe things will be as they should be* is _____

UNDERSTANDING THE ARTICLE
There may be more than one correct answer in each exercise.

1. This article by Jack Gould seeks to
   a. Explain why the F.C.C. has banned Pay TV.   a. _____
   b. Present some of the problems faced by Pay TV.   b. _____
   c. Prove the dangers of Pay TV.   c. _____
   d. Present facts that prove Pay TV is illegal.   d. _____

2. As the marginal notes indicate, the first six paragraphs
   a. Present the case against Pay TV.   a. _____
   b. Present the background of the debate.   b. _____
   c. Briefly present some arguments of both sides.   c. _____
   d. Explain why the F.C.C. has banned Pay TV.   d. _____

3. As the marginal notes indicate, Paragraphs 7 through 14
   a. Present the arguments for Pay TV.   a. _____
   b. Present the views of the F.C.C.   b. _____
   c. Present the views of a nationwide survey.   c. _____
   d. Present the arguments against Pay TV.   d. _____

4. As the marginal notes indicate, Paragraphs 15 through 19
   a. Present the arguments against Pay TV.   a. _____
   b. Present the arguments for Pay TV.   b. _____
   c. Present some problems facing Pay TV.   c. _____
   d. Present a plea to the public to fight Pay TV.   d. _____

5. The arguments presented against Pay TV include these items:
   a. It will not do away with commercials at all.   a. _____
   b. It will end up controlling all the airwaves.   b. _____
   c. It will make the public pay for what it now gets free.   c. _____
   d. It will seek huge audiences and ignore public service
      programs.   d. _____

6. If Pay TV were allowed, it is feared regular broadcasters would be unable to present public service programs because

    a. The government would give all the entertainment programs to Pay TV.   a. _____

    b. They could not match the money offered by Pay TV.   b. _____

    c. Advertisers would no longer give them enough business.   c. _____

    d. The top talent would be lured to Pay TV.   d. _____

7. Pay TV, it is claimed, will really offer nothing new because

    a. It will seek the largest audience possible.   a. _____

    b. High quality programs will not make enough money.   b. _____

    c. Regular TV has a great variety of programs already.   c. _____

    d. It will tend to ignore public service programs.   d. _____

8. If Pay TV were allowed, it is feared that

    a. Commercials in movie houses would increase.   a. _____

    b. Commercials will disappear from regular TV.   b. _____

    c. Commercials will still be carried on Pay TV.   c. _____

    d. Sponsors would tempt Pay TV operators with huge offers.   d. _____

9. In short, then, it is argued that if Pay TV were adopted

    a. It would be a monopoly.   a. _____

    b. It would prove to be illegal.   b. _____

    c. It would not be much different than regular TV and would cost the viewer more money.   c. _____

    d. It would use up all the TV channels.   d. _____

10. According to Mr. Gould, one problem facing Pay TV is

    a. Finding a way to transmit the programs.   a. _____

    b. Getting enough money to operate before it has proved to be a success.   b. _____

    c. Getting Congress to lift its ban on Pay TV.   c. _____

    d. Getting the Congress to provide government funds.   d. _____

The Real Delinquent—The Parent?

VOCABULARY STUDY

1. In Par. 1 the word that means *in an indirect way* is _____

2. In Par. 1 the word that means *to restore to mental and moral health* is _____

3. In Par. 2 the word that means *destroy, wipe out* is _____

4. In Par. 2 the word that means *having the characteristics of a city* is _____

5. In Par. 5 the word that means *argument, claim* is _____

6. In Par. 6 the word that means *partially change* is _____

7. In Par. 7 the word that means *brothers or sisters* is _____

8. In Par. 9 the word that means *a tendency to show off* is _____

9. In Par. 9 the word that means *make up for* is _____

10. In Par. 9 the word that means *fond of the company of others* is _____

11. In Par. 11 the word that means *not social, withdrawn from society, though not necessarily opposed to it* is _____

12. In Par. 17 the word that means *poorly fitted to society's demand* is _____

13. In Par. 22 the word that means *future, likely* is _____

14. In Par. 22 the word that means *the condition of being obligated, accountable for, having duties* is _____

15. In Par. 23 the word that means *including much or all* is _____

UNDERSTANDING THE ARTICLE
There may be more than one correct answer in each exercise.

1. In examining the causes of juvenile delinquency, Judge Panken wants to prove that

    a. Delinquent parents are the chief cause.   a. _____

    b. The parent of today is not really negligent at all.   b. _____

    c. Poverty is the chief cause.   c. _____

    d. Our society's lack of moral certainties is the chief cause. d. _____

2. So far, he claims, our attempts to combat delinquency

    a. Have not directly hit at the chief cause.   a. _____

    b. Have produced surprisingly successful results.   b. _____

    c. Have tried to remold delinquents after they're found.   c. _____

    d. Have not prevented a rise in delinquency.   d. _____

3. Panken focusses on the parents because

    a. No child is born bad.   a. _____

    b. Something shapes children to be good or bad.   b. _____

    c. Bad tendencies are shaped early in life.   c. _____

    d. The parents are the most important force in a child's early life.   d. _____

4. Neglect of children most basically and importantly involves

    a. Lack of clothing.   a. _____

    b. Lack of medical care.   b. _____

    c. Lack of supervision and guidance.   c. _____

    d. Lack of community assistance.   d. _____

5. Children, Judge Panken believes, almost always

    a. Have a single tendency toward good or bad.   a. _____

    b. Are torn between good and bad impulses.   b. _____

    c. Want to belong to some group.   c. _____

    d. Can be guided by their parents.   d. _____

6. Panken finds evidence that most delinquents

    a. Are opposed quite directly to society.   a. _____

    b. Are incapable of developing a moral sense.   b. _____

    c. Have not been taught certain essentials.   c. _____

    d. Have parents with overly strong attitudes.   d. _____

7. The best solution for delinquency, Panken believes, is

    a. To throw more parents into jail.   a. _____

    b. To strengthen the penalties against delinquents. b. _____

    c. To send delinquents to special schools.   c. _____

    d. To train people specifically for parenthood.   d. _____

8. Panken believes that the best way to improve the nation's parents is

    a. To send all parents to school at night.   a. _____

    b. To teach less science and mathematics in high school. b. _____

    c. To teach courses in proper parenthood in high school. c. _____

    d. To change the laws about the responsibilities of parents. d. _____

9. A course in how to be a good parent should include

    a. How to pick a mate.   a. _____

    b. How to choose a profession or occupation.   b. _____

    c. How to encourage a child's interests and talents. c. _____

    d. How to make clear to a child his social duties.   d. _____

10. In addition to this new program, we should continue

    a. To increase penalties against delinquent parents. a. _____

    b. To eliminate poverty and slums.   b. _____

    c. To get children to enjoy and understand reading. c. _____

    d. To demand that all children attend twelve years of school. d. _____

Parents and Juvenile Delinquency

VOCABULARY STUDY

1. In Par. 1 the word that means *to explain as being caused by* is   _____

2. In Par. 1 the word that means *narrowly self-satisfied* is   _____

3. In Par. 2 the word that means *a nicer word* is   _____

4. In Par. 3 the word that means *customary, usual* is   _____

5. In Par. 4 the word that means *unsound, without support of evidence* is   _____

6. In Par. 6 the word that means *torment* is   _____

7. In Par. 7 the word that means *misconceptions or false beliefs* is   _____

8. In Par. 7 the word that means *silly and unrealistic* is   _____

9. In Par. 10 the word that means *means of control* is   _____

10. In Par. 11 the word that means *creates* is   _____

11. In Par. 11 the word that means *the standard* is   _____

12. In Par. 14 the word that means *severely beaten* is   _____

13. In Par. 15 the word that means *a full crew* is   _____

14. In Par. 17 the word that means *agrees or matches* is   _____

15. In Par. 18 the word that means *claimed as a basic truth* is   _____

UNDERSTANDING THE ARTICLE
There may be more than one correct answer in each exercise.

1. In examining the causes of juvenile delinquency, Bergen Evans wants to prove that

    a. Delinquent parents are the chief cause.　　　　　a. ＿＿＿

    b. The parent of today is not really negligent at all.　　b. ＿＿＿

    c. Poverty is a chief cause.　　　　　　　　　　c. ＿＿＿

    d. Our society's lack of moral certainties is the chief cause.　d. ＿＿＿

2. In comparing the present to the past, Evans claims that

    a. There were always delinquents, but they weren't always so classified.　　　　　　　　　　　　　a. ＿＿＿

    b. Modern parents feel more responsibility toward their children.　　　　　　　　　　　　　　　b. ＿＿＿

    c. Modern children feel less responsibility toward their parents.　　　　　　　　　　　　　　　c. ＿＿＿

    d. Parents in the past were more certain about moral values.　d. ＿＿＿

3. According to the 1957 Senate Investigation,

    a. Sports are a sure cure for juvenile delinquency.　　a. ＿＿＿

    b. Housing projects prevent the spread of juvenile delinquency.　　　　　　　　　　　　　　　b. ＿＿＿

    c. Poverty determines juvenile delinquency.　　　c. ＿＿＿

    d. Most conventional explanations of delinquency are not valid.　　　　　　　　　　　　　　　d. ＿＿＿

4. A child's conflicts with his parents

    a. Are stressed as causes by many experts in the field.　a. ＿＿＿

    b. Are seen by Evans as only part of a larger story.　　b. ＿＿＿

    c. Are seen by Evans as having no connection with juvenile delinquency.　　　　　　　　　　　　c. ＿＿＿

    d. Are often described as important by delinquents.　　d. ＿＿＿

5. Evans believes that the moral certainty of parents of the old days

    a. Is no longer possible for the modern parent.   a. _____

    b. Was always based on the truth.   b. _____

    c. Was effective even if ignorant and mistaken.   c. _____

    d. Was not accepted by the children of the past.   d. _____

6. According to Evans, the intelligent parent of today

    a. Constantly has to tell his child he doesn't know.   a. _____

    b. Feels the world is too uncertain and changing for absolute rules.   b. _____

    c. Believes his child should reject authority.   c. _____

    d. Is negligent because he is not firm enough with his children.   d. _____

7. Evans believes that insistence by today's parents on the values they themselves were taught

    a. Is the best solution to the problem.   a. _____

    b. Will not meet the problems of the modern world.   b. _____

    c. Is at least better than saying they don't know.   c. _____

    d. Will often turn children against their parents.   d. _____

8. Evans believes that the claim of a great increase in religion

    a. May help stop juvenile delinquency.   a. _____

    b. Does not seem to be supported by the evidence of a rise in delinquency.   b. _____

    c. Does not seem to fit our current lack of certain values.   c. _____

    d. May help explain the rise in juvenile delinquency.   d. _____

9. The Senate report shows that delinquents

    a. Are more interested in sports than non-delinquents.   a. _____

    b. Are less interested in sports than non-delinquents.   b. _____

    c. Are often led into gangs through sports activities.   c. _____

    d. Are often reformed by playground supervisors.   d. _____

10. In the past juvenile delinquency was often spoken of as

    a. "Boys will be boys."   a. _____

    b. The work of the Devil.   b. _____

    c. The reason for child labor.   c. _____

    d. The cause of revolutions.   d. _____

Why Are Americans Unhappy?

VOCABULARY STUDY

1. In Par. 1 the word that means *pleasantly perfect* is   _____

2. In Par. 6 the word that means *mental* is   _____

3. In Par. 6 the word that means *matching, equal* is   _____

4. In Par. 7 the word that means *proved right* is   _____

5. In Par. 9 the word that means *making specific, pinning down* is   _____

6. In Par. 9 the word that means *a disturbing oversupply* is   _____

7. In Par. 9 the word that means *arranged in layers or levels* is   _____

8. In Par. 11 the word that means *that cannot be satisfied* is   _____

9. In Par. 11 the word that means *diseased, abnormal* is   _____

10. In Par. 12 the word that means *the necessary element* is   _____

11. In Par. 16 the word that means *the direct opposite* is   _____

12. In Par. 17 the word that means *obstruction, hindrance* is   _____

13. In Par. 22 the word that means *weakening and destructive* is   _____

14. In Par. 27 the word that means *startlingly contradictory* is   _____

15. In Par. 34 the word that means *falseness and artificiality* is   _____

16. In Par. 39 the word that means *a basic split or division* is   _____

17. In Par. 40 the word that means *the basic cause or reason* is   _____

18. In Par. 41 the word that means *simple and easy* is   _____

19. In Par. 42 the word that means *vastly increased production* is   _____

20. In Par. 44 the word that means *an object of fear or dread* is   _____

237

UNDERSTANDING THE ARTICLE
There may be more than one correct answer in each exercise.

1. Mr. Dutscher wants to prove that we are unhappy because of

    a. The effects on us of our emphasis on material progress.   a. _____

    b. The slowness of our material progress for all the people.   b. _____

    c. The shortage of leisure time.   c. _____

    d. The specter of depressions.   d. _____

2. Dutscher believes that the rising standard of living produces

    a. A harmful vulgarity.   a. _____

    b. A valuable comfort.   b. _____

    c. A harmful excess of goods.   c. _____

    d. A threat to the quality of our personal and social lives.   d. _____

3. Dutscher's basic question about the rising standard of living is first specifically stated in

    a. Paragraph 1.   a. _____

    b. Paragraph 26.   b. _____

    c. Paragraph 13.   c. _____

    d. Paragraph 4.   d. _____

4. According to the marginal notes, Paragraphs 6 through 12

    a. Examine the necessity of the rising economy.   a. _____

    b. Illustrate the rise in vulgarity.   b. _____

    c. Criticize the nature of our comfort.   c. _____

    d. Examine the difference in our current unrest.   d. _____

5. According to the marginal notes, Paragraphs 14 through 19

    a. Examine the boredom produced by the rise in the economy.   a. _____

    b. Examine the problems of an uneven rise in the economy.   b. _____

    c. Examine the vulgarity produced by the rise of the economy.   c. _____

    d. Examine the necessity of the rise of the economy.   d. _____

6. According to the marginal notes, Paragraphs 20 through 25

    a. Question the reality of the rise of the economy.   a. _____

    b. Question the extent of our lack of taste.   b. _____

    c. Question the reality of our unhappiness.   c. _____

    d. Question the benefits of increased leisure time.   d. _____

7. According to the marginal notes, Paragraphs 28 through 32

    a. Examine the extent of our vulgarity.   a. _____

    b. Examine the reality of the rise in the economy.   b. _____

    c. Examine the comforts produced by the rise in the economy.   c. _____

    d. Examine the literature of our age.   d. _____

8. The question of the necessity of the rise in the economy is examined

    a. From Paragraph 1 to 5.   a. _____

    b. From Paragraph 41 on.   b. _____

    c. From Paragraph 13 on.   c. _____

    d. From Paragraph 44 on.   d. _____

9. Our present unrest is said to be different because

    a. We can blame it on ourselves.   a. _____

    b. We can't pin it down to specific, concrete problems.   b. _____

    c. We suffer from having too much.   c. _____

    d. We suffer from having too much balance.   d. _____

10. The vulgarity that Dutscher criticizes

    a. Involves poor taste and decay of the spirit.   a. _____

    b. Is caused by having too few items to choose from.   b. _____

    c. Applies only to fashions.   c. _____

    d. Threatens the nature of our civilization.   d. _____

11. Dutscher's evidence in questioning how real the rise in the economy is includes

    a. The problem of poor taste.   a. _____

    b. The problem of credit.   b. _____

    c. The problem of obsolescence.   c. _____

    d. The problem of useless and harmful commodities.   d. _____

12. Dutscher is not impressed by the comforts of our society because

    a. Comfort itself is not necessarily valuable.   a. _____

    b. The time we save is often wasted anyway.   b. _____

    c. Easier jobs are not necessarily more meaningful.   c. _____

    d. Workers must still work much too hard.   d. _____

13. Dutscher finds in our literature evidence of

    a. Our need for continued expansion.   a. _____

    b. The dangers of commodities, conformity and security.   b. _____

    c. The phoniness of our goals and desires.   c. _____

    d. The limitation of our real freedom.   d. _____

14. Dutscher decides that increased economic activity

    a. Is a good in itself.   a. _____

    b. Must be allowed to go on unplanned.   b. _____

    c. Must be directed toward satisfying human needs.   c. _____

    d. Must be prevented from "moronizing" us.   d. _____

15. At the end Dutscher emphasizes as the cause of all the rest

    a. Vulgarity.   a. _____

    b. Comfort.   b. _____

    c. Phoniness.   c. _____

    d. Surplus.   d. _____